The Art of Public Prayer

NOT FOR CLERGY ONLY

2nd Edition

Lawrence A. Hoffman

SkyLight Paths Publishing
Woodstock, Vermont

Grateful acknowledgment is extended to the following for permission to reprint excerpted material: Simon & Schuster, from *The Human Cycle* by Colin M. Turnbull, Copyright © 1983 by Colin M. Turnbull; Pantheon Books, from *Family Networks* by Russ V. Speck and Carolyn Attenave; and the Aaron Copland Fund for Music, Inc.

Library of Congress Cataloging-in-Publication Data
Hoffman, Lawrence A., 1942–
　　The art of public prayer : not for clergy only / by Lawrence A.
Hoffman.—2nd ed.
　　　　p.　　cm.
　　Includes bibliographical references and index.
　　ISBN 1-893361-06-3
　　1. United States—Religious life and customs. 2. Public worship.
3. Public worship—Judaism.   I. Title.
BL2525.H64 1999
291.3'8—dc21   98-33128
　　　　　　　　　　　　　　　　　　　　　　　　　　　　　　　CIP

Second Edition

10 9 8 7 6 5 4 3 2

Manufactured in the United States of America
Cover design: Bridgett Taylor
Text design: Chelsea Dippel

Walking Together, Finding the Way
Published by SkyLight Paths Publishing
A Division of LongHill Partners, Inc.
Sunset Farm Offices, Route 4
P.O. Box 237
Woodstock, VT 05091
Tel: (802) 457-4000   Fax: (802) 457-4004
www.skylightpaths.com

Contents

102439

Is Ecstasy Enough?

> I can see it now as plainly as I saw it thirty years ago, every day I was at Banaras, for two years. Young and old go down to the water's edge at dawn and stand there, each alone . . . but all together as one greater Self. One by one, as they feel ready, they walk out into the water until they stand waist-deep. Some stand there for half an hour. It is their time of mantra. Then as the sun rises above the green fields on the far side of the Ganga, its first rays reaching across and touching with warmth the ancient palaces and temples of Banaras, thousands of pairs of hands, cupped together like begging bowls, raise the water to the sky, and thousands of voices recite the sacred *gayatri mantra* so silently, you feel it rather than hear it. As they let the water trickle back into the holy river the sun catches it, and a million sunlit drops add their beauty to the beauty of the sound of the temple bells and the voices of devotees singing *kirtan* all in one single greeting to another day of life. . . . Is that ecstasy enough at the beginning of every day of youth, every day of adulthood, and every day of old age? And what might we have been if we had been taught such an art as this?
>
> —Colin M. Turnbull, *The Human Cycle*

Picture the early morning gathering at the river, but with yourself among the loyal thousands gathered there. Would any of us presume to doubt the efficacy of the rite? Who wouldn't gladly drop a hundred years of sophistication to stand by a sacred stream with the meaning of life shining through a million sacred droplets glittering in the morning sun? Or, if you don't like Turnbull's example, choose from thousands of others. Bathing in the Ganges at Banaras is only one of many stories of religious rituals that impress their adherents with the unmistakable conviction that worship matters.

By contrast, the worship we Jews and Christians know best in our North American sanctuaries seems like a pale imitation of the real thing. Only yesterday, it seems, Vatican II opened up the possibility of liturgical renewal for Roman Catholics, and overnight, Protestants and Jews too were promising new liturgies that would make public prayer compelling. Those were the heady 1960s and 1970s, when anything seemed possible. By the 1980s, even though new worship books had been introduced in churches and synagogues everywhere, it was becoming clear that the problem was not just literary. The question shifted from, "How do we write new liturgies?" to "How do we restore meaningful public prayer to our churches and synagogues? How do we make true worship happen?"

This book is for the worship care committees that I see functioning in every church and synagogue, intent on discovering how to better the spiritual state of public prayer. The descriptions of dysfunctional worship in chapter 3 ought to evoke smiles (and tears) of recognition, since they are composite cases drawn from the experience of Everyman and Everywoman. The chapters on language, music, and space empower ordinary men and women to know enough to take an active part in determining their own liturgical future. The book empowers lay people and clergy to work together to develop worshiping communities where individuals are nurtured by the power and depth of the rituals of their past.

You Just Open Your Mouth

When I was still a rabbinic student, I asked my teacher, Dr. John Tepfer, of blessed memory, if he would offer a course in Yiddish, the folk tongue of eastern European Jews that was fast dying out. Professor Tepfer, it was rumored, knew everything. So why not Yiddish?

In fact, he knew Yiddish very well. He had been raised on the language—spoke it, I am sure, before he learned English. Nonetheless, he refused my request. His somewhat serious, somewhat tongue-in-cheek explanation I remember to this day. "Teach you Yiddish, Hoffman? Why, you don't teach Yiddish. You just open your mouth and it comes out."

Alas, though I have never been shy about opening my mouth, Yiddish does not come out. We know now also that worship, which we once took for granted, does not happen automatically—even with the new and better liturgy books that the last thirty years have given us. "Teach worship?" my teacher would also have replied. "Why, you just open your mouth and it comes out." He would have been wrong there too. What our ancestors not many generations ago took for granted, we struggle with. We now teach worship in our seminaries. And we should teach it in our synagogues and churches.

This is a book to do just that. When I wrote it in 1988, it became a standard manual, used by Christians and Jews, in parishes, congregations, and classrooms. Now, ten years later, some revision is called for. Rather than reprint the old edition, I decided to bring the book up to date, integrating what we have learned about worship in the last decade. I have streamlined it as well, not just adding material, but omitting it whenever possible, so as to produce a serious but workable handbook for people concerned about the life of congregational prayer.

Watch My Language: Worship, Sanctuaries, Theology, and Such ⊛

The hardest task in writing has been to find some common language to address Jews, Catholics, and Protestants—all at the same time. Our several worshiping communities use words differently. Take "sanctuary," for instance. For Jews and Protestants, the sanctuary is the entire worship space; for Catholics, it is the area immediately around the altar, and older Catholic usage applied it only to the area reserved for the clergy.

Or take "clergy." Some confessions (a Protestant term roughly equivalent to denominations, but what Jews call movements) have no clergy at all, strictly speaking. Jews do have clergy, but debate rages over whether cantors, not just rabbis, fit that category. In some synagogues, rabbis who are recognized as clergy do not lead worship, while cantors who may still be striving for that recognition do.

More important than misunderstanding is the mistaken impression that the wrong word may have upon readers. Until recently (and still today, in many synagogues) Jews, who know what worship is, rarely use the word because it sounds "too Christian." So as not to alienate Jewish readers from the outset, I have therefore entitled my book *The Art of Public Prayer*, not *The Art of Public Worship*. Nonetheless, Christians will readily recognize that my topic is worship.

I have, however, held steadfastly to Christian practice by retaining the word "theology." Jews do have theologies, of course, and they know they do. But they do not readily connect them with religious decisions the way Christians do. For Jews, proper worship practice is deduced from *halakhah* (Jewish law). This book describes what you have to know about such things as sacred music, sacred space, religious symbols, and systems thinking to make worship meaningful today. I do not mean to tinker with age-old forms of prayer just for the sake of bringing in the masses or pandering to current fads. I have the highest regard for inherited traditions that ultimately govern what we do. Serious religious planners never lose sight of age-old verities, which they balance against the need to make those verities speak to the current generation of the faithful (another word used by Christians, but not by Jews). But what word should I use to characterize those verities? In the end, I decided on "theology," not only because it is the word most Christians would select, but because what Jews think about Jewish law must ultimately be consistent with what they believe about God. In addition, if worship *is* worship, it should somehow relate to the knowledge of God's presence in our midst.

Some Jews would question even that assumption, however. An old Jewish joke pictures two elderly gentlemen, Schwartz and Cohen, leaving synagogue. Cohen is accosted by his teenage son who wonders why his father, an atheist, attends services regularly.

The son: "Why do you go to pray? Can you really say that you go to talk to God?"

The father: "No. I do not go to talk to God. But Schwartz goes to talk to God, and I go to talk to Schwartz."

There are plenty of Jews (and Christians too) who do not expect that worship will be spiritual. They go to talk to Schwartz, not God. Still others go out of habit: "What else do you do on a *Shabbat* [Sabbath] morning?" Or out of obligation: "This is just something Jews do—like giving charity and keeping holidays." The idea that there is a theological reason to pray or that the presence of God ought to be manifest in worship never arises.

Obligation differs from plain habit or coming to talk to Schwartz. I will return here, again and again, to the theme of making worship matter so that people will want to attend and will report spiritual meaning in worship after they have attended. But I do not at all denigrate the motive of religious obligation. We do some things because we *should*, whether it feels good or not. Nonetheless, doing what we *should* ought not necessarily feel bad. Moreover, people have a right to truth-in-advertising: If worship purports to be a dialogue with God, it should at least make good on that claim. At any rate, it would be folly to imagine that large numbers of people will continue worshiping out of mere habit—or as a way to talk to Schwartz. The crux of this book may well be the discussion on how we learn again to talk to God, not to Schwartz; or, as I will describe it later, how we revise our expectations on what it means to know God in our time.

For People Who Wish They Could Pray   ◉

This book is very much for people who will not go to talk to Schwartz and cannot go to talk to God; for people, that is, who have experienced the damp chill of knowing they cannot go home again to the particular Banaras of their youth, but who still want to be able to pray. It is for people who find themselves by habit or inclination in church or synagogue, at least on holy days, and who wonder afterward, given the relative failure of the services to speak convincingly to their lives, why they even bothered.

If you are happily engaged in daily, or even weekly, communal worship, you are among the blessed few in this land where the masses get up at the crack of dawn to jog, not to pray. The officially churched and those who belong to synagogues make up only a small minority of our citizens. Only a minority of that minority actually live religious lives according to the dictates of the faith they espouse, and not all of those people go regularly to Sabbath worship.

This book differs from some others on the subject of public prayer in that it does not blame people for the failure of worship to move them. Indeed, it tries not to blame anyone. It admits from the outset that much that passes for worship in church or synagogue is baffling or banal to most of the people who find their way there. This judgment will come as no surprise to most Americans who stay away from regular worship in droves. It may shock the regulars—those who attend with commendable regularity—and even some of the professionals who are there out of necessity, habit, and love, but whose very calling can easily blind them to the true state of affairs. Still, I suspect that even they know the truth. Surely they must wonder why the closest thing we have to the mass ritual of the Banaras bathing is the Super Bowl or a local high school homecoming weekend. I have been to clergy conventions where many of the gathered clergy did not attend their own convention worship services. And I, like every reader of this book, have found myself on too many occasions in dutiful attendance at worship services where my predominant thought was how slowly the time ticked by, as the proceedings threatened never to come to a merciful conclusion.

The underlying postulate of this book is that prayer is not just for those who attended seminaries. Without consulting with one another, Protestants, Catholics, and Jews have all moved toward more involvement of the people—all the people—in worship. They are invited now to claim their worship as their own: to sing, chant, speak, and even direct and organize their liturgies, rather than let a privileged clerical class do so for them. That is why I adopted the subtitle *Not for Clergy Only.*

In the first part of the book, I demonstrate that ritual in general is alive and well in modern life, and that only religious ritual is in trouble. I carefully avoid blaming anyone for that sorry fact, since I believe that the best way to right a wrong is to see it as arising from a badly functioning system and to summon all the members of the system to work together to achieve change. Yelling at people to drive safer, eat healthier, work harder, dress neater, or act fairer doesn't usually get us as far as analyzing the entire context in which the "unhealthy" behavior emerges. Similarly, then, rather than yelling at worshipers to pray harder, I prefer to analyze the system we call worship in modern America, and ask why it malfunctions as it does.

Chapters 1 through 4 outline what I call the worship system. By and large, religious ritual does not work for us. Why not? How do symbols function in prayer? What elementary understanding of communications do we need if we are to alter hardened worship patterns that stand in the way of spirituality? Chapters 6 through 8 analyze the words we say, the songs we sing, and the spaces we occupy during our communal liturgies. Chapter 5 provides the theological reasoning that lies behind the suggestions in chapters 6 through 8. Chapter 9 concludes the book by returning to the practical side of system intervention: How indeed does change come about in a venerable institution like worship, which has resisted renewal so steadfastly, so successfully, and for so long?

I know that my analysis does not do justice to many Americans whose worship comes very close to the Banaras bathing rite of India's faithful. I especially have in mind the Orthodox Jewish services I attended while growing up in a small Jewish community in southern Ontario. For many years I attended Sabbath worship in a traditional milieu where the same men—never women—met to go through their traditional liturgical text with anything but attention to the matters I cite as necessary for meaningful public prayer. With the exception of the rabbi, they understood little, if anything, of a Hebrew text that they rattled through at breakneck speed from beginning to end. The Torah was read, but very quickly and purely by rote. Unable to understand the reading, the people engaged in steady congregational crosstalk. They paid no heed whatever to the role of music, preferring to have the old-time melodies chanted rather than sung, and poorly at that, by a self-proclaimed cantor who had little vocal skill, and who was joined here and there by a few straggling voices that were not necessarily in the same key. They had never heard of sacred space. In fact, in a cabinet under the ark they kept some very unholy whiskey bottles from which they liked to imbibe after services. At almost exactly the same time that the congregation rose to sing the final hymn of God's ultimate reign (not that anyone knew that was what the hymn was about), the old man who was charged with preparing the liquid refreshments was bending over to collect the whiskey from the cabinet below the very ark we faced. It must have looked to an outsider as if we were praying to his backside.

By every standard of western worship, their rite was a failure. Except for one thing: They are still doing it. If it is a failure, they certainly don't know it! What can they learn from my book? Perhaps nothing. They are like the Armenian churchgoers I once visited in Jerusalem. There, behind the walls that set the ancient sect apart from the rest of the world, you find daily worship in which old priests and child acolytes go through motions, words, and melodies hallowed by age—in fearless disregard of what we moderns think they ought to do. I make no claim to speak to or for them. They need a book on worship no more than the Hindu morning bathers and the Orthodox Jews of Ontario do. In that regard, they are the lucky ones. So too, I suppose, are "born-agains" of any religious stamp—Jews call them *ba'alei t'shuvah*, "penitents who return"—who manage somehow to rediscover verities that command their allegiance despite their dissonance with modern life.

I mean no disrespect to any of these people when I say as a simple matter of observable fact that the majority of would-be religious Canadians and Americans are not like them. We are more like the young Muslim student from Morocco described by the anthropologist Clifford Geertz.

Both Hands Full

He is on an airplane bound for New York, his first trip away from home, where he will study at an American university. Frightened, as well he might be, by the experience of flying (as well as the thought of what awaits him when he lands), he passes the entire trip with the Koran gripped in one hand and a glass of scotch in the other.

Like him, most of us have discovered not scotch but the elixir of modernity, which we do not easily let slip from our grasp, even as we hold equally fast to the texts and forms of our premodern youth. As they say, "You can't go home again."

The Jerusalem Armenians, the southern Ontario Jewish Orthodox, the born-agains, and the *ba'alei t'shuvah* can all do without this book. But for the rest of us, worship is not just something we do; it is a form of art. If public prayer is done with care, it successfully defines an alternative universe of reality for people adrift in an unrelenting secular stream of consciousness. It helps us suspend the disbelief of the secular sphere while we attend to the religious stories that our grand-parents once believed without question. I call it an art because art is the means by which alternative universes of being have been forged since time began. The traditionalists I've already mentioned live in only one world to start with, and in that world, it is the secular rites and symbols that seem strange, not the other way around. They need no self-conscious artistry to effect the illusion of alternative visions of their world. It was inconceivable to the old men in my hometown *not* to come to pray every Saturday morning, and where they kept the liquor for the midday "schnapps" was irrelevant to them. By contrast, if most of us want to adopt a religious vision of the world, we must do so against the grain of secularity. We keep the whiskey out of sight, as if, in the moment of prayer, secular appetites do not exist.

So to those who find their age-old traditions of worship totally satisfying, I have little to say. But those who are not so blessed should not make the mistake of blaming themselves for life's complexity. They have done no wrong in accepting the compelling message of history's march into the twentieth and twenty-first centuries. The good old days may be old, but they weren't always good. To all those who, like myself, hold modernity in one hand and tradition in the other, who cannot return to yesterday's unquestioned certainties, who refuse to part with their intellectual curiosity but want also to retain the spirituality of prayer, I dedicate this book. May it help transform the tired forms of public prayer into the beauty of holiness.

one

Structuring Time

Not all moments of our lives are the same. All may be equally lasting, but some mean more than others. When we say that we are "killing time" or that "time flies," we recognize the qualitative distinction between some moments and others. There really are such things as momentous decisions, momentary lapses, affairs of the moment, and moments of truth.

Our understanding of time suffers from at least two misconceptions. The first is that we imagine time to be a straight line moving from the beginning to the end. The line is stretched taut so that each point or moment on it is the same as any other. That may be so for the scientific world, where laboratory experiments must be replicable whether today is Tuesday or Thursday. But it is most definitely not true for the everyday world of ordinary people, for whom Tuesday may be magnificent and Thursday disastrous.

So we would do better to chart our graph of time as if it were a curve moving up and down the page over and over again, like the diagram of a sound wave. Time has high points and low points; as we sometimes say, "I was on a high," or "I felt low." Drugs are described as uppers or downers, depending on the direction time will take as a result of their medication. We may spend hours or even days building up to some high point or hurtling downward to the low point on the graph. Some people allow the extremities of high and low to move so far away from each other that we say they suffer from a bipolar disorder. But manic-depressives (as they are also known) differ only in degree. We all experience a qualitative difference in life's moments. We learn to recognize our lows and to bear with them until the graph swings upward again. And we work at creating those moments of exhilaration that make life exciting, challenging, and significant.

Our second misconception is that we think time should be measured by the span of our lives. To be sure, that makes sense from the perspective of our being born, living so long, and then dying; and to that extent such customs as counting birthdays and remembering things by how old we were at the time are sensible. Not every culture, though, has been so individualistically oriented; many would have laughed at making individuals the measure of time. And even in our culture, it is generally people in their middle age and upward, people, that is, who are aware of their mortality, who carry the American message that a lifetime is a discrete block of time that must be planned. Groups not fully in the mainstream of the American work ethic may see things differently. They may live for today as if it had no relation to tomorrow, blowing all their savings on a momentary whim, for example, instead of salting it away for the future. They endure the scorn and wrath of others who fail to comprehend how anyone could be so foolish as to waste the promise of future achievement by indulging in transitory pleasures.

The truth is, however, that only in retrospect do the combined moments of a lifetime take on a character of their own. The entirety of life turns out to be too much for any of us to handle all at once. Though we may maintain a general notion of working toward some ultimate goal, we live day by day, or even hour by hour, breaking up our years into much smaller and manageable units, each with its own rules and its own graph of highs and lows.

Take something as simple as a lunch break. Office workers who go out to lunch every day develop habitual ways of spending their lunchtime. A few people discover friends in the neighborhood and meet daily, at a certain table, at a certain time. Each gets to know what the others order, so that when one of them alters the usual order, the others look on, astonished. Soon this lunch becomes a unit of time unto itself, a social setting where other units of time (such as the board meeting or family dinner) are put aside, dismissed from consciousness.

As a unit of time in and of itself, it can be graphed upward and downward, and, to the extent that the script is fixed, the high and low points can be predicted. If the people meet at their table every day and immediately greet each other profusely while ordering cocktails and celebrating their togetherness, we might consider that the high point. Serious conversation may deliberately, though not officially, be delayed until all the people get there. During that waiting time, expectations build—the graph is on its way up—but with the arrival of the last person, cocktails are ordered, greetings are shared, glasses are clinked: The high moment is reached.

Not everyone spends lunch this way, but those who do are adding meaning to moments. Each moment in the hour-long lunch break is tied to the moment before and the moment after. A loose script defines who sits where, who orders what, who pays, and so on. The participants have managed to force time into a frame of meaning by ritualizing it, defining what is done and said for every moment of it, and then repeating the script with but minor variations each and every day.

❀ **Ritual is how we play out prearranged scripts of behavior to shape specific durations of time. Since each script is repeated regularly, it prepares us to anticipate the high and low points of our lives. Without ritual there would be no meaningful use of time, except for accidental events that force us to laugh or cry on occasion. Ritual helps us minimize our dependence on chance. It arranges our life into relatively small packages of moments that matter.**

If ritual is successful, a high point will be reached. After much waiting and anticipating, for instance, the lunch partners will finally all arrive and drink to each other's health, while they temporarily forget the fight with the boss, the sick kids at home, or whatever else might otherwise have been on their mind had those moments not been ritualistically reserved for their special role in the script. At the moment of mutual satisfaction—the cocktail glasses clinking, perhaps—the ritual climaxes. If, as in our example, this is a lunch ritual, we can call that high point the "lunch moment."

Wanted: Ritual Moments ◉

Lunch may seem too trivial an event to be characterized as ritualistic, but it is not. Lunch time is an hour a day, let us say, when we have the possibility of writing a ritual script together and playing it out to mutual satisfaction. It is but one example of many.

A mother nursing her child is another. She goes about her task with regularized routine, saying favorite things to the baby, then finding the proper chair, and finally nursing her child. Is her act any different from the people going to lunch at the same time every day? Certainly not. Both nursing and lunching have become ritualized so that one act invariably follows another. Anticipation of what is to come builds to the climax of the ritual script. As the child takes the nipple and the mother feels the crying infant being soothed, or when the nursing is over and the baby falls asleep at the mother's breast—whichever has become the high point in the mother's definition of the graph of moments that make up the nursing time—we find the "nursing moment."

Unfortunately the word "ritual" has taken on a negative connotation. Ritualism is equated with the hocus-pocus magic of some presumably backward tribes practicing local superstition. This attitude is seen in popular literature where an author describes an old-fashioned, stereotypical chairman of the board going through the "empty ritual" of lighting the cigar before calling the meeting to order. This evaluation misses the whole point: Lighting the cigar is a ritual, but not an empty one. It is indeed ritualistic in that it precedes the formal call to order, but it serves in this very way as a readily recognizable means of setting the stage, cueing the players in this particular ritual, and keying them up to the expectations demanded of them. So outsiders are wrong to speak of either the "witch doctor" or the board chairman as performing "mere" rituals. Real rituals are never "mere"!

Of course, rituals that once mattered deeply to the people who kept them can degenerate into sterility. Let us call such empty rituals *ritualizations.* The script is played out, but the actors' minds and hearts are elsewhere. The lunch partners may have seen half their group retire, and the old restaurant change hands so that the familiar table isn't there anymore. New people may have joined the group, bringing new behavior, new personal relationships, and, thus, a changed script. It is hard to reproduce the same lunch moment now. Similarly, the mother nursing her baby may be tired of it after some time. Sleepless nights, visions of a career thwarted, loneliness as her husband leaves early and comes home late—any one of a number of things may make it difficult for her to achieve the psychological satisfaction she once enjoyed in nursing her flesh and blood. For her, now, there is no nursing moment. The graph never goes very high, because despite her efforts to do the same things in the same way, she finds her mind wandering and her patience wearing thin; she cannot wait for this block of nursing time to go. She will then move happily to another time block that may still be a meaningful ritual—perhaps meeting other mothers of similar temperament in the park.

So whether the chairman who lights a cigar is going through a meaningful ritual or an empty ritualization depends on the psychological expectations of the ritual's participants and the degree to which they are able to recognize and to enjoy the ritualistic high point, in this case, the board meeting moment. Let us assume it is the reading of the bottom line on the quarterly economic statement and the mutual awarding of kudos to all present. When the company first started, only a few people made up the board. When they met, they brought high personal investment in this company that they were building. So successful were they, that years later the company became a multimillion-dollar corporate giant. Of the original founders, only the president remains. He still begins by lighting his cigar, and the meeting still concludes with reading the statement and congratulating the department heads. But the latter are all new now, and the sense of personal involvement is gone. The executives attend out of corporate responsibility and cannot wait for the ritualistic sign that they may leave. There is no high point on the graph any more, no moment toward which the script can move and the actors aspire. Ritual has become ritualization.

So there are empty rituals—ritualizations we now call them—and they are what we think they are: boring, meaningless, seemingly silly in the way the participants do a multitude of things with no inherent pragmatic connection to the job at hand. The ritualistic cues once pregnant with meaning are now vacant words, empty gestures, vacuous activity. But there are also rituals, real rituals, where the opposite is the case, and on these we depend to convert structureless time and necessary tasks into meaningful and satisfying experiences. For each such ritual, whether it be as simple as eating lunch with some friends or as serious as getting married, we follow a script and build to a high point, the moment, which we share together because we have been taught to recognize the symbolic behavior of the script as a series of connected signposts along the way. What is necessary in each case is the common acceptance of the script; the common decision to see symbolic significance in behavior that would otherwise appear secondary or even foolish; and the consensus to invest oneself psychologically in the

❂ **Our days are filled with rituals, one following on the heels of another, as we carve up time and compartmentalize it around events that involve us. Ritualizations are indeed empty, but real rituals are not. Ritualism is neither good nor bad, advanced nor primitive, but human.**

whole drama, waiting for what everyone accepts as the high point in the ritual's curve, the moment that makes it all worth while.

I began by discussing such mundane matters as going to lunch or lighting a cigar before a board meeting. By taking the event around which the ritual has been built, we can classify the ritual itself as a lunch ritual, a board meeting ritual, or a nursing ritual. And by noting that the ritualistic flow of events does move in a graphlike fashion toward a culminating moment, we can call that moment the ritual moment, further classifying it as the lunch moment, the board meeting moment, or the nursing moment.

Once we concede that even such apparently mundane and daily tasks as these are played out in ritual ways, we should have no trouble at all imagining more "serious" public pursuits as being of like character. Thus public schools open each day with a ritual that may include the Pledge of Allegiance. When public schools functioned primarily to socialize immigrants into American values, the pledge was part of what was once a more extended script of considerable importance. Today the pledge may be empty (a ritualization) or full (a ritual). Congress, too, opens each seating with a ritual, and the president of the United States is sworn in ritually, just as the queen or king of England is ritually crowned. These latter displays of public pomp and circumstance are certainly not empty to most people, who watch them on television or even travel halfway across the world to catch a glimpse of the event from among a throng of thousands. The 1997 funeral of Princess Diana attracted television audiences around the globe who wanted to be part of saying goodbye to a popular heroine.

A similar example of a public ritual is a nationally televised Republican or Democratic convention, where the roll call of states is ritualistically performed. Sometimes everyone knows in advance who the presidential candidate will be, but just as on Broadway, the show must go on. State by state the count is given, as one "great state" yields to another. Slowly, inexorably, tension mounts and muted cheers are silenced by a pounding gavel and a call for order. Finally the count reaches the magic number; someone is over the mark. The band breaks into song; pent-up emotion erupts in carefully choreographed "spontaneous demonstrations"; television personnel scurry back and forth interviewing the winner's key supporters, who respond to predictable questions with equally predictable answers. By now the climax of the ritual is over, and the interviews are merely denouement, a winding down from the moment, in this case, the political moment. The graph is moving downward now toward the neutral horizontal axis where it began.

Still, there was a moment of intense excitation, a crescendo toward which the whole evening built. Everyone knew in advance what it was, and what would happen once it occurred. At each stage along the way, a political pro could read the signs of the script that were equally transparent to the delegates, who performed with all the polish and verve expected of them. These symbolic gestures necessary to the political ritual were sent and received, until at last the political moment was at hand.

Examples could be multiplied. From the world of sports, one could consider the annual grudge match between the University of Michigan Wolverines and the Ohio State Buckeyes; or the Super Bowl madness that sweeps the country every year; or the homecoming pep rally at the local high school. Can anyone doubt the ritual nature of these events? And they are certainly not empty rituals, not for the thousands upon thousands of fans who know the ritual's language inside out, who see the signs and follow the symbols as they occur, who recognize the actors and their roles, and who explode together at the attainment of the sports moment no less than do party loyalists at the political moment.

The last few examples from the worlds of politics and sports have culminating moments of cathartic outbursts of emotion. At some soccer games, the emotional exuberance may even spill over into pitched battle. But ecstatic joy, aggressive shouting, and loud singing are not necessary components of the ritual moment. These occur only when called for by the particular ritual script being enacted. Other rituals climax in other ways.

Consider for a moment a ritual that no one will dispute: a funeral. Some religious traditions feature songs and shouts of joy at funerals, but for most Americans, funerals seem to move climactically downward to a low point on the graph rather than to a high one. People play roles: the mourners, the mortician, the clergy, the friends and relatives, who can be arranged, theoretically, in concentric circles of closeness to the mourners, and who behave in ways befitting the circle they inhabit. The members of the inside circle are practically mourners themselves; they are confidants, aides, helpers, mainstays. Those of the outermost circle, on the other hand, merely take time off from work to attend the funeral ceremonies, adding only their physical presence as a sign of the event's significance. From the moment of death to the time when the bereaved resume normal activities, a lengthy ritual of death unfolds.

Within that ritual, there are subrituals: the funeral itself, for example, or the negotiations at the funeral parlor regarding the details of the burial. At one point though, usually at the funeral ceremony, the climax begins to mount. For the first and only time, all the actors in the ritual are present under one roof: mourners, intimate friends, distant acquaintances, professionals. Now the ritual roles are enacted according to the script. The widowed spouse cries and is supported by the helpers, those within the first circle of friends and relatives. But the crying is kept in check to some extent, and the other real-life actors enter the scene. People offer consolation. The crowd gathers. The casket is closed and readied for burial. Religious services are read. The eulogy is given. At last, at the grave side, the coffin descends into the bowels of the earth, and the moment occurs. Now even the professionals, the clergy and the mortician's staff, may be moved to tears, whether or not they knew the deceased. The funeral ritual has culminated in the funeral moment.

The notion of culminating moments was anticipated many years ago by the psychologist Abraham Maslow, who named such experiences "peak moments." His interest was not religious worship or even ritual, but human psychology as it applies to religious experience in general. Maslow wrote in the 1960s, when all institutions—including churches and synagogues—were under attack by a younger generation that considered them sterile. He tried to replace organized religion with a sort of humanistic personalism, in that he denied the need for any institutionalized format to bring out the religious impulse within us. Instead, he felt that every human being has the potential for religious experience, since religion is an intrinsic element in our psychological makeup. Nevertheless, some people tend toward religious realization more than others, in that they are innate "peakers," while their opposites find peaking distinctly foreign. Maslow made no attempt to hide his own bias in favor of people who can peak, so he maintained that true spirituality is demonstrated in an attitude toward the world that enables peaking to occur. The mystics, prophets, and seers of religious history are famous peakers; the bureaucrats who run true religion into the ground, Maslow thought, are ruinous for religious identity.

Later, Maslow amended his theory somewhat. He realized that many spiritually sensitive people never reach peak moments, and that not everyone is an Elijah-like miracle worker, a striver after speaking in tongues, or even a seeker after emotional highs. So he altered his expectations of true religion, explaining that sometimes, instead of peak experiences, one might expect only plateau experiences: not a genuine momentary high, that is, but a longer-lasting sensation of more moderate satisfaction.

Despite surface similarities, the position I am outlining here is very different from Maslow's. I have borrowed his basic realization that people do not experience every moment in time exactly the same way; we do have highs, and most of us can recall times when the exhilaration we felt was similar to what Maslow must have meant by peaking. But Maslow was wrong to think that the goal of life is always to attain a high, and he was correct to scale down that unrealistic expectation when he recognized the equal validity of a plateau experience as well. Moreover, I recognize equal validity in low points in human emotion— the satisfying sigh of the funeral moment, for example. Not that we live for the days when we can attend funerals, certainly, but sadness is no less inherent to human life than happiness. We learn from both, and we develop a mature and balanced character by integrating both into our repertoire of states through which we pass in the normal course of our lives.

Religion is the category of life's pursuits that best integrates these highs and lows, and religious ritual is how we structure sad and happy moments so that they occur within a framework that we understand and appreciate. Other institutional rituals work in similar fashion to structure personal experience in socially desirable ways. My second deviation from Maslow, then, is my insistence that psychological states depend more on the groups with which we identify than on any inherent psychological ability. Individuals die, but churches structure funerals and tell us when to cry. Individuals seek out glory, but political parties channel that search into the political process. Even individual mothers nursing their babies learn how to do it from other mothers, who follow rules laid down by culture, class, and ethnic group patterns of which they may be only dimly aware. Who among us would give up life in society to live on a desert island? Sports fans watch baseball games on television in the privacy of their living rooms, but they would rather invite friends over to share the joy of watching together. We need the company of others to enjoy the peaks and the plateaus.

Like Maslow, I am highly critical of that bureaucratic, spiritless approach to religion that stymies attempts at successful communal prayer. But unlike Maslow, I don't believe that leaving organized religion for some imagined state of total individualism is a real option.

❋ **Rituals require ritualizing groups, without which our inner yearnings to make the most of life would be reduced to the elemental and elementary levels of emotional frustration that we associate with infants.**

Rating Rituals by Type and Style ◉

We have already seen that rituals can be divided in various ways. But we can add to the catalogue of ritual types and styles.

1 ▪ Rituals may be empty (ritualizations) or full (actual rituals).

Theoretically, only rituals that work are actual rituals; but in practice, any particular synagogue or church may well feature prayer that is so bad that everyone just seems to be going through the motions, and yet, people speak of it as their ritual anyway. With imagination and thought, congregations or parishes can rescue their ritual from its doldrums.

2 ▪ Culminating ritual moments vary in emotional tone.

As we saw, rituals may culminate in moments of joy (a wedding) or of sadness (a funeral) or of any other emotional state that characterizes our existence. There are such things as intellectual rituals, for instance, which culminate with solving a particular problem. This is more joyful than sad, but hardly has the same emotional flavor as celebrating a wedding. Classes tend to become intellectual rituals, in that a teacher may customarily pose a problem and work through the classroom hour until a solution is reached. Students who attend class regularly get used to a certain ritualized flow of time, and may even mimic the teacher's way of always conducting the class in the same way.

What all the moments have in common, regardless of their diverse emotions, is that they *satisfy*. They provide a pleasing sensation of having completed what we began. I recall a wedding at which I officiated where I neglected to say, "By the authority vested in me . . . I hereby declare you husband and wife." That declaration is not part of the Jewish wedding ceremony, and so I had never told the couple that it would be lacking. But they had attended countless weddings and seen lots more on television, and they were anxiously waiting for me to "declare them married." As the wedding reached its conclusion and I reached forward to take their hands and offer a final benediction, the groom whispered painfully to me, "When do we get to be 'declared' husband and wife?" I quickly improvised the words he was waiting for, and they smiled in beautiful satisfaction. The moment for which they were waiting had arrived.

3 ▪ The culminating emotive state may be experienced privately or demonstrated publicly.

It is not always easy to know if a ritual works. Some ritual is extroverted, some not so. It is always tempting to judge other people's rituals by the standards that we have for our own, but it is wiser to ask the people involved in the ritual what counts for success. The ritual of classical Reform Judaism, for instance (the kind of Judaism favored by most German Jews in the nineteenth and early twentieth century) frowned on demonstrating high emotion. This was especially true in some parts of Canada, where British understatement was the norm anyway.

An American Rabbi in Canada

An American rabbi tells of the time he was hired by a classical Reform congregation in Canada. With ritualistic predictability, he had gone from interview to interview, fielding the usual questions with the usual answers. Late in the day, the interviewing committee asked him to wait outside the board room while they deliberated his candidacy. After only five minutes, the committee chair admitted the rabbi and announced with all due gravity, "We are proud to say that you have been elected to be our rabbi"—at which time the committee members tapped the table gently with two fingers of their right hand and said quietly, "Hear, hear. Hear, hear." The hiring ritual had reached its moment, but the American rabbi, unaccustomed to British-style understatement, wasn't sure it had. Like the groom in the wedding, he was still waiting for the right declaration in a show of emotion with which he could identify.

4 ▪ Ritual scripts may be inherited or newly created; they may be open or closed.

The participants may have developed the script entirely on their own over a course of years, or they may be bound by the limitations of a script composed far before their time, and to which they must generally comply.

In either case, scripts may be open or closed. A closed script is fully predictable; it has no freedom for personal improvisation. An open script is the opposite; while it is governed by some rules, it depends greatly on what the individuals who perform it feel like doing. A traditional Catholic mass is relatively closed because the priest feels obliged to follow the regulations of the rite in every detail. Worship at a Quaker meeting house or in the Pentecostal tradition (where people speak in tongues) is relatively open, because in both cases, it is assumed that worshipers are responding to the unpredictable impact of the Holy Spirit speaking through them. Traditions that consider themselves liturgical (Catholic, Lutheran, or Jewish, for example) have relatively closed scripts that have been handed down through the ages and make radical improvisation difficult. (Jews, for instance, cannot just skip the *Sh'ma* if they feel like it, and Catholics cannot forego the Lord's Prayer.) Traditions that consider themselves nonliturgical (Baptists and most independent evangelical churches, for example) are relatively free to do whatever they want. They have no strict series of scriptural readings; they choose whatever hymns, songs, or psalms they want; and they make up novel prayers at will.

Open-script worship in the Protestant tradition is usually driven by the sermon. At the so-called megachurches, for instance, the pastor of the morning may elect a particular message based on a biblical passage that may never have been featured before and may never be used again. The songs and prayers are freely composed to elucidate the message. In closed-script worship, the sermon depends on the fixed lectionary—that is, the order of biblical readings that the rules of worship prescribe. Many a rabbi has sighed deeply when Leviticus comes around, since sermons are supposed to be drawn from readings of the day, but the readings of Leviticus deal largely with priestly regulations and cultic minutiae that seem, at first glance, irrelevant to modern life. The art of the sermon, however, consists precisely in finding meaning there.

The art of public prayer varies for each of these two groups. As we shall see, while certain principles for successful ritual hold for both, liturgical faiths have to balance the desires of the moment with the responsibility to remain true to the script of the centuries and the rules of the liturgy.

In either case, however, since public prayer is a ritual, it has a beginning, a middle, and an end. Even open scripts *are* scripts, and those in the know recognize the flow of the ritual as it builds to a ritual moment and recedes from it. As the ritual begins, participants begin closing out other activities from their minds. They follow the symbolic signposts telling them that the graph is approaching the climactic moment. And when the moment arrives, they do not miss it.

At least *most* people do not miss it. My description of ritual that works may not hold for churches and synagogues where the ritual style is less than ideal. A further way to analyze ritual, then, is to think through the ritual style that any particular worship setting tends to feature.

5 ▪ Worship styles vary; some of them get in our way.

Psychotherapy is a wonderful example of ritual for people who often say they do not believe in ritual. Evan Imber-Black and Janine Roberts are two family therapists who use ritual in their practice to help people work through issues and resolve problems. They differentiate personal ritual styles that may tend to get in the way of using ritual effectively. What they say about individuals and their families is also true of churches and synagogues. The extent to which we convert empty ritualizing into meaningful ritual, or how we make the most of our ritual script, or whether we manage altogether to create a ritual moment may depend ultimately on our ritual style.

Three ritual styles that get in the way are known as *minimalist*, *rigid*, and *obligatory*.

- *Minimalist* style uses ritual sparingly and with suspicion.

At a conference once, I sat next to an African-American pastor who lost patience with my concern for ritual because he saw no connection between ritual and social justice. As a liberationist theologian, he was committed to using religion to free the masses of people still suffering from servitude around the globe. He saw ritual as a religious opiate that deflects attention away from the work of liberation that ought to engage us.

But ritual can help accomplish social justice, not impede it. My colleague in dialogue that day was illustrating a minimalist style. He officiated at rituals when he had to, but preferred other expressions of religious fervor, and had almost no expectations about the little ritual he did observe. Many Reform rabbis also think of religion as a way to bring justice to the world, and were never taught that ritual matters very much. Each week they read through the script of Sabbath worship, but mostly because they have to. They skip whatever they can, because the important thing for them is the sermon, which calls people to arms in a world that awaits their social action. The parallel trend in some Conservative and Orthodox synagogues is to rush through the ritual without expecting anything of it, but to linger while rabbi and congregants engage in an open discussion of the Torah portion. The worship may be dull, but at least the discussion can be scintillating. To be sure, a lively discussion of God's word may be desirable, as may a sermon that moves its hearers to action. But these are no substitute for ritual that works its magic on those who experience it.

- *Rigid* style arises from the fear that tradition, habit, and precedent prevent even minimal change.

Many synagogues feature a sign above the ark in the sanctuary that says, "Know before whom you stand." Congregations with rigid style operate as if it said, "But we've always done it this way!" Actually, customs that people think go back centuries are often much more recent, and would never have come about at all if the people who initiated them had let rigid style get in their way. Ritual tends toward conservatism, precisely because it is ritual—it follows patterns. During the 1960s and 1970s, countercultural Jews and Christians attacked traditional ritual with a passion, but what they created often became as orthodox and unbending as the orthodoxies that they reformed. In one synagogue I know of, services were moved out of the sanctuary and into an unimposing social hall where people could sit in a circle and play the guitar. After several months of this, someone tried adding a flute, only to be castigated for ignoring the "tradition" of having a guitar singalong.

Ritual requires a reverence for tradition, not a slavish adherence to it. Mordecai Kaplan, the founder of the movement in Judaism called Reconstructionism, once remarked, "Tradition should get a vote, not a veto."

- Closely allied to rigid style is *obligatory* style. Obligatory style sees ritual only as what we have to do out of mere obligation.

Ritual becomes something to get through, to live through, or to rip through (as fast as possible). Christian ritual suffered from obligatory style in the Middle Ages, when the mass was privatized as something that priests or monks did out of obligation, even to the point where lay people were not expected to show up. Churches were built with tiny celllike apertures all around the walls where priests took turns celebrating mass all day.

Pure Obligation?

On New York's Lower East Side, I once encountered a prayer service in the middle of a dilapidated Jewish bookstore. I had been hunting for books for several hours, when, just before dark, people started arriving one by one. Since the store had been empty but for myself all afternoon, I wondered why there was a sudden crowd, especially since several of the newcomers were just leaning against the wall with no apparent interest in buying anything at all. The store turned out to be the local haunt for the Orthodox men who worked in the area—a convenient get-together for *Minchah* and *Ma'ariv*, the requisite late afternoon and early evening prayers. It quickly became clear that people were there out of sheer obligation. They mumbled rapidly through the service, and one of the men did so while continuing to read the book he had taken off the shelf. The owner of the store actually said his prayers while adding up the price of my books and announcing between lines of prayer what the cost of each book was and how much I finally owed him.

None of these styles—minimalist, rigid, or obligatory—is inherently evil. In appropriate measure, they are desirable. Ritual should not take the place of ethics. Proper regard for the past is commendable. I especially want to say that the discipline of taking obligatory worship seriously is praiseworthy. By no means do I wish to convert religious obligation into optional theater. I use the model of theater and the analogy of art throughout this book only to insist that even when public prayer is necessary, even when its rules make demands on us, it is still possible to infuse necessity with meaning. In the Jewish-Christian tradition, the mandatory nature of public prayer was laid down first by Rabbis who insisted also on being inwardly attentive to prayer, as well as to performing commandments in a beautiful way. The first of these two "corrections" to acting out of pure necessity (inward attentiveness) is equal to the modern insistence on spirituality; the second (beautiful performance) is the aesthetic sense that goes into a good play or work of art. For Jews and Christians, public prayer is indeed a requirement. But it ought also to be seen as an art that is filled with spiritual significance, not as the rote reiteration of an act that has little meaning for those doing it. Dismissing ritual as insignificant, venerating worship as beyond our power to change, or treating prayer as *only* obligatory robs us of the chance to make religious services come alive with all that they can do for us. And there is much that they can do.

Handling Doubters: Why Bother with Religious Ritual?

I do not think that most people would dispute the existence of ritual in general. PTA meetings, the annual Little League opening, putting the kids to bed, making love—everything from the most ordinary to the most sublime may be programmed as a ritual in which what each participant does is determined by a script and everyone is an actor. We play out our roles hoping for the moment that signals success, now in a supreme shout for joy, now in a quiet good-night kiss, now in a satisfied nod. Ritual moments are real things that we have experienced regularly. So most people would not, I think, question the general scheme I have provided.

But oddly enough, people often do question applying that scheme to religion. They recognize the ritual moment when the object of activity is physically present—as when a person is buried, or a bride and groom are married, for example. They came to take part in a funeral or wedding, and that is what they got. But, they argue, why mistake that for religion? Isn't religious ritual just primitive nonsense? Imagine the priest worrying about holding his hands just like that! Why is the choir dressed so formally? Why spend hours reciting empty words and singing stupid songs? These are conceded to be ritual, but *dead* ritual. At a regular worship service, no one gets married and no one gets buried, so why bother?

To the question, "Why bother?" every religion has its own answer. Theologians work out theological justifications that explain why we should bother. But theologians don't always get through to the real doubters. Theologians experience God, so they may argue that rituals make sense simply because God wants them. If the doubters had experienced God, however, they would have had no plaguing doubt to begin with.

The problem is that doubters lack the experience necessary to make sense out of any theological retort; they cannot see the ritual as anything but empty words and gestures going nowhere. It looks to them like vestiges of a piety that may once have characterized medievals, but surely should be uprooted in the space age. These critics may dabble in religion. They don't dismiss it altogether. They usually want some religious upbringing for their children, for example, and even for themselves. When it comes to lifecycle celebration, they are apt to prefer a religious way of marking it. They may even attend church or synagogue, at least on important days like Easter Sunday or Yom Kippur. But the worship that they find there reminds them all over again that regular religious ritual is anachronistic and empty. To make matters worse, they stand in judgment of their ancestors, assuming either that the ritual made equally little sense for them, or that times have changed so much that the kind of sense it did make is irrelevant to conditions today.

This last point deserves closer attention. Most people wonder casually how it is that a given prayer came into existence. And if we extend our imagination, picturing a community of individuals in a given time and place praying that prayer, we might even inquire what they were thinking about while they were praying. Put another way, we wonder how worship rituals developed and what people saw in them before they lost their fullness of significance.

The answer to the first question ("How did the ritual begin?") is often available from scholarly analysis of our traditional texts. The Jewish practice of breaking a glass at weddings, for example, probably emerged in France about the eleventh century; it was practiced by a relatively wealthy class of merchants who often made their living marketing wine that they produced from their own vineyards.

The second question ("What did the ritual mean?") is more challenging. When those Jewish merchants broke a glass, what did they see in that act? It seems patently ridiculous to say that they saw nothing in it, so thoughtful doubters must come up with a rationale that makes sense for the initial ritual celebrants but not for modern skeptics. There are two kinds of answers that satisfy this requirement, and both have had their day in court. They can be encountered regularly in both scholarly and popular accounts of religious ritual.

The first response assumes that people were really religious once upon a time: They broke the glass as a symbol of the destruction of the Temple in Jerusalem, and they believed that God would someday rebuild it and return them to Zion. But to many people, the days when you could believe such things have been put to rest by science. We may bemoan this loss of naiveté, but innocence once abandoned cannot be retrieved. So our forebears are now "exposed" as simpleminded but well-meaning folk who did the best they could to tackle a difficult existence. To do this, they developed a simplistic religious faith that had equally simplistic rituals.

The second response stops short of impugning the wisdom and maturity of ages past. Plato, after all, believed in ritual. So did Aristotle. Many of the greatest champions of religious observance turn out to be brilliant philosophers and theoreticians. Sir Isaac Newton believed he was unraveling the mind of God. So, the skeptics argue, earlier geniuses may have been motivated by extraneous reasoning having nothing to do with religion. Maybe rituals came about because religious leaders wanted to polemicize against heretics or to extract profit from (or reinforce power over) the masses. Maybe the sacrificial cult in Jerusalem was really designed to line the pockets of the priests who lived off the donations and sacrifices. To be sure, explanations like this one may be correct, but the evidence for their validity is usually slim or nonexistent. Their truth or falsity is less significant than their function in maintaining the fiction that our forebears participated in religious ritual without actually being religious.

Sometimes that reductionist explanation fails, however, and we are left with evidence of a highly esteemed religious leader, a man or a woman of monumental intelligence, taking part in a ritual and attaining what I call the *ritual moment*. Now another prong of the attack is launched. Such an individual is labeled a "mystic" and assumed to be beyond the pale of rationality and ordinary behavior. Once again the skeptics are saved: They admit that our forebears appreciated religious ritual, but only because they were "uniquely gifted," which is a euphemistic way of saying they were somewhat demented.

We ritualize our activities to express their significance; we do so religiously to express religious significance. If religious ritual is empty, if the words sound hollow and the actions seem comic, many possible causes come to mind. But none of these has to cast aspersion on religious ritual per se. The problem, if there is one, lies in the complex conditions of modern existence, which make religious ritual harder to observe and the religious moment harder to recognize than happens, say, with politics, sports, or family life.

Now it must be admitted that if people today say that religious ritual is empty, then for them it *is* empty. But it does not follow that it was empty in ages past. Nor is there any evidence that Greek philosophers or medieval scholastics were less intelligent than we are; or that a Machiavellian mind burrowing in the background of religious history cleverly derived ritual from politics or economics; or that mentally competent religious people of the past must have been virtual lunatics. The truth is that whatever people once saw or now see in *religious* ritual must be compatible with what people see in ritual *in general*.

Religious rituals can still speak to people. Among other things, they can heal our aching souls, provide us with celebration, create closure on our past, and move us to live meaningful lives. Religious moments are as vital now as they have ever been.

## Ritual Check List 	⊛

Words and Concepts You Should Know

- **Ritual shapes time.** It arranges our life into packages of moments that matter.

- **"Ritualizations" are empty; "ritual" is not.** Ritual is neither good nor bad, advanced nor primitive. It is human through and through. It can remind us of our humanity, and move us to act humanely.

- **Ritual culminates in ritual moments** that provide the satisfaction of closure and allow us to move on to another activity with a greater sense that life matters.

- **Culminating ritual moments vary in emotional tone.** They may be happy, sad, poignant, cathartic, or just inwardly satisfying. They may be experienced privately or demonstrated publicly.

- **Ritual scripts may be inherited or newly created.** They may be open or closed.

- **Style matters.** Minimalist, rigid, and obligatory worship styles can impede ritual satisfaction.

- **Jews and Christians treat public prayer as a necessity, not an option.** Viewing it as an obligation does not mean that it is meaningless or must be poorly done. Seeing it also as an art—a sacred drama, in particular—allows us to apply considerations of artistry to it, and thereby to do it better.

## Conversation Points for Making Worship Work 	⊛

1 ▪ Is your script open or closed? What do you absolutely require? What can you change? To answer these questions, consider the following story.

The Sacred Cat

Once upon a time, there was a guru in the mountains of Asia who gathered around him a band of monks dedicated to prayer. The guru owned a cat, which he loved deeply. He took the cat with him everywhere, even to morning prayer. When the disciples complained that the cat's prowling distracted them, the guru bought a leash and tied the cat to a post at the entrance to the prayer room. Years later, when the guru died, his disciples continued to care for the cat. But, as they say, cats have nine lives, so the cat outlived even the disciples. By then the disciples had their own disciples, who began caring for the cat, but without recalling anymore why the cat was present during prayer. When the cat's leash wore out, they knitted another one in the sacred colors of the sky and the earth; and when the post wore down, they built a beautiful new one that they began calling the sacred cat stand. During this third generation of disciples, the cat died, and the disciples wasted no time in buying another sacred cat to accompany them in prayer. Their worship was eventually expanded to include the sacred actions of tying the cat to the leash and affixing the leash to the sacred cat stand.

What we assume to be necessary in our worship may just be cats, leashes, and cat stands—encumbrances that grew up once upon a time but could just as easily be gotten rid of.

Look at your worship and decide: What is really necessary and what is mere cats.

2 ▪ What is your congregation's style of worship? Does it get in the way? Most congregations listen to the people with the loudest voices. Who determines what your congregation's style is, and who never gets listened to? If you could adopt any style of worship at all, and if you could give it a name, what would it be?

two

Lost Symbols

The most important characteristic of ritualized time is that the people who participate in the ritual give time its meaning. The people who go out for lunch every day know when things happen according to schedule and when they do not. They develop signals that let everyone know what stage of the ritual they have reached and what to do next. Individual moments of time now cease being equal in importance because of the cues that mark them off from one another. Some of these cues are signs and others are symbols.

Symbolism has been studied by philosophers, literary critics, logicians, and social scientists. By and large, they agree on the existence of symbols, but on no single definition of what a symbol is or how it functions. For our purposes, we can adopt the relatively simple understanding of C. G. Jung, whose concept of symbol is easily grasped. He came across it by a simple psychological experiment: an association test. Jung would say certain words or point to certain shapes or designs and ask people to say whatever came to mind. He didn't much care what they said, however; rather, he was interested in the timing of their responses. When people hesitated before responding or seemed ambivalent about what they were about to say, he assumed that there was some deep-seated resistance to the word or shape in question. Words and shapes that elicit easy responses because their meaning does not go deep inside the human psyche are mere *signs*. *Symbols* are words, objects, or acts of behavior that suggest some deeper level of meaning.

Jung went farther than I am prepared to go, by trying to identify what symbols point to. He thought they indicated deep-seated universal human complexes called archetypes. For instance, the squared circle (a circle inside a square, used by medieval alchemists) and the Christian cross (which points to all four compass points) were said to be forms of a more general symbol called the mandala, which symbolizes wholeness. As attractive as that suggestion may be, other symbols, which Jung believed were equally universal, are less appealing and more dubious. For example, the labyrinth where mythical heroes get lost on their way to heroic accomplishment was explained as betraying a man's entanglement with his mother, and his escape was interpreted as freeing himself from the feminine side of his character so that he could relate positively to women. Jung attributed the immediacy of all symbolic suggestion to the archetypes' universality, which made every human being share an innate awareness of them.

Jung was right to say that certain things evoke especially deep responses in us, and that these are the things that we should call symbols. He was wrong in thinking that the deep response is due to the universal psychological conditioning of every human being. Symbols do not necessarily point to universal archetypes. Instead, members of any society or culture share certain values or experiences that they see reflected in the symbol.

A true symbol (unlike a sign) has the following qualities:

- *It evokes its response automatically.* If people feel constrained to explain what a thing symbolizes, then that thing is not a symbol, but a sign.

- *Verbal description of a symbol's significance is by definition superfluous and inadequate.* When, for example, Reform Jews say (in their Friday night liturgy), "Light is the symbol of the Divine," or "Light is the symbol of Israel's mission," they use the word "symbol" loosely. If light really symbolized either entity, we would not have to say so, and to the extent that the Divine and Israel's mission are part of what light suggests, they do not exhaust its symbolic content.

- *In a ritual that deals with group experience, the symbol's significance must be shared by the members of the group.* A prime indication that various individuals really do constitute a group is their ability to respond similarly to a common symbol. They do not have to agree on the symbol's content, however, since symbolic content is always greater than what people are able to verbalize about it.

  ❋ **A group's ritual symbol is an item that directs its participants immediately and with absolutely no commentary or explanation to an awareness of an experience or value that they hold in common, and to which they are attracted or from which they are repelled, even though they cannot explain or agree on the reason why.**

- *True symbols are immediately apprehended and seem self-evident, so people hold to them with considerable emotional tenacity.* They may disagree about a symbol's meaning, but they will not readily give up their emotional response to the symbol itself.

Once people adopt symbols, they feel that they ought to justify their strong feelings about them by developing explanations in terms of *sign values*. This can happen in two ways.

If the objects to which we are symbolically attached are part of the official religious repertoire of our faith, we can say that they are *official* symbols. That means they have an *official meaning* that "explains" their symbolic appeal. For example, Christians explain the appeal of the cross as their favorite symbol by saying, "Jesus died on the cross"; similarly, Jews explain their strong attachment to the Torah scroll by saying, "The Torah was given at Sinai." Both "Jesus died on the cross" and "The Torah was given on Sinai" are official interpretations of the cross and the Torah. Both cross and Torah are symbols; but the explanations are only sign values that the two religions arbitrarily assign to them.

Sometimes, we become attached by chance to things that are not already part of our religion. They just happen to be in the vicinity while we are in the midst of a deeply felt emotional experience. In such cases, the symbolic objects have no public theological association at all; they are *incidental* symbols—that is, they were there that one time, by accident, and came to be associated with the event in question. Incidental symbols are held by individuals, not groups, since they depend on personal experience. But to individuals who hold them, incidental symbols are as real as the public ones that they learn about from their cultural or religious groups. They work the same way: They remind us of the events and experiences that we hold dear. The only difference is that they attract no official interpretations. Thus, for example, I have a papier-mâché sculpture of a bird, sitting on my desk at work. It means a lot to me, not because it has any official religious meaning, but because my daughter made it when she was in elementary school, and I recall the love that passed between us the day she gave it to me.

Symbols can be positive or negative. A prime example of a negative symbol for Jews is the swastika, which automatically evokes recollection of the six million Jews slain by the Nazis. Jews never feel compelled to explain the swastika to each other. Even if they tried, they would not be able to verbalize what it conjures up for them, precisely because what it denotes is symbolic by its very nature. So the swastika fulfills our criteria: Response to it is automatic; verbal description is superfluous; it is shared by the whole community; and Jews react emotionally just by looking at it. Scholars who know the swastika's pre-Nazi history may explain that it was used by ancient cultures for purposes entirely remote from the Nazi context. But such logic is irrelevant to Jews, for whom the swastika symbolizes what mere words cannot begin to approach.

For most Americans, the national flag is a positive symbol. It conjures up the freedoms of American citizenship and the pride we feel in living in a free country. We may have warm memories also of carrying flags for parades through Main Street on Fourth of July celebrations. The media regularly bombard us with images of the flag along with moving music, like *America the Beautiful*. Sporting events begin with salutes to the flag, and the flag appears more frequently than any other image on the postage stamps we use. As the most available positive national symbol, the flag became the focus of debate during the Vietnam War years. It became common for students bent on civil disobedience to trample on the flag or sometimes even to burn it. Predictably, their more conservative elders denounced their flag burning as a criminal act. Fights broke out between police and demonstrators over the way the flag was treated. We almost passed a constitutional amendment to protect the flag from desecration.

Rituals are full of symbolic items whose symbolism is, by definition, never fully explained, since as soon as we feel we have fully captured their meaning in words, we can be sure they are no longer symbols. The only means of identifying whether a term has symbolic force is to scrutinize how ritual participants react to it.

Any number of things may be symbols, but we are usually aware only of the strong feelings we have about them. So debates over symbols usually revert to irrational arguments, with neither party to the debate understanding the depth of the other's emotional commitment.

Symbols and "Sign-ificance": What Do Symbols Symbolize? ❀

If symbols do not actually point to universal archetypes (as Jung imagined), what exactly do they symbolize? And why do we find it so hard to explain that meaning to others? For the first question, we might consult a popular account of religious symbolism. I read, for example, that there are different types of crosses, each with its own significance. The cross that we usually see in North American churches is a Latin cross. An alternative shape is the Ansate cross, in which the top of the cross forms a loop. This, we are told, is an ancient Egyptian symbol denoting life. It was taken over into Christianity and used on Christmas to denote life made possible with the birth of Christ. Shall we say, then, that because the Ansate cross is a symbol of life, Christians who attend church for Christmas immediately recognize in it the promise of life everlasting?

Alternatively, I read that particular flowers have their own symbolic significance. The myrtle, for example, which symbolizes peace and love, is used in wedding bouquets. Does that mean that the people attending a wedding ceremony see the myrtle and, recognizing its symbolism, find their hearts turning to love?

Or take a more common example: holly. Since people hang it up as a Christmas decoration, we would imagine that it symbolizes Christmas somehow. Actually though, our handbook on Christian symbolism tells us that because of its thorns and red berries, holly represents Christ's Passion. The thorns are his crown of thorns and the berries are the blood that he shed upon the cross. Is holly, therefore, a symbol of Jesus' death rather than his birth? When Christians hang holly at Christmas, should we correct their "error" and have them take it down until Easter? Do we let them continue their practice and theologize that, for example, Christmas and Easter are so closely related that a symbol of Christ's resurrection is permissible or desirable even at the feast celebrating his birth? Or should we decide that, regardless of its prickly thorns and red berries, holly symbolizes Christmas, simply because that is when people use it? Our book on Christian symbols may define accurately how holly is used in Christian art, or what church authorities have seen fit to find in holly. But in terms of a behavioral cue in ordering a ritual and achieving the ritual moment, holly is linked to Christmas and has nothing whatsoever to do with the scholarly or artistic use of the plant.

Finally, to take an example from Jewish symbolism, I was once asked for the symbolism behind the six-pointed Jewish star (the Star of David, as it is called; in Hebrew, the *Magen David*).

Why Jewish Stars Have Six Points

How happy I was that beautiful morning in May when the president of my student pulpit asked me for the story behind the six-pointed Star of David. Having just finished reading a scholarly monograph on that very subject, I launched a copious explanation of when Jews first started using the star, how they used it, and so on. I told her that Muslims had used it too, and called it the Star of Solomon; that Jews began putting it on their tombstones in the High Middle Ages; that it was taken over by mystics in the sixteenth century; and that in modern times, it was chiseled on synagogue walls, primarily because its straight-line design made it easy for stone masons to work with. Churches had crosses; synagogues had stars.

The woman who asked the question was impatient with me and quickly shrugged off everything I had to say. "Rabbi," she retorted, "the Star of David symbolizes the Jewish People. It has six points, you see, so no matter how you stand it up, it will always have two points on which to balance. From such a firm base, it cannot be toppled. Just so, we Jews are firmly entrenched, no matter what history brings us."

Who was right, the woman or the scholar? Recalling the distinction between symbol and sign, we should ask if the cross, myrtle, holly, and Star of David are really symbols or just signs. When scholars assign them meanings, they are discussing them as signs. Their official sign meanings are simply what an elite group of experts has agreed to recognize in them. When most of us look at a painting from the twelfth century, say, we can barely tell the difference between the various plants and animals displayed there. The expert, though, recognizes each one as a particular entity chosen deliberately by the painter to represent something special. Holly brings to mind the Passion, while myrtle evokes thoughts of love. But these are not yet symbols, since the link between holly and blood and thorns is merely an arbitrary convention passed on culturally from one generation to the next and learned as a matter of rote by a minority of the faithful. Having read the handbook of symbols, I too can now spot holly in medieval art or in contemporary homes, and even though my aesthetic appreciation of the artist's handiwork is increased, I feel no sense of the kind of immediate personal significance that accompanies symbols. I don't care very much about what holly is supposed to represent. At best I am now able to say what the experts say it stands for.

Imagine, however, a Christian for whom Christ's Passion is of such constant importance that it informs every moment of that person's life.

Justin and Christine

Justin was raised in Europe. He came from a pious and learned Roman Catholic family of the old school. He almost became a priest, but studied art instead, believing that the goal of the visual arts is to inculcate spiritual truths in the faithful. Early on, therefore, he internalized the symbolic significance of holly, and now, many decades later, Justin never sees holly without being reminded of the central religious mystery that guides his every step. No one dares disagree with him when he explains the history of holly in Christian art. For him, holly is indeed a symbol, and he speaks the truth when he tells us that historically, holly has been used to symbolize the Passion.

Christine is much younger, a modern Catholic raised in Baltimore. She decorates her home with holly every Christmas. Like most Catholics today, she knows nothing of the history of holly. It has never even occurred to her that holly might mean something artistically. She just knows that her parents used holly every Christmas, and so does she. She never fails to see it without warm memories of Christmas flooding her mind. As with mistletoe and Christmas trees, it wouldn't be Christmas without it.

Our two Christians met at Christmas, and Justin asked Christine why she hung holly at Christmas. As the conversation developed, Christine discovered that holly stands for the Passion and belongs, correctly speaking, to Easter, not Christmas.

He quoted chapter and verse to prove his point, while Christine knew only what her parents used to do, and that they didn't know a whole lot anyway. Nevertheless, the possibility that her parents might be wrong was irrelevant. When Justin practically insisted that Christine remove the holly until Easter, he forced her into an untenable position. Rationally, Christine was prepared to admit that Justin might be right. But deep inside, Christine felt that Christmas would not be Christmas without holly, regardless of doctrine, theory, and catechism.

The problem is that from Christine's perspective, Justin was right in terms of *sign* and her parents were right in terms of *symbol*. The significance—"sign-ificance"—of the holly may well be what Justin told her. But nobody changes behavior because of "sign-ificance"! And what is symbol to one person (Justin) is sign to another (Christine).

These two points need some elaboration. First, no one changes behavior because of a mere sign. Every advertising executive knows this. For the purposes of marketing, a sign is the surface content of what appears on billboards. But we all recognize by now that telling everyone how cigarette smoking causes cancer does not by itself lead people to stop smoking. The surgeon general who wants to get this point across will have to hire an advertising agency, which will connect the message with something deeper and more immediate to people's motivation. That is, the message will be associated with something symbolic. Then, and only then, will people change their habits.

Ritual moments are akin to changing habits. Indeed, the ritual moments I am describing really do change people, as devotees of religions have always known. Christians speak of conversionary moments, when a spiritual truth suddenly becomes patently clear. Jews describe moments of *t'shuvah*, literally turning from old and sinful ways and returning to God in true repentance. In Christian worship, the liturgy features a penitential rite early on so that communion can occur only after worshipers are cleansed of sin; and the early synagogue service featured a confession every day, not just in the High Holy Day period. Ritual has always been known to have the potential to change habits for the better.

But rituals do not change people's habits automatically. Presenting worshipers with ritual signs will never open them to an appreciation of the ritual's potential. Only symbols will do that. Ritual signs are the things the experts *tell* you during worship—the words of the prayer book or the sermon, for instance. Maybe they ought to mean a lot, but they rarely do. They are like billboards urging you to stop smoking. They have little impact, even if they are right. Yet religious leaders constantly confront problems in religion as if they were problems in signs. Why don't people come to church? They would, it is said, if only they knew that avoiding communion means courting sin! So we tell them, and still they don't come. Why don't Christians practice Christian charity? They would, we argue, if they only knew the importance of clothing the poor and feeding the hungry. So we preach to them, but they don't become charitable. Why don't Jews come every *Shabbat* to pray? It is a *mitzvah* (divine commandment). So we explain all this, but the sanctuary remains half-empty week after week. Why do children graduate from synagogue religious school with little commitment to religious values and practice? There must be something wrong with our curriculum, we argue. So we move Jewish history from sixth to eighth grade and create a course on symbols (by which we mean signs) that will tell ninth graders the sign-ificance of prayers, synagogue objects, and Jewish art. But children aren't fooled by the mere reshuffling of signs.

❀ **Signs multiplied (more school hours), signs altered (more relevance), and signs redistributed (new curricular order) are still just signs. And nobody changes behavior because of signs.**

The only exception to that general rule is when signs are accompanied by relatively immediate threats of punishment. We do, in fact, slow down if we are speeding when police cars are in sight. And if frightened sufficiently, we may even stop smoking for a while rather than risk contracting cancer. But as the police car fades into the horizon, or as the threat of cancer recedes, we speed up to a dangerous level or light up a cigarette. In the past, when religious societies could enforce their signs with threats of punishment, people followed religious signs. "Go to Church" was the same kind of message as our own "Speed Limit 30." No longer is that the case, at least not in America. We need to rediscover the power of *symbols*, not signs, for they alone have the power to lead people to change their habits; only under the influence of symbols will they want to.

So we return to the second moral of our story about the hypothetical conversation between the Justin and Christine over the meaning of holly. What was symbol to one person was mere sign to the other.

Not Facts but Personal Memories   ✸

If asked what something symbolizes, most people will bow to the authority of the expert. They assume that symbolism, like most other things in our technological society, is the realm of specialists. There ought to be experts in symbols just as there are experts in law (lawyers) or experts in medicine (doctors). If you want to know what symbols are, ask the experts. Justin was such an expert. He had memorized everything the books had to say about holly. But that does not mean that Christine had nothing to say about the matter. Justin (it turns out) was really an expert on signs, not on symbols. Sometimes expert theory is not very useful for what we want to know.

Most expert debate has boiled down to arguments regarding what a given symbol symbolizes. Is holly a symbol for Easter or Christmas? What is the symbolism of Lady Macbeth washing her hands from the crime? What does the number three symbolize? Or the color red? But expert opinion differs on all such points, so we need to know how to decide which expert is right. It would be nice if there were some necessary connection between the symbol and what it symbolizes. When confronted with the symbol (holly) and two or more possible items being symbolized (Christmas or Easter), we would know automatically that only one of the two (Christmas or Easter) is correct. If enough such rules are established, we could theoretically have no difficulty discovering what things symbolize.

Unfortunately, no set of rules has proved self-evidently correct or so convincing that it makes regular converts out of adherents of rival theories. When all is said and done, we know at most some distinguishing features of some symbols. There are those, for example, that seem to share a physical quality of that for which they stand, as red is more apt to symbolize blood and white to symbolize milk. Others are arbitrary, as, for instance, the donkey represents the Democrats and the elephant represents the Republicans. Was Jung right after all, when he claimed that symbols derive from common human archetypes, so that what seems arbitrary to the outsider has careful logic behind it from the psyche's perspective? Is the human mind programmed to dichotomize existence into opposites, for example, so that symbols represent one or another of the opposites or the unification of them both? Do things have their own inherent symbols, or do we determine symbols arbitrarily, even haphazardly? These are the sorts of questions that have filled pages of discussions on symbolism for over a century now. Unfortunately, I see no way of solving any of them, so I find myself returning again and again to the realization that what counts is not a thorough understanding by the experts, but a simple observation of what actually happens when people use the symbols that they most love.

Try the following experiment. Invite a dozen people to a discussion on symbols, telling them that they are each to bring something symbolic from home. Let us imagine the setting is a synagogue, and the things that people bring will be items they identify as Jewish symbols. When the people arrive, each puts his or her symbol on the table, and you now go around the room asking each participant, "What did you bring and why?"

I have conducted this experiment on numerous occasions, and the results don't vary much. The items are normal household ritual objects, like Sabbath candlesticks or the tray used for a Passover Seder. A few people bring nothing, saying that they forgot, or that they didn't know what to choose, or that the only thing they might have selected is immovable or unavailable, but that they will describe it. Some people bring items that could never have been predicted.

The conversation almost always begins on the level of sign. "I brought these candlesticks," says one woman "because they symbolize the Divine. Isn't that what we say each Friday night in services?" A neighbor who also brought candlesticks responds, "I thought that light symbolized creation." The two people now discuss the relative merits of light's presumed symbolism, but neither really cares what the "right" answer is. Their discussion is purely academic. I now ask the first woman who brought the candlesticks, "If light symbolized creation rather than the Divine, would you still have brought candlesticks?" Her reply invariably is affirmative. Her argument about light's meaning, as well as her neighbor's argument, was rooted in the fact that they happened to have learned, somewhere in their education, to parrot back different explanations of light that existed as readily available *official meanings;* neither person had ever stopped to consider whether what she learned was correct. And now each is perfectly willing to entertain the notion that another symbolic value is the correct one. If, at the end of the discussion, the first woman has been convinced that light symbolizes creation, not the Divine (as she first thought), she will still bring her candlesticks as her favorite symbol. The reason is that she has not given up their symbolic importance at all. She has simply substituted one *sign* (creation) for another (the Divine), and predictably, she does not change behavior (bringing candlesticks) because of a change in signs.

Apparently, the candlesticks were brought regardless of what they stood for, because the woman says she would have brought them even if they stood for something else. So we ask again, "Why did you bring them?" Eventually the woman answers in personal terms. Her mother gave them to her. Or she recalls, fondly, sitting as a child at the *Shabbat* table with the candles glowing. Or she was a war orphan, and she came to America with nothing that belonged to her parents but this single set of candlesticks, which she swore to cherish.

 Symbolism always evokes personal memories of something. It is precisely because symbols are so personally relevant that we insist on asking what they mean, as if anything that evokes such emotion from us must have some grand religious or cosmic meaning beyond ourselves.

The candlestick must mean something, it seems to us, so when by chance we read one night in the liturgy that light is the symbol of the Divine, we readily accept that interpretation as the true meaning of our symbol. "So that's what it symbolizes," we say to ourselves. "That explains its attraction." There is, however, nothing inherent in light that makes it a necessary symbol for the Divine. It may remind us of God, but only if we work at making that connection.

Symbol generally comes before sign; sign is the intellectual rationale for symbol.

Symbols turn out to be crucial for all of our ritual moments. Every ritual has them.

Harry's Ashtray

Though he didn't know it was a ritual, Harry had been a member of a lunch ritual nonetheless. He used to own a furniture store in New York, and every day for years, he and some friends who operated other stores nearby would go to their favorite haunt for lunch. They would sit at the same table and have the same waiter wait on them. They always ordered the same thing, even joked around in the same way with the waiter, who got used to their jibes about the old-fashioned restaurant, and gave as good as he got.

Then the restaurant was sold to a new owner who decided to capitalize on the fact that the old part of town was being gentrified. He changed the menu to *nouvelle cuisine*, replaced the round tables with smaller, square ones, altered the decor, and warned the waiter not to waste so much time talking with the customers. By the time the final renovations had been finished, however, Harry had decided to retire anyway. He sold his store, bid the boys (as he called his lunchtime friends) a last good-bye, and moved to Florida.

If you visit him in his condominium there, you will see an old and battered ashtray sitting on his desk. But Harry doesn't smoke; he never has. Just before he moved south, his friends met him one last time at the restaurant, and on the way out the door, he took the ashtray as a visible reminder of his years of friendship with the lunch crowd. If asked about the ashtray, he will smile sheepishly and explain all about the lunch moment.

A major difference between lunch and religion is that lunch makes no claims of absolute sign-ificance; it develops no sacred narratives and no theologians. Merely an *incidental* symbol, the ashtray will not be singled out by later interpreters and given meaning in terms of sign. No one will think to call it a symbol of the Divine, of creation, of salvation, or of anything at all. It remains just an item of accidental symbolic sign-ificance to the few members of the lunch group, and serves as a reminder of their good times together.

How Symbols Really Work 🔅

Now we can see how symbolism really works, how, that is, the body of knowledge that we call symbols is applied in real life. People develop meaningful relationships with other people and play out these relationships in ritualized blocks of time, punctuated by verbal or nonverbal cues for behavior. These otherwise meaningless entities that punctuate ritual space—the menu at lunch, the special chair for the nursing mother, the holly over the fireplace, the candlesticks at Sabbath eve—become personally significant and come to be reminiscent of the ritual moment around which the ritual revolved.

> ❋ **Symbols do not really symbolize anything. They just symbolize. Only our insistence on linking everything up with signs, as if symbols must always refer to something ritually significant (creation, the Divine, the Passion, love, and so on), prevents us from seeing symbols as they really are. Symbols are otherwise meaningless words, gestures, or things endowed with great personal significance because they have accompanied ritual moments that are important to us.**

In the case of the lunch group, the symbols will remain just that. In the case of organized religion, or, for that matter, any other institution that has developed its notions of specialized items (the gavel for debating societies, or trophies for athletic clubs), symbolic objects will be invested also with "sign-ificance," that is, with sign importance. Children who are exposed to the ritual will probably select one of its ritual objects as their symbol and will then be told its sign importance. But maybe not. In the experiment I mentioned earlier, one man brought some gold cuff links as his symbol of Judaism, explaining that his grandfather had given them to him at his bar mitzvah. Since cuff links have no a priori religious sign importance, he was never told that the cuff links meant anything other than what they were, a gift from a treasured grandfather at an emotional occasion. Had he chosen a ritual object that already had sign importance in the Jewish cultural repertoire—the prayer book, for example—someone would have told him what its sign importance was, and he would have grown up thinking, "Prayer books symbolize talking to God," instead of the much truer explanation: "Prayer books symbolize; that is, they awaken in me fond memories of a ritual moment. In terms of their sign value ("sign-ificance") however, prayer books signify talking to God." This truer axiom could then produce the following corollary: "Even if I stop believing in talking to God—even if, that is, the sign value loses importance for me—the symbolic value of prayer books will remain the same."

We are now in a position to understand why people cannot explain their depth of emotion regarding symbols. When they are asked for an explanation, they revert to a discussion of signs. Suppose this man who loved prayer books remains convinced that prayer books do mean talking to God. He then meets a woman who meditates, and who suggests that worship services be altered to exclude the prayer book entirely, as meditation is far more successful in that nothing gets in the way. The man will react with predictable hostility at the prospect of his prayer book being taken away from him. When challenged, the two debaters discuss the altogether irrelevant issue of whether prayer should consist principally of talking to God or whether it should be the opportunity for free-flowing meditation, and the presumed connection between those two "rival" activities and a prayer book. They are like Justin and Christine discussing holly. They too differed on the symbolism of an object but could come to no agreement as long as they limited their discussion to sign values, Christmas versus Easter. It would have been much better if Christine had announced that, having grown up with holly in her house every Christmas, she was unable to bear the thought of doing without it at that time of the year; and likewise, let the lover of prayer books say that he recalls the joy of holding his own book during children's services when he was young. That kind of argument cannot be lost, since no one can deny another's experience. But if Christine is drawn into an argument over the sign value of holly, Justin (the scholar) may prove she is wrong; just as the meditation expert may demonstrate with eminent clarity that prayer books get in the way. But the woman will not let go of her holly, nor the man his prayer book. They cannot explain their stubbornness, since apparently they are being unreasonable, having lost the argument of signs. Let them know, however, that the sign value was never the issue.

❈ Sign value, or "sign-ificance," is only the prop for symbol value or symbolism, and it is symbolism that we humans cannot allow to come crashing down. Once symbolism goes, all our recollections of ritual moments go too; and without ritual moments all time is leveled to meaninglessness. That we cannot bear.

Symbols Evoke Memories of Moments ❈

We now see that the problem underlying most symbol theories is that their proponents insist on asking, "What does a symbol symbolize?" They expect the answer that it symbolizes some particular object and they look for necessary relationships between the symbol and the object. But there is no object! The answer to the question, "What does a symbol symbolize?" is simply, "It symbolizes." It evokes memories of moments.

Since behavior depends on symbols, not on signs, our most critical challenge is helping people relate to sacred objects in a symbolic way. People must come into contact with sacred objects in positively experienced situations that culminate in ritual moments. Those ritual moments must be memorable. If they are marked by sheer boredom, we can be sure that people will be indifferent to what religious traditions hold dear. And if they are experienced negatively, the items that they feature may even become negative symbols, evoking only bad memories. I do not mean extreme cases only, like the swastika (for Jews) or burning crosses and white hoods (for African-Americans). I mean the thousands of men and women who feel uncomfortable in churches or synagogues because these remind them of unsatisfactory childhood experiences. The task for those who wish to facilitate religious moments is to be sure that children in their formative years identify positively with their religious experiences and to multiply the positive experiences that occur in religious environments.

Alas, that almost never happens today. Most religious schools deal, at best, in signs. Children generally forget signs, but even if they learn them, they rarely invest themselves emotionally in them. The signs do not become symbols. How can they become symbols as long as we isolate the learning experience from symbol-producing ritual moments? To take but one example: If we consistently separate little children from their parents at times of prayer—as I see some churches and synagogues do— the children may learn by rote the rules of how to function as

> We should reshape religious education to deal with symbols, not signs.

worshipers, but they will never achieve the warmth that comes from being with their parents at sacred times. If their highest emotional peaks are reached while watching a parade with mom and dad or riding a bike with other kids, then parades and bike riding will become symbols of ritual moments—as the menu was to the lunch crowd, or as Harry's ashtray was to Harry.

A second challenge is the lost generation of the adults, not the children. These are the adults who have already been raised on religious school curricula of signs, not symbols. Having experienced symbols only elsewhere, they look for ritual moments in anything but religion: jogging with friends, watching the ball game, celebrating New Year's Eve, going bowling, attending cocktail parties, joining committees, psychotherapy—any of these may be ritually programmed with endless care to provide symbolic depth and the experience of ritual moments.

> If we want religion to compete, we need emotionally satisfying experiences within religious environments. Only then will religious, rather than secular, symbols become part of people's lives; only then will people return to religious rituals for the satisfaction that comes from ritual moments; and only then will they really want to know the accepted religious sign value ("sign-ificance") of their symbols, and discover also what intellectual depth religion carries.

In sum, symbols do not symbolize anything; they just symbolize. They remind us of ritual moments in which we have invested intense emotion at one time or another. Though we share symbols, we may differ on the sign value attached to them without doubting the supreme importance of their common symbolic significance. Using these shared symbols, we can take time that is utterly meaningless in itself and program its flow on the ritual graph until the ritual moment is attained. Without shared symbols we can do no more than force or embarrass people to go through the motions. The result is depressing, as most clergy can tell you. Most worship services assemble people who share practically *no* symbols (though they may have been taught some signs) and have nearly no emotional investment in what transpires. Clergy are symbolically aware. They see things as supremely important that non-clerical worshipers find boring. The worshipers will leave church or synagogue without comprehending that a religious moment has passed.

Ritual Check List　◉

Words and Concepts You Should Know

- **A thing is a symbol if:**
  It evokes its response automatically.
  Verbal description of its sign-ificance is superfluous and inadequate.
  People feel strongly about it, regardless of what it means.
- **Some symbols are *official*; others are *incidental*.** Official symbols attract theological explanations that serve as their sign value (their "sign-ificance"). Sign is the intellectual rationale for symbol.
- **Rituals are full of symbols** that, by definition, are never fully explained, because if we can capture their meaning in words, they are no longer symbols.

- **Signs multiplied** (more school hours), signs altered (more relevance), and signs redistributed (new curricular order) are still just signs. Nobody changes behavior because of signs.

- **Symbols do not symbolize anything.** They just symbolize. They are words, gestures, or things that we endow with great personal significance because they have accompanied ritual moments that are important to us.

- **Religious education should be reshaped** to deal with symbols, not signs.

- **If we provide emotionally satisfying experiences** within religious environments, people will experience religious symbols as positively as they now do secular ones, and they will seek satisfaction in religious ritual. Only then will they care about the sign values of their religious symbols and discover what intellectual depth religion carries.

Conversation Points for Making Worship Work   ❀

1 ▪ Invite a group of people to bring their favorite religious symbols from home, and ask them what each symbolizes. Differentiate sign values from personal anecdotes that explain why people are really so attached to the particular symbol they bring. They may say that they like candlesticks because light has some theological meaning (the sign value). But why do they bring *this particular* set of candlesticks? There is probably a personal story connected to it. Once you hear that story, you will know why *this* set of candlesticks is a symbol, from which they may also generalize to other candlesticks.

2 ▪ Take your group into the room in your church or synagogue where worship normally occurs, and ask people to stand as close as they can to their favorite symbol there. Have everyone explain

their choice. Try to get at the personal stories behind these choices. Recollect the story (from chapter 1) of the sacred cat. For some people, a thing is a symbol about which they feel passionately; for others, who have no such passionate associations, it is just a cat, an item with no special importance. Liturgical "wars" occur when people who think things are only cats come into conflict with the people for whom those same things are symbols.

three

Worship Systems

The Law Firm and the Secretary

A certain law firm has just fired its second secretary in eight months. The firm's history indicates that this year is typical of others. Though old, reputable, and competent, the firm finds that for some reason secretaries are hard to keep. The partners don't know how to explain their constant search for able secretaries: The pay is adequate, benefits are substantial, and no undue demands seem to be placed on whoever holds the position. Yet letters do not get written well, legal briefs are sometimes late, and, in general, no one is satisfied with the clerical department. The firm concludes that the difficulty must have something to do with the sorry state of the work force these days.

The law firm is not unlike a synagogue that complains how hard it is to find good teachers for an eighth-grade Hebrew class that meets for an hour on Sunday mornings. Every year the pattern is the same: Lots of people apply, and on paper, at least, many seem qualified. But when the course gets under way, and the kids finally get to class, not many weeks elapse before parents start complaining about the noticeable absence of learning. By May or June, members of the Sunday school committee find themselves agreeing once again that the new teacher has not done the job. A subcommittee will spend the summer advertising for a new teacher. Résumés will arrive, and the annual Hebrew teacher hunt will be under way. Oddly enough, no one on the committee stops to ponder the sign-ificance of the fact that committee members who grew up in this particular congregation never learned Hebrew here either. The problem is so old that it is entering its second generation. After twenty years or more of hiring and firing teachers, the "right" teacher has yet to come along.

The experience of perennial problems that somehow never get solved is familiar to everyone. Competent people find themselves embroiled in seemingly insoluble difficulties that just will not go away. Public schools, for example, take their educational pulse every so often and decry the fact that "Janie and Johnnie can't read." They change the textbooks or the teaching method or the audiovisual aids or even the teaching staff and discover five years later that the new Janies and Johnnies in their system still can't read. Universities bemoan their graduates who are abysmally ignorant of basic skills and knowledge. So they alter curricula, fire deans, publish new catalogues, and get (alternatively) tough or soft, again to find that the kind of education everyone wants never quite becomes the norm.

What goes wrong? Why can't the law firm get its clerical work done? Why can't the synagogue school teach Hebrew? Why do public schools and universities fail to live up to their own expectations?

More important than asking, "What goes wrong?" is the observation, "Look at how the problem is attacked." In each case, an institution resorts to solutions that have failed before and will fail again. That is, they blame the problem on someone or something. Secretaries are no good; Hebrew teachers can't teach; the reading textbook is outdated; the curriculum is too strict (or too lenient). Those in charge then exchange the designated culprit for another secretary, teacher, book, or curriculum. And when that fails (as of course it always does), they go through the same exercise of identifying and replacing a villain all over again.

✹ The process of finding someone or something to blame is called *scapegoating*. Scapegoating never solves the problem, but it allows the people who make up the institution to avoid locating the real problem, which is so pervasive and so deeply rooted in the institution's life that trying to apply a real solution would prove very painful.

A true solution might mean rethinking basic institutional assumptions or reshuffling essential departmental relations. So it is much easier to imagine that some single entity in the organization is at fault: secretaries, teachers, textbooks, curricula. Perhaps everyone's favorite scapegoat is "the times." People aren't as responsible these days. Kids are too spoiled nowadays. By deciding that "the times" are the problem, people avoid working on the real but painful source of ineffectiveness.

It may seem as if we have strayed far afield from the subject of ritual, but we haven't. Ritual too is often perceived as ineffective and failing. But rather than truly try to solve the problem of the failing ritual, people generally scapegoat someone or something. The alternative, after all, is to reevaluate the very essence of religious life and the very institutional substructure on which religions are built.

Let me take a case in point: congregational singing in Reform Jewish congregations. Reform Judaism was born as a sort of Jewish Reformation in the nineteenth century. For many Jews in western Europe, the dawn of modernity opened up the opportunity to achieve civil rights and to enjoy the normal amenities of citizenship that hitherto had been denied them. Though full equality was not nearly as close as they imagined, these Jews did learn the modes of behavior that normally marked the non-Jewish world, including its religious ritual life. They instituted the reform of traditional rituals, systematically reworking old ceremonies to fit modern sensitivities. That process continued in North America, where Jewish immigrants from Germany attempted to make age-old rituals fit contemporary aesthetics.

One change in ritual they called for was the institution of congregational singing. In traditional Jewish worship, congregational singing had not been unknown. But it differed substantially from the characteristic singing practices that we associate with modern houses of worship, since the old style had been marked by spontaneous singing of folk melodies, entirely in Hebrew (which few understood), and without musical scores or sophisticated musical settings and trained choirs. So by the end of the nineteenth century, American Reform rabbis were anxious to encourage modern congregational singing. Since that seemed tantamount to hymns, they began compiling hymnals, col lecting modern scores, training choirs, and introducing aesthetically acceptable but singable music into the worship ritual.

The primary parties to this long and agonizing process are two Reform organizations: the Central Conference of American Rabbis and the Cantors' Association of America (later renamed the American Conference of Cantors). Both were in their infancy in the 1890s, and as part of their agenda of fostering the success of American Judaism, they felt compelled to encourage modern religious music in the synagogue.

At their annual convention in 1892, the rabbis held an extended debate on the topic, noting that "the Jewish synagogue is indeed sadly in need of Jewish music." In the absence of Jewish music, many congregations had borrowed Christian hymns, particularly from the Methodists. Some rabbis had compiled hymnals containing those offerings they liked best, but no single uniform book was available for all congregations to buy. The "fault," in other words, was declared to be in the non-Jewish music and the lack of uniformity in the extant books. The rabbis recommended that as soon as possible, the cantors compose music for a variety of Jewish prayer texts that individual rabbis would submit; these new hymns would become an official Jewish hymnal.

The cantors, however, were loath to do this. There was no guarantee that the lyrics forwarded by the individual rabbis would ultimately be accepted by the rabbinic body. Without such a guarantee in advance, the cantors were unwilling to proceed with the arduous task of musical composition. But the next year, tired of waiting, the rabbis voted to collect whatever music they could find and to issue that as an interim hymnal. This step prodded the reluctant cantors into composing some new tunes, and a hymnal was finally produced. An introductory volume appeared in 1893, and a definitive hymnal was published in 1897.

Reform congregations should now have been able to sing hymns. Indeed, if sales are any indication of success, success was guaranteed. Even the 1893 volume, which its editors declared had been so hastily produced that it contained "little of permanent value," was (to everyone's surprise) received enthusiastically. By 1911 it was practically a best seller, but again to everyone's surprise, even though most congregants had a copy, almost no one used it.

So the next year yet another discussion was scheduled for the rabbis' convention. A speaker concluded that it was "rather strange" that, in spite of the publication of the hymnal, "in few, if any, of our large congregations do even a minority of those assembled on Sabbaths or Holidays really sing the hymns." He was right. A survey taken the following November revealed "the most surprising result . . . that the hymnal is even less generally used than had been assumed."

This sorry pattern was to be repeated time and time again. In 1930, for example, the rabbis met to figure out how to stimulate congregational singing. In 1932, and again in 1960, new hymnals were produced, but the "full-volumed joyful noise" called for back in 1912 never materialized. Again, people blamed the hymnal, or the kind of music, or the cantors, or the choirs, or anyone and anything they could conveniently scapegoat.

As recently as 1977, the old hymnals were deemed outmoded, and plans made for a new one. That very year, an interim edition with a flashy, inviting cover was published. But almost no one used it. Though a few cantors or musical directors may have looked in it at times to find a particular song, congregational members did not own the hymnal, and temples had no copies in their pews; 90 percent of them probably never even knew that the book existed. So the interim hymnal too managed to do absolutely nothing to encourage communal singing. Undaunted by evidence that 1979 was no different from 1892—new hymnals did not communal singers make—the editorial board that year proceeded on the final edition. In November 1987 the book finally saw the light of day. Its publication was heralded at the biennial convention of Reform synagogue leaders meeting in Chicago. Every single one of the four thousand delegates was given a free copy to take back home, in the hope that the gift would promote mass sales around the country. But the 1987 hymnal was no more successful than the 1897 one had been.

It seems abundantly clear that no new book, no matter how well conceived, will *by itself* solve the problem of getting people to sing their prayers. When we simply declare the hymnal the culprit and change it every so often, we scapegoat the song book; and scapegoating the song-book is no different from scapegoating anything else. It ignores the basic, underlying problem.

In all these instances, we would be better off stopping our futile search for an imaginary culprit responsible for undermining our efforts. No amount of scapegoating will correct what is essentially a much deeper defect going beyond what particular hymnal is in use or what particular Hebrew teacher or secretary is now being employed. The underlying fault does not lie in any one entity in the prayer service, the law firm, or the Sunday school. In each case the culprit is the institution as a whole. Put another way, the problem lies in the very system of things of which it is a part. The problem, then, is *systemic*.

Why Things Don't Work   ◈

The notion of a systemic problem has been around for so long that it is amazing to see how little it is applied to ritual. All that is required is an elementary understanding of systems.

In *The Bourgeois Gentleman*, a famous comedy by Molière, the chief character, Monsieur Jourdain, thinks himself very learned, but actually insists on making a regular fool of himself. When he learns the word "prose," he remarks with absurd self-congratulation, "Imagine, I have been speaking prose all my life, but never knew it!" Similarly, we all know what systems are; we would not get through the average day without dealing with them. We just take them for granted. They are the prose of our daily, routine tasks.

Imagine, for instance, that you take your son to the playground, where he jumps onto one end of a seesaw. On the other end is a much lighter child, so your son finds himself on the ground with no way to get his end of the seesaw into the air. After trying in vain to push himself up, he calls you to help. Now, you could reason that the problem lies with your son, who must be pushed up. This diagnosis would lead you to lift up his end of the seesaw and force the other end down. But only a fool would do that, because it is much harder to lean down and pull up than it is to reach out and push down. It is easier to address the weight inequity by going to the other end (where the lighter child sits perched up high) and pushing that end down.

We do that because we know instinctively that the seesaw is a system, and that what we are dealing with is the relationship between the system's constituent parts (in this case, the light child, the heavy one, and the position of the fulcrum that distributes force). So a malfunction in one of the parts can be solved without ever going near that part.

Choosing where to apply the corrective measure depends on how the parts are related. We would never think to push down on the middle—the fulcrum—for example, since that wouldn't change the relationship between the ends. We must also know what part within the system is most available for adjustment. We could have pulled the heavier child up, but that would have been harder, which is to say, less available to us. The problem, in any case, is the way the parts of the system relate to each other; the problem is with the seesaw and its two inhabitants (seen as a whole), not with the single rider who happens to sit on one of the ends.

The seesaw is a mechanical system, and the relationship between its parts is easier to recognize than in those systems that involve people only. But there are *people systems* too, where the relationship between the parts (the people) is mediated not by an observable mechanical entity, but by less tangible relationships.

A People System

The son of a renowned physicist entered college bent on emulating his father. To everyone's surprise, the son, who did extremely well in high school, could not master science at the college level. The anxious father virtually drove himself crazy trying to help his son, but in vain. At last, deciding that the son must be suffering from some emotional block, the father scheduled the young man for psychiatric counseling. But the psychiatrist insisted on talking to the father too, and eventually convinced the father just to leave the son alone—not even to inquire how he was doing or what he was studying. Amazingly, nothing was prescribed for the perceived problem: the son. Yet, two things happened. The father discovered he could live without having to bear the burden of his son's successful completion of college, and the son, freed from the anxious parent who obviously excelled in the very area that he himself wanted to master, began doing as well as his aptitudes had indicated he would.

This too illustrates a system, one involving an apparently "sick" part (the son), and other parts (like the father) presumed to be "healthy." The psychiatrist recognized the relationship between the parts and knew that, even though the "sick" part was not amenable to corrective measures, a remedy could still be applied to the other part (the father) so that the benefits could extend back to the son. Without recognizing the system, the psychiatrist might have scapegoated the son and had him spend years in therapy, by which time he would have failed school.

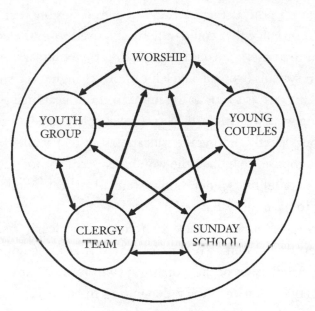

Fig. 3.1. Church or Synagogue System

So let's take a look at the rituals of communal worship from the perspective of systems.

Our *worship system* is a part of a larger system, which we can call the *church* or *synagogue system* (see Fig. 3.1).

Worship is one of several subsystems of this larger whole, the others being such systems as the young couples club, the men's club, the sisterhood, the Sunday school, the clergy team, and so on. Frequently, rituals that go wrong in the worship system can best be handled by doing something to one of these other subsystems of the parent church or synagogue system. (Let's call these subsystems *first-generation systems*). There is input from one system to another, so that, for example, by changing the Sunday school system in certain prescribed ways, we would alter the way children perceive worship, and rituals within the worship context might work more successfully. Similarly, recall a problem mentioned earlier. The synagogue that couldn't teach Hebrew might have found success if it had altered the worship system by including the regular singing of certain Hebrew prayers; people would have learned that participation in the attractive ritual of group singing demanded the Hebrew knowledge that could only be acquired from the educational system. In this case, we would be adjusting the boundary of two first-generation systems (worship and education), changing the worship system in such a way as to adjust the input to the educational system, and thus solving what was originally perceived as solely an educational problem without directly altering the educational system at all.

But suppose we look at the worship system without considering its other, parallel first-generation systems. Like the simple seesaw, it turns out to have subsystems of its own—we'll call them *second-generation systems*—though these are by no means as clearly visible as the first-generation system, worship, of which they are components. In fact, the very division of the worship system into its constituent subsystems may be quite arbitrary, depending in large part on what will be helpful in the end in meeting our long-range goal: understanding how ritual works and creating rituals that satisfy us.

The Individual at Prayer █

We begin with the individuals who make up the system, the people who have come to pray. Each person has a distinct personality, aptitudes, moods, and so on. Moreover, each participant in prayer has come from other systems: their particular families, for example, or their jobs, or neighborhoods. Each of these will have had an effect on what is expected from prayer, and consequently, on how much knowledge or emotional commitment each person can or will invest in the ritual about to occur. The extent of concentration, the appreciation of the music or sermon, the very ability to recognize what the ritual is about and to participate in it—all these are affected by the various systems out of which our worshipers have emerged and in which they participate at other times, perhaps that very day. Each individual, then, can be isolated as a complete *individual-system*.

Before we move on to the second subsystem, however, we must recall the nature of the particular first-generation system of which the individual-system is a part: It is worship. Hence, though we could be interested in anything that makes up each complex individual, the focus of our interest here is not how a person functions, say, at work or in leisure time, but how he or she relates to the act of worship. We don't have to define right now what worship is. That will come later. All we need to say is that, by definition, we have isolated a system called worship, and either our title is meaningless or there must really be something called worship.

Too many people have spent their lives at empty rituals and concluded that they have no need or desire to participate in public prayer. Others may be more positively disposed toward it, they imagine, but their own experience is that when they go to services, worship does not occur. They mouth the prayers, sing the songs, and go through the necessary actions of standing and sitting on cue, but to some extent, the whole thing is a charade. They don't come to pray but to hear the sermon, or to enjoy the company of friends, or to respond to an invitation from a family celebrating a first communion or a bar mitzvah. If they are correct, they are really not part of a worship system, and we would be better off giving the system a name that better expresses what they are doing there.

But there is no reason to assume they are correct.

When people say that they personally do not need to pray, that they cannot pray, or that they have never even experienced public prayer, they are unknowingly scapegoating themselves, mistakenly (though understandably) blaming themselves for a system failure.

To be sure, their past experience in a worship system that has broken down into empty ritualization without ritual moments cannot— and should not—be denied. But it does not follow that these people are congenitally incapable of experiencing ritual in a smoothly functioning ritual system, any more than it follows that people who have never gone to a good art gallery would not appreciate art if they were given the chance to see it. Of course, if they have been led to think that tiny magazine reproductions, which they *have* seen, are what you get in art galleries, they will surely claim that art is of no interest to them. But here too they would be scapegoating themselves. The problem lies not with them but with the "art system," which has led them to identify non-art as art.

The situation with people who say they cannot pray is identical. Substitute "church or synagogue" for "art gallery," and we find people who have experienced empty ritualization (= non-art) instead of ritual (= art). Mistaking ritualization for ritual, they conclude that religious ritual is meaningless. Since, however, they hear that other people appreciate religion, they blame their incapacity to respond to prayer on themselves.

> ◉ But if the word "worship" is to have any semantic reality at all, it must correspond to some genuine human experience. There is no reason to assume that the ability to pray is not as general a human aspiration as the desire to eat, talk, or play. A need to worship is common to everyone, though that need may rarely—or even never— have been met.

To be absolutely clear about what we mean by worship, we have to say something about God. We need not to get bogged down in theological debates, but it seems pretty clear that when Jews and Christians speak of worship, they have in mind some kind of communication with (or apprehension of) God. When we say that the individual worshiper has a need to worship, we mean that a man or woman in prayer must be able to encounter God; then to recognize the divine encounter for what it is; and, finally, to learn to express that encounter in communication, verbal or otherwise. Later (chapter 5) we shall see that one of the causes for the breakdown in worship is a misunderstanding regarding the appropriate metaphor to express the divine-human encounter in our time, and a consequent failure to recognize that encounter, even when it occurs. Rather than fumble for the right words now, let it just be said that I have no intention of avoiding what most people consider the real issue of worship: the presence of God. A later chapter will be devoted to it.

There are other individual needs too, certainly: the need to socialize, or to receive communal recognition, for example; and they too may be met in the worship setting. But they may also be met elsewhere. What we are interested in here is what makes public prayer different from football rallies, study groups, and family reunions. Worship enables people to encounter God. So for worship to be worship, the individual need requiring discussion is precisely what the title of the system says: worship.

The Worshiping Group ✸

✸ **When people come together in public prayer, they are transformed from individuals into a worshiping community that constitutes its own system. If the individual-system is the domain of the psychologist, the *group system* is the realm of the sociologist.**

The worshiping group exists only because individuals make it up; if the individuals didn't come, there would be no group. But precisely because the individuals depend on the group to meet whatever individual needs they have, there arise certain group needs too. If, for example, the group possesses no common language, individuals will be unable to communicate; if it has no structure, people won't know what they should be doing. In either case, the group will not satisfy the needs of its members, who will stop coming, and the group will disband.

When we were talking about the needs of individuals, we distinguished worship from other activities that people enjoy. This led us to identify the recognition of a divine-human encounter as the particular need most pertinent to worship. Here, too, as we discuss our worship group, we should ask how a group meeting for worship differs from a group meeting to play bridge or to hear a concert. What special needs does the worship group have if it is really to be a congregation at prayer?

Before answering that question, we have to step back for a moment and consider how religious groups differ from nonreligious ones. Imagine the following conversation. The scene is the conclusion of a church social.

A Conversation on Duty: I

Allan: As your organizer for this wonderful evening, I have a request of you all. Please help us take all the dirty dishes into the kitchen and move all the tables to the side. Thank you. (Everyone begins helping, except George.)

George: Why should I help?

Allan: Because the Sunday school needs this room tomorrow morning at 9:00 A.M., and it doesn't seem fair to ask the maintenance staff to do all the work cleaning it up.

George: Why not? That's their job.

Allan: True, but it's only right to help out when we can.

George: Why?

Allan: Well that's what Christianity is all about, isn't it? Haven't you ever heard of Christian charity?

What makes the conversation interesting is that George keeps receiving different answers to what sounds like the same question: "Why should I help?" At first, Allan gives him the *practical* answer: "Because we need the room tomorrow morning." That fact is undeniable. But George doesn't see what that has to do with whether he should help or not, so Allan ups the ante, so to speak, and reverts to an *ethical* answer: "Because it's not right to make the maintenance people do all the work." Ethical advice is deniable, however, so George retorts that it is right to let the maintenance people do the work for which they contracted. Now Allan feels the need to justify his own ethical judgment by recourse to a *religious* notion that both he and George surely must share as members of the same church. This final answer, "Christian charity," is unarguable. You either believe it or you don't.

Arguments regularly progress through these three stages: from (1) disagreement over *facts*, which are empirically demonstrable; to (2) disagreement over *logical deduction* from those facts, which is rationally arguable; to (3) disagreement over *first principles*, which are assumed to be self-evident.

The problem with identifying a group as religious is the cultural bias that Jews and Christians bring to the word "religion." We would like to say that a religion ought at least to have a belief in God, and in fact we have actually done just that insofar as we have identified a particular individual need that we called the divine-human encounter. This book is addressed to Christians and Jews in whose tradition that encounter is real. But what do we do about such great religions as classical Confucianism or Buddhism, which do not have a concept of God in the same way that western faiths do? Yet there are Confucian and Buddhist religious rituals, which function the way our own worship does. Similarly, closer to home, some American religions like Ethical Culture Societies, branches of the Unitarian Universalist Association, and classical Reconstructionist Judaism deny the existence of a personal God who literally hears our prayers. Yet these faith communities have religious services.

Two consequences flow from the recognition that there are world religions with rituals equivalent to what we call worship, but that do not have a concept of a personal God. The first is that their rituals are indeed worship, as long as they have their own definition of worship's goal that is functionally equivalent to what we call the divine-human encounter. Secondly, the realization that groups identify God differently lets us look not at God, but at the groups themselves, in the hope that we can find some common feature to them all that is independent of the particular God-concept that they espouse. If we can thereby avoid limiting our analysis to traditionally theistic Jews and Christians, we can hope to say something useful about the worship (or the worship equivalent) of all groups in all religions that satisfy the human need to be in touch with the Ultimate Power we call God. Even here among us, we might otherwise wonder what, for example, Reform Jews, Mennonites, Quakers, and Orthodox Jews have in common. Obviously, it is useful to work with a generic identification of all such groups, so as to be able to make comparisons among them.

There are two group needs. The first is inherent in the nature of the group experience itself. The second is the way in which the group connects its members with the Divine. We have to phrase both in terms that are free of the bias associated with this or that church or doctrine.

Let us begin with the nature of the group experience and the attempt to define what makes a group religious. Based on what we saw regarding the ultimate basis of arguments in first principles and the common need for people to have a group that provides those principles, we can say that a group functions religiously to the extent that it governs itself and its members by what it and they consider a set of ultimate principles, which are used to justify behavior on the highest possible level, that is, on a level beyond argument. You either accept them or you don't. Since we all have to justify what we do, we all have such ultimate concepts, and all of us are part of one religion or another, though we may not recognize it.

To the extent that any group has such ultimates, it functions religiously in the lives of its members. If, for example, a business held firmly to a final principle like, "The bottom line is the annual profit statement," it would have to be considered religious, even though the Jewish or Christian ethic would hardly applaud its religion. If a member of the board objected to the profit/loss calculus as the final word, citing biblical ethics as justification for the objection, other board members would likely rule the religious argument out of order. "Business is business," they would observe, meaning, in effect, "You can't mix religions." If the board member persisted, he or she might be forced to resign for holding principles incompatible with the business charter, or, as religionists would put the same thing, for the sin of heresy. Heretics are banned because their objection goes beyond the two elementary stages of fact and logic. They question first principles, which by definition are beyond question for anyone who wants to stay in the group.

We can go even further and recast the imaginary conversation on duty as part of a supper meeting of a chapter of the Communist Party, somewhere in the former USSR.

A Conversation on Duty: II

Alexei: As your organizer for this wonderful evening, I have a request of you all. Please help us take all the dirty dishes into the kitchen and move all the tables to the side. Thank you. (Everyone begins helping, except Georgei.)

Georgei: Why should I help?

Alexei: Because the Lenin study group needs this room tomorrow at 9:00 A.M., and it doesn't seem fair to ask the maintenance staff to do all the work cleaning it up.

Georgei: Why not? That's their job.

Alexei: True, but it's only right to help out when we can.

Georgei: Why?

Alexei: What kind of Communist are you? Haven't you read anything Lenin has to say about helping each other in a classless society?

Though Alexei would be the first to deny it, he is giving a religious answer to a religious question. Why help others? Because ultimately that is the right thing to do. How do you know it is right? Because Lenin said so. The difference between Allan the Christian and Alexei the Communist is the set of ultimate reasons selected. The former believes in God, so he quotes Christian doctrine. The latter is an atheist, and cites Communist dogma. Both rely on ultimate sources of authority of one sort or another.

Technically speaking, both men belong to religions. Allan will

probably call Alexei a godless Communist, this being our modern linguistic equivalent of such older labels as heretic, pagan, heathen, and
idolater. Jews and Christians surely will agree that Alexei's ultimate
source of authority is unacceptable; even though it is used in this case
to justify perfectly legitimate Jewish or Christian behavior, there are
other cases where Communism diverges enough from Judaism and
Christianity that it must be considered by them as misguided. Still, it
cannot be denied that from a purely formal point of view, both Allan
and Alexei belong to groups that claim to know ultimate truths and to
justify ways of life on a level of final principle, where further argument is not possible. So I have to call both systems religious, even
though I, personally, deny the truth of the Communist "religion."

Is it possible then that even Communists worship? Yes and no.
Insofar as we define worship as implying the presence of God, obviously Communists do not worship. On the other hand, they have some
notion of something ultimate, perhaps party solidarity or the memory
of Lenin; and they have rituals, too, a May Day parade, for instance. To
the extent that they provide rituals that invoke these ultimates, they
participate in religious rituals (which we might consider idolatrous)
designed to satisfy the individual needs of Communists (whom we
might call idolaters) by setting up a group ritual in which their particular ultimates (which we might call idols) are confronted.

> ❈ Any group that provides ultimate answers is by defi-
> nition a religion. Every such group provides religious
> rituals that satisfy the individual member's need to confront
> the ultimate. We call our rituals of this kind, *worship*, and
> our ultimate, *God*.

We are ready now to return to the question of the group needs.
We have already said that, like every other group, worship groups
require all the things that make groups viable vehicles to fulfill members' needs. But these are personal needs of individual members. What
more can we say about the specifically group-oriented needs—needs,
that is, for the group as a group?

We can answer that question on the basis of our definition of religious groups. Since religious groups provide ultimate values that guarantee personal worth, the worship group must be cohesive enough to be able to foster the members' shared affirmation of ideals that are ultimately valuable from a religious perspective.

> **Worship does more than evoke the presence of God. It provides religious identification, declares what is right and what is wrong, and explains why being a Christian or a Jew is ultimately valuable. Worship defines a world of values that group members share; it both mirrors and directs the social order in which the group lives.**

Later, I will call this the creation of an *alternative world of experience* that individuals internalize from their rituals and then enforce on their further perception of life's circumstances as they leave their rituals to enter the world at large. As the worship ritual is played out, individual members of the group give and receive messages that support their decision to affiliate with their religion. They return home with their own value reinforced and their identity within the amorphous mass of humanity clearly established. The group need is whatever it takes for the worshiping community to function effectively at achieving these ends.

A second diagram (Fig. 3.2) will illustrate what we have been describing. First we draw an oval, representing a group at prayer. At various points on it, we draw individuals, each of whom belongs to the group; the boundary that constitutes the oval passes through each

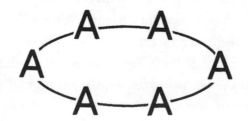

Fig. 3.2. Group System

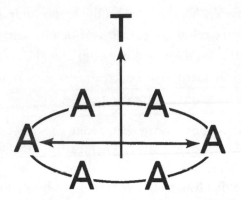

Fig. 3.3. Group System with Horizontal Axis (Group
Identity) and Vertical Axis (Link to the Transcendent)

member and represents the fact that the individuals are united in the
unique constellation that we call the "worshiping community."

Now let's recall the two individual needs that we noted before.
The first was an actual sense that God was somehow present, that worship really *is* worship, not just socializing. Since people usually picture
God as being "up there," we can diagram this need by adding a vertical arrow from the group upward (Fig. 3.3). This vertical axis represents the generic equivalent of the divine-human encounter. In
Jewish and Christian parlance, it is the sense we have, when we leave
worship, that we have indeed prayed. For the time being we can call the
vertical axis "the transcendent" (represented by the letter T), allowing
for a variety of religious experiences through which worshipers are prepared to say that they have transcended themselves and encountered
the Divine. The second need of the worshiping group is to bond the
worshipers together in such a way that the sense of their ultimate
shared identity is linked somehow to the Ultimate Power we call God.

The two needs are intertwined. We saw that when we pray
together we provide a mirror image of ourselves, sending and receiving
messages about the nature of reality, the values and aspirations that
we hold in common; and we bind ourselves together as an actual group
rather than as sole individuals, united in our commitment to ultimate

purposes, respectful and affirming of each other's worth. In contrast to the vertical axis by which we relate to God "above," this need can be represented as a horizontal arrow running through the oval and connecting the individual members together. The horizontal axis is the process of group identity, the means by which individuals define and affirm who they are and what they stand for.

One more element must be added to our diagram before it is complete. Group identity has a positive and a negative aspect. When we say who we are, we also say who we are not. Imagine, for example, a world in which there were only men but no women. In such a universe we would have no word "man," since "man" and "human being" would be synonymous. The word "man" is necessary only because we want sometimes to say that "man" equals "not a woman." Similarly, the term "human being" means "not an animal or a vegetable"; the word "animal" means "not a human being or a vegetable"—and so on. So every positive, definitive term implies other things that are ruled out.

Moreover, the items ruled out are not just things chosen at random. "Man," for example, does not imply "not a desk." "Man" means only "not those things that might conceivably make sense in context," which must consequently be overruled, for example, "man" equals "not a woman," since human beings may be either men or women (though not desks).

Hence the horizontal axis of group definition states who we are, but does so in precise ways that also state who we are not. Who we are not is not chosen randomly, but with care, to select out of the infinite range of possibilities only those alternative groups that conceivably we might be. So we must add to the diagram two heavy vertical lines representing the boundary of the worshiping group. And on the other side we draw other ovals to stand for the range of possible alternative group identities that our group deliberately sets bounds against. These we label arbitrarily as W, X, Y, and Z. (See Fig. 3.4.)

Liturgies are full of statements that reinforce positive identification with our own group by showing how it differs from other com-

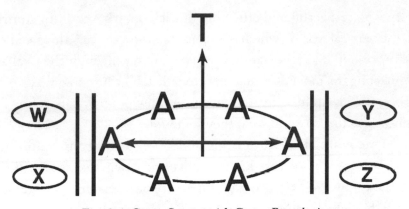

Fig. 3.4. Group System with Group Boundaries
That Mark It Off from Other Similar Groups

peting groups. The Nicene Creed, for example, reflects the orthodox definition of God the Father and God the Son as separate but equal entities, according to a decision reached in the Council of Nicaea in 325. It was adopted in 473 in the city of Antioch as a boundary against a Christian group known as Monophysites. And in 589 it was similarly recited as a distinguishing mark against Arians, another Christian group that the orthodox church saw as heretical.

In Judaism, a blessing against a variety of alternatives, including Christianity, was added around the end of the first century, the very time when some Jews might have identified with Christianity. The blessing announced, in effect, that one could not be both a Christian and a Jew at the same time. It thereby relegated Christianity as an option beyond the double boundary line, making it one of the W-X-Y-Z network of groups that were beyond the pale.

I could go on at length, indicating the many prayers now in worship services that began as subtle or outright denials of alternative group identities, but the examples given should suffice to illustrate the point. Though the groups that compose W, X, Y, or Z change with time, the process of defining our religious community against some alternative is constant. These polemical prayers (or for that matter, actions—consider the way some people baptize indicates the church to which they belong) may drop out once the alternative against which they were directed is no longer a reality, but sometimes they remain; or people get used to them and eventually forget how they got started. New prayers or actions will in any case be added as boundary markers against new alternatives. The horizontal axis of group identity cannot be understood without comprehending at the same time who the reasonable alternatives across the boundary are.

The Physical Environment: Worship Props ❀

❀ The final subsystem of worship is the physical environment, particularly the set of worship props: the prayer books, hymnals, pews, cups, crosses, Torah scrolls, flowers, and special clothing such as robes.

Obviously, the entities that compose the *prop system* are not people and can have no needs in the sense that human beings do. But even an inanimate system is a system; it can function well or poorly and therefore has needs or conditions that must be met for it to work. To take two obvious examples, both the eucharist and the *Kiddush* for *Shabbat* (the prayer in Judaism that introduces the Sabbath by announcing the day's holiness), require a cup with wine in it.

The prop system is not unlike the seesaw seen independently of the people riding it. Both are subsystems of a larger whole; each is a mechanism for achieving its own appropriate ends. The seesaw is a simple device that even little children can figure out. The prop system for worship, however, is complex, composed of many items with built-in rules governing how they will be manipulated. Clergy spend considerable time memorizing the rules and practicing the art of using the worship props. They know that competent handling of the props enhances the possibility of achieving both individual and group needs. In other words, proper use of the objects of worship fosters a sense of God's presence and builds a firm sense of group identity.

The worship props must be congruent with the nature of the congregation using them. People raised in a High Church tradition are taught to identify religion with the replete regalia that go into worship. They may be distressed in a Quaker meeting house, and say that they have trouble finding God there. Jews may be unable to pray effectively in a room containing a cross, since the cross is so thoroughly identifiable with Christianity. They will say, "This just doesn't feel like a synagogue," by which they mean, "We cannot achieve Jewish group consciousness here."

> ❂ **The prop system consists of items with which the worshipers identify. In successful worship, they identify with them on the emotive level of symbol. The use of these props according to the right rules reminds us of who we are, tells us that our group and its values are supremely important, and suggests the possibility of God's presence among us.**

When a group finds its self-image changing, the first thing it generally does is change the props, since it identifies them as "just things," and it is easier to tamper with things than with the group members, who are people. Sometimes they are right. The church architecture may be too barren, the seating too impersonal, the ritual objects meaningless. A more proper explanation of the problem, however, is that the worshipers, not the props, have changed. The props are the same but they no longer suggest what the group's identity has become. Much of our problem with worship today is that the traditional props are not compatible with the emerging religious identity of the worshiping group. If they no longer have personal significance or suggest the presence of the Divine, they thwart the needs of individuals. When people say they cannot pray, one way to help them discover that they can may be to change the props. Exactly how the environment of prayer should be changed will concern us later (chapter 8), when we know more about today's religious identity.

In sum, all phenomena are systems that must be treated as wholes.

Worship too is a system, and can be divided into three subsystems: each individual who comes to pray; the worshiping group; and the environment (with the worship props) where worship occurs—everything from the layout of the space to the design of the books. The prop system, too, has needs if it is to function smoothly: Carpets need cleaning and hymnals require storage space, for example. But props serve people, so our focus is still the individual worshipers, who need to achieve a sense of God's presence (the vertical axis) and a feeling that they belong to a group that expresses their ultimate values (the horizontal axis). These two goals of worship are the two axes on which successful worship rests. Horizontally speaking, members of the worship group identify with each other and draw moral guidance as well as human sustenance. Vertically speaking, they relate to God in a way they call prayer.

The most common reason why these two eminently desirable goals are not always achieved is the next subject to concern us.

Ritual Check List   ✺

Words and Concepts You Should Know

- **When problems seem to be intractable,** it may be because they are systemic in nature. The system as a whole needs change.

- **Rather than face the fact that the entire system needs overhauling,** it is more convenient to find some part of the system to blame, and to constantly go about changing it. This is the common process of scapegoating.

- **A church or synagogue is a system.** It has various subsystems, including the worship system, which has three parts: (1) the individuals who make it up; (2) those individuals seen as a group; and (3) the environment with its worship props.

- **When individuals say that it is their own fault** that they cannot pray, or that they have never experienced prayer, they are often scapegoating themselves when it is really the worship system that is broken.

- **When the worship system is working efficiently,** individuals who comprise it experience the Divine and enjoy the security of group identity.

- **Group identity involves** not only knowing who you are but also who you are not.

- **The worship props must be congruent** with the nature of the congregation using them. People should identify with them on the deep level of symbols. When a group finds its self-image changing, the first thing it generally does is change the worship environment.

Conversation Points for Making Worship Work

1 ▪ If you have a worship care group (see p. 250), go into the room where communal worship generally occurs. Divide the members of your group according to the number of years that they have been in your synagogue or church. Ask those who have been there the longest to recall how the group has changed, and how the props have changed alongside it. What kind of worship used to be here ten, twenty, thirty years ago? How did the props make that kind of worship possible? (Was the seating or the general spatial arrangement different? Did people dress differently?) When and why were the props changed? What happened to make people want to change them? Did the changes have any impact on the way worship worked? How did worship change when the props did?

2 ▪ Ask for people who have prayed in very different environments: other cities, different movements, other religions. Without actu-

ally comparing the details of the liturgy, find out how the feel of prayer might have differed there, and whether the feel had anything to do with the worship props that were used.

3 ▪ Does your worship polemicize against other groups? What groups? How does your group differ from others that are in your own denomination, confession, or movement; or from those outside of it? Does the worship make those differences clear, so that a stranger who wandered in would know who you are and who you are not?

four

Mistaking the Code, Mixing Messages, and Managing Change ✸

Successful ritual demands successful communication. Delegates at a political convention, for instance, recognize the cues telling them when to applaud, when to wave signs, and when to be quiet. The mother about to nurse her child has learned to recognize a cry of hunger, and then to respond by preparing her baby and herself in ways that tell the child that food is on the way. In worship too, people have the satisfaction of successfully completing the ritual only if communication appropriate to the experience of worship is successfully sent and received.

✸ **Communication about the ritual tells participants what to do, when to do it, and how to respond to each other; it is the energy that makes the ritual system run.**

A common impediment to getting the ritual message through is the inability of worshipers to decode the message properly. It is not exactly that they do not know what is being said, so much as they do not interpret what they hear as having anything to do with worship. If worship were music, we would say that they were tone-deaf: They hear the music, but do not even recognize it as a melody. They have been away from worship for so long that they do not recognize it even when they are part of it.

David's Job

David has belonged to his synagogue for over ten years. He comes from a synagogue-oriented family and attended a Sunday school much like the one whose policy he now decides in his capacity as Sunday school chairperson. He feels personally dedicated to transmitting his religious heritage to the next generation, just as his parents bequeathed it to him. In all ways, David is an admirable synagogue member: active, concerned, Jewishly sensitive, highly motivated.

But David rarely comes to synagogue to pray. Truth be told, even when he comes to prayer services, he still does not come to pray. People rarely discuss this, so he has never had to confront this anomaly. David's friends would be surprised to hear that he has never taken worship seriously. He feels at home in the sanctuary and knows the ritual script inside out, but worship bores him. His mind wanders even while his lips move in mechanical recitation of the text. Occasionally, the sermon or the discussion around the Torah reading makes him think a little, and sometimes he is moved by a particularly artistic cantorial rendition. But generally, he passes the time looking around the room to see who else is present, and he looks forward to the chance to talk with friends during the coffee hour that he knows will follow the service. Sometimes he uses the time when others are praying to plan presentations that he will make during services by virtue of being chairperson of the Sunday school committee.

That is what David is doing now. He is in synagogue because it is his job to represent the committee at tonight's special event: Scout Sabbath, an annual Sabbath service honoring the scout movement. On the pulpit is a row of chairs where uniformed scout leaders are sitting. The congregation is fuller than usual, its regular worshipers augmented by faces of strangers who have come only because their children who are scouts are being honored. David's job is to offer a word of greeting. As the congregation rises to take the Torah scroll from the ark, he has just about finished figuring out what he will say.

David doesn't know it, but he suffers from "false decoding." Unknowingly, he decodes worship messages as if they were not really about prayer at all, but about something altogether different. Though he goes through the motions, he never actually prays.

David is the product of a religious school system that dealt only in signs, never symbols. If it ever dealt with worship at all, it taught it as a cognitive discipline with certain facts and lessons to be committed to memory. When he was young, he memorized important prayers and responses and internalized general notions about what Jewish prayers said. The actual expression of his own religious feeling, however, had no place in the curriculum, so even if as a child David had really experienced worship, he never learned how to talk about it, and therefore he never had his sense of spirituality in worship reinforced.

In our vocabulary of systems, we should say that the educational system got the best of him. Taught to accept only rationally provable concepts and rewarded for critical acumen, he now reads the prayer book as if its words were treatises *on* prayer rather than prayer itself; if he is occasionally moved emotionally, he explains his feelings by his ability to appreciate aesthetics. He sits back in detached admiration of the cantor's voice or the religious poetry. He can read about worship, he can judge sermons on worship, and he can appreciate the poetry that is the stuff of worship. But he cannot worship.

Moreover, this is Scout Sabbath. There is an entire network of new people present simply because they are involved in scouting, so there are two systems at work simultaneously: the scout system and the worship system. And they are not coupled very well, since most of the scout system members never come to synagogue and can barely follow the prayer service. To complicate matters, the normal ritual of the evening has been altered drastically to include the scouts' pledge and a color guard—activities relevant to scouting but not to Sabbath worship. So a large percentage of the messages being sent from pulpit to pew are irrelevant to worship to start with. By sitting through the prayer service and concentrating on what he will say to the visiting scouts, David has correctly perceived that this service is more of a scouting ritual than a worship ritual. He knows that his role in the drama now being enacted is to send a message to the scouts that validates their presence in a setting that is unfamiliar to them.

If special Sabbaths like the Scout Sabbath occurred only once or twice a year, it might still be possible for those people who attend worship regularly to celebrate the worship ritual and to achieve the worship moment at least most of the time. But special Sabbaths have become the norm in this synagogue, where scouting is not the only outside system to invade the sanctuary. David typifies the synagogue leaders: Though uncomfortable with real worship, they appreciate intellectual or aesthetic events. So the ritual committee has begun to program academic lectures and artistic performances within the worship context. Throughout the year, special speakers or singers are announced in the temple bulletin and city newspapers, and predictably, new faces, drawn by the guest personalities, continually come and go. A high proportion of the messages during the worship service itself regularly focus on the intruding "attraction" rather than on prayer, and the worship service, or script, insofar as it is followed at all, will not be seen as worship—surely not by the newcomers, who have come solely to enjoy the speaker. And not by many of the regulars either, who come because they expect good programming by now.

Ironically, anyone who really appreciates prayer has probably decided to stay home. Rival systems have so taken over the worship system that the prayer service has become an empty vessel into which a host of extraneous activities have been poured. Week after week, the men's club, the young couples club, the new members' group, the youth group, the interfaith committee, or a visiting folk choir invade the sanctuary and play out their own ritual. In effect, they have usurped worship.

No wonder that David has never experienced worship and finds prayer dull or meaningless. As we said at the outset, people who say they do not appreciate religious ritual should be taken with the utmost seriousness. Religious ritual, in this case worship, is not even represented at their churches and synagogues. The systems to which it is interfaced have sabotaged it to the point where words may look like worship, but the people saying them decode them as an excuse for whatever else is happening tonight. When religious moments are described by others, people here correctly report that they have not experienced them.

A starting point, then, to providing the religious moments that characterize real worship, is to synchronize the connections between parallel systems that prevent the worship system from functioning in the first place. Educational systems should deal with symbols, not signs; children and adults should be encouraged to recognize their own religiously rooted emotions for what they are, rather than explain them away as something else. Groups irrelevant to prayer should not be allowed to intrude on the worship system, even though this decision may cause many regulars to start going elsewhere for their entertainment. Sermons and choir performances should take a back seat to worship, which should occur without apology so that congregants can learn again to pray. Just as surely as there are nursing moments or sports moments, there are also worship moments—if we would only let the worship system function without trying to turn it into what it is not.

We send mixed messages by preaching about prayer but ignoring prayer when it conflicts with something else. We need to look more carefully at how mixed messages come about, and the role they play in obscuring true worship. To do this, we can examine the difference between communication and metacommunication.

Metacommunication: Communication about Communication ◉

Reading the Talmud

When I was in rabbinical school, I learned to read a most difficult literature known as Talmud: some twenty volumes of tightly woven rabbinic argumentation that were edited about the sixth or seventh century, and that synthesize five centuries of rabbinic thinking on every conceivable subject. What made it so hard was that the Aramaic words were written without punctuation. That meant that even if I knew each word's meaning, I still had trouble combining them into sentences. And without question marks or periods, even after I knew the sentences, I was never sure whether I had a question, an answer, a declarative statement, or an emphatic conclusion. Worse still, if it was a question, let us say, I had to determine whether that question was serious, a passing jest, a sarcastic objection to what someone else had said, or mere rhetoric. If the question was serious, then the sentence after it was probably an equally serious attempt at an answer. If the question was a joke, it might receive no response at all. If the question was sarcastic, the next line might be a comparable biting remark by someone else. A rhetorical question, on the other hand, might elicit an answer by that very questioner or not be answered at all. I later learned that the Talmud does have its own form of punctuation: special words in the text that are not meant to be translated; they are inserted by the editor to tell the reader *how* to read the words they introduce.

✵ **Words by themselves are not communication. We convert words into communication by providing cues about how our words should be interpreted. In writing, these interpretive cues are called punctuation. What punctuation is to writing, metacommunication is to communication.**

Here is an example of metacommunication. When my children were little, they told me that when they asked me to do a favor for them and I said, "Maybe," that really meant, "No." I thought about that for a while and decided they were right. If I was working and they asked to play a game of Monopoly, I would think vaguely to myself, "Maybe I'll finish in time to play," even when I know I probably wouldn't, and I would answer, "Maybe." What I really meant was, "Probably not," and in practice, "Maybe" meant more than "Probably not"; it almost always meant "No."

Shortly after the kids told me about my use of "Maybe," one of them asked if we could see the circus. For a variety of reasons, I was pretty sure we could. But not being sure that we could obtain tickets, I answered, "Maybe." According to their own theory, the kids should have walked away depressed, but instead they were elated. How did they know that "Maybe" with regard to the circus meant "Probably yes," while "Maybe" with regard to most other requests meant "No"?

They knew because of metacommunication. In some subtle way, I indicated how they should understand my latest "Maybe." We cue our own communication all the time, so people can read us. Sometimes it is in the way we talk (verbal punctuation). Sometimes it is through body language, such as a smile that indicates a joke or a shrug of the shoulders that means we don't care. If I say of the budget deficit, "The president will balance it," I may accompany my statement with the kind of determined look that shows I mean the remark as a serious vote of confidence in the current administration. Or I may smile knowingly or even sneer, which would signal that I mean exactly the reverse of what the words themselves say.

Metacommunication determines how we respond to the communication. If I really mean that the president will balance the budget, you may reply, "I certainly hope so," or "I don't have as much faith in him as you do," or "What presidential policy leads you to say that?" If I am being sarcastic, you may say nothing verbally, but nod knowingly or join me in my disdainful look to indicate that my sarcasm is not lost on you and that you agree with me. By replicating my metacommunicative punctuation, you make my words stand for yours, just as surely as if (in writing) you were adding a ditto mark to the conversation. In either case, *how* you know what I mean depends on the metacommunicative cues sent and received. People who do not send or receive these cues very well are in a constant state of embarrassment. They and the people they talk to never know whether something being said is serious or a joke.

As a form of communication, worship too depends on metacommunicative cues. I know of a particular synagogue where every Friday night, the organist begins playing softly before anyone arrives for services. The ushers, who may have been joking in the corridors until now, suddenly become serious and greet new arrivals with a somber face. The words of greeting are the same as they were two minutes ago, but the ushers' visual cue has changed. The arrivals nod a curt hello and proceed quietly to their seats.

On most Saturday mornings, the rabbi of this congregation can be found orchestrating the ritual script of a bar or bat mitzvah, part of which calls for him to address the young man or woman who is officially entering adulthood. The entrant is barely thirteen, however, so the rabbi usually begins his charge with a metacommunicative smile meaning, "Relax. We're friends. Don't worry. This will be painless." But eventually he gets carried away—surely he should say something significant on this occasion—and at that moment, his voice rises as his smile disappears. The metacommunication is clear: "Joke time is over. This is a religious message that you better take seriously." Throughout the address, the child responds not to the rabbi's words, (which, as often as not, he or she barely comprehends), but to the metacommunicative cue accompanying them.

The actual communication in worship is generally very clear. The words from the prayer book and the accompanying instructions (for example, "The congregation rises") are usually obvious—and deliberately so, since the congregation on any given day is made up partly of people who would not know the rules otherwise. Some may be here just for a special program (like Scout Sabbath) or because of personal circumstances (someone in the family just died, or they know someone being confirmed today). So extra care is built into the ritual to tell people what they are to do. It is as if, knowing in advance that the ritual's actors will not know their lines, modern liturgies see to it that the cue cards, so to speak, are readily visible. Some synagogues even have a knowledgeable person walk around during services, telling individuals with special roles in the service what to do and when to do it.

("Go up to the pulpit now. Stand beside the rabbi. She'll nod to you when it's time to read your prayer.")

So if it were only a matter of communication, everything would proceed without a hitch. The problem occurs when the metacommunicative cue contradicts the patently obvious meaning of the communication that it punctuates.

Congregational singing is the best example of such a conflict. In scores of places the singing is done by paid professionals who are aspiring opera singers moonlighting in churches and synagogues. Their credentials for the job consist primarily in their ability to sing well, although they may be completely untrained in the art of leading people in congregational singing. It happens frequently that in keeping with current trends of increasing congregational participation, worship goers express an interest in singing, and the soloists are asked to invite the congregation to sing along. This they dutifully do, but their tone of voice, the music selected, and the key in which it is sung make it obvious to everyone that they really do not welcome congregational singing. Predictably, only a few people join in singing, and they do so practically to themselves.

The most important point about all of this is that if the worshiping group really wishes to avoid congregational singing, the discrepancy between the communication and the metacommunication is not bad. Far from causing a problem, it solves one. The metacommunicative message—"We are not serious about telling you to sing"—overrides the content of the communication itself. The *real* purpose, which is to maintain the status quo, will be accomplished. The system will function smoothly despite the lip service paid to changing values. Success or failure in communication depends entirely on what we define as the goal of the system fueled by that communication. If the goal is to overcome a populism that threatens to replace the tradition of entrusting artistically excellent music to trained soloists, the system works beautifully: It successfully keeps out accessible melodies that the congregation might actually sing. It even defuses a potential challenge from those who want to convert listeners into singers. The soloist can always blame the congregants who, after all, were invited to sing but chose not to do so. Only if the goal of the system is worship and if worship is defined as participatory, can we can judge the system a failure. So the success or failure of a system depends on the arbitrary definition of what the system is supposed to do in the first place.

In success or failure, however, the dissonance between communication and metacommunication causes problems for at least *some* of the individuals who take the communication seriously and then are cued not to. This is called a *double bind* because they cannot obey either set of communications without simultaneously disobeying the other. Thus when the cantor or music director says (but doesn't mean), "Please join in the singing of . . . ," there may be people who do not read the metacommunicative cue properly. Perhaps one man who enjoys singing doesn't come frequently enough to know the music director's views, or is the kind of person who takes things literally. To the dismay of those who do recognize the cue, and who know better than to follow the explicit instructions, this man joins in the singing with a booming voice. Systems have built-in safeguards against such "miscreants." The people sitting near him give the man an icy look. If he doesn't notice these sidewise glances, his family will, and they can be counted on to shush the old boy up. If need be, people around him will say, "Shhhh!" kindly and gently at first without actually looking his way. If that fails, they will escalate their warning by staring directly at him. Eventually special "police," who go by the title "ushers," may have to step in to enforce the rule. Things rarely go that far, but no matter what stage is reached before the would-be singer is silenced, he ends up frustrated, embarrassed, and perhaps even ostracized from the group.

> ❀ **Metacommunication, not communication, determines what we do in public prayer. When these two conflict, some people will mistakenly follow the communication, only to get hurt in the process. They will probably not**

return to worship, since few people willingly get clobbered twice. Instead they will join the ranks of the multitude who say that religious ritual is cold, barren, and uninspiring.

The proposition that people confronted with mutually exclusive communication and metacommunication will not return to the scene of the conflict is worth more than a casual sentence. Over 50 percent—and in some cases almost 90 percent—of nominal synagogue or church members do not attend weekly worship services on any regular basis. Among other things, it is mixed messages that have chased them off to other activities where the rules are clearer.

Worshipers face mixed messages regularly. In our example above, the clergy tell them, "You should sing" (the communication), but also, "Don't sing too loud, if at all" (the metacommunication). But in many ways, clergy are to lay people as parents are to children. Priests are called "Father," for instance, and "backsliding children" confess to them. Worshipers who get conflicting instructions from clergy are structurally identical to children who are told, simultaneously, "You may," as well as, "You may not."

Everyone tries to avoid no-win situations. So our would-be worshipers will probably opt to stay clear of worship services whenever possible. They may, of course, show up whenever overriding needs present themselves. For life-cycle events, like funerals or baptisms, the family will dutifully do what they must; and on major holidays, when prayer is sensed to be absolutely necessary, congregants will sit uncomfortably for hours, if that is what it takes. But they won't come regularly. And when they do come, they will sit passively, probably in the pews nearest the door, where they can observe without being truly involved.

❀ **All this indicates that even in otherwise good American churches and synagogues, the worship system has broken down. Having been taught to scapegoat themselves, the worshipers confess, "I'm sorry, but religious ritual doesn't mean anything to *me*." Their admission gets** us nowhere. What they say is absolutely correct, but the blame lies elsewhere. The problem is systemic.

Preaching at people will not correct the situation. We need to treat the breakdown systemically.

Worship Pathology: Regulars, Watchers, Movers, and Professionals ◉

Sometimes, the fault does indeed lie with an individual, in which case, the analogy is a sick cell within an organism. Though the organism as a whole is healthy, a single deviant cell is not. The cell may grow malignantly until the entire organism stops functioning. In the face of potential malignancy, we resort to radical surgery, if necessary, to save the organism. We remove the pathological cell to save the organism as a whole.

Worship pathology is when a single worshiper ruins worship for everyone else. There is nothing otherwise wrong with the individual, but from the viewpoint of the group, he or she is pathological. Usually, social pressure inhibits outright pathological behavior. Worshipers who stand out as pathological usually recognize that they are outsiders and do not return to services. The system has performed surgery on a potentially malignant cell, whose pathology turns out to have been benign.

A problem occurs only when the pathological person moves from being benign to being malignant—like a man who really believes the communication inviting him to sing loudly, even though everyone else does not sing. If he corrects his misconception, saying in effect, "I missed the metacommunication," and stops singing, he is still pathological, but inhibited and benign. Alternatively, he may perceive the metacommunication clearly, but disagree with it. Having a personal need to sing, he may rationalize his own pathological presence in the group by saying, "Singing together is good for worship. This congregation must be taught to sing. I shall teach them." Again the built-in corrective measures of the group will be called into play, but this time the pathological individual will resist them, escalating his behavior to the point where it prohibits the other worshipers from accomplishing their worship moment.

Fortunately, malignant pathological defiance is rare, and when it does occur, the guilty party is rarely an average worshiper. Most worshipers fear the social ostracism that comes from challenging the group's corrective mechanisms. So pathology is usually limited to its benign manifestations: people who find themselves uncomfortably out of place, but who do nothing about it (except, of course, not return).

⊛ **Aggressive pathological behavior almost always emanates from a certain subgroup of worshipers: those who are so comfortably established in the group that they feel free to tamper with the communication energy that makes it work.**

Judaism and Christianity preach that all are equal before God. The social systems of real people are never so egalitarian, however. When a handful of people first come together to form a religious community, they may relate to each other as equals. But eventually some establish themselves as decision makers, while others become decision followers. Groups at prayer are no different, in that some people act as if they belong there and have the right to determine the rules, while others avoid overt acts that challenge what people are doing.

I have already referred to this phenomenon by observing that some people who come to pray are regular attendees, while some come infrequently enough that they are only observers, content to watch the proceedings from the sidelines. It is time we analyzed more clearly the subgroups into which a worshiping community should be divided. Looking out at those who come on any given Sabbath service, a pastor, priest, or rabbi can distinguish four categories of worshiper, each with its own degree of propensity for initiating action and for challenging the rules in a pathological way. The subgroups can be plotted diagrammatically, as if they were four concentric circles radiating out from a center where the *liturgical action* occurs.

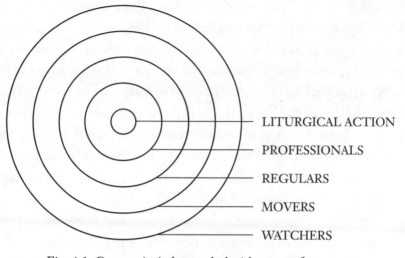

Fig. 4.1. Concentric circles marked with names of groups

The circle farthest from the center is the *watchers*. Watchers almost never come to worship, so if they are here today, they must have a special reason. They may be intimately involved in some other system that draws them here: They are the parents of the scouts on Scout Sabbath, for example; or they are relatives of the guest preacher, come to honor family commitment and hear their advertised famous visitor; or they have come to celebrate their own life-cycle events.

This last category is especially evident in synagogues that have subtly been transformed into bar or bat mitzvah "factories." These are usually large congregations that find themselves featuring a different bar or bat mitzvah (or even more than one) every Saturday morning. The celebrating families and friends may have taken over the congregation, to the point where almost no one else is there. The regular worshiping group, if there ever was one, long decided to go elsewhere or stay home rather than put up every week with a new set of strangers who are likely to sit blankly throughout the service, completely uninterested in it until the appearance midway through the morning of the featured bar or bat mitzvah child. At the front of the sanctuary sits the immediate family, waiting and watching nervously,

their only prayers being that everything will go smoothly in this baffling religious service that they know nothing about. At the back are
the bar or bat mitzvah child's school friends; their entire year is being
spent going to each other's bar or bat mitzvah celebrations, where they
gather as only adolescents can, dressed like adults, but acting like children, giggling in the back row until the ushers tell them to please be
quiet. In between sit row upon row of family, close friends, casual
acquaintances, and obligatory invitees from the neighborhood or from
work, most of whom may never go to synagogue at all, except when bar
or bat mitzvah invitations summon them to do so.

Shabbat morning worship has virtually ceased here; in its place is
a programmed bar or bat mitzvah ritual designed to reinforce individual family systems. Saturday after Saturday, a different family plays
the role, inviting its own network of watchers for the occasion.

Watchers come to other services also, and are immediately recognizable because they know little, if anything, about worship. They
are handed books they have never seen, and listen to music they have
never heard. They must be told explicitly what to do, and when and
how to do it. They generally prefer seats near the back, where they
can slip in and out without drawing attention to themselves. They
harbor deep fears of being asked to do something that will reveal their
ignorance, in a ritual milieu that rarely goes out of its way to make
them feel comfortable. If they must play a role in the ritual scripts, such
as godparents at a baptism or grandparents of the bat mitzvah girl, they
may be moved to the front of the ritual stage, told in advance what to
do, and then prompted when the time comes to do it. Watchers want
mostly to get through the proceedings and return home safely. They
almost never consider tampering with the system's communication.
As long as they are allowed to remain relatively invisible, they can usually be counted on to do whatever they are told and not make trouble.

The watchers are the fourth and farthest circle from the action.
Let's skip over the third circle for a moment and describe the second,
the *regulars*. At the very opposite pole from watchers, regulars come

all the time, not only to worship services, but to almost everything else that the church or synagogue features. They are the lay board, the decision makers, the chairs of committees, the volunteers, organizers, and attenders of most events, the folk you can count on to make a function work. As regulars, they have completely internalized worship communications. Handling the props and sending and receiving messages are second nature for them. Unlike the watchers who sit at the back of the room, regulars sit up front. Within the confines of acceptability, they may even leave their seat and move around—something watchers would never do, since watchers don't know what those confines are. Becoming a regular means accepting a code of conduct that is nowhere spelled out, but is part of the rules governing the many settings in which regulars meet. By the time a man or woman achieves regular status in the worship system, he or she has fully assimilated the communications rules, and though in a position to challenge them, rarely does so. Still, the regulars have great latitude of action, so they can stretch the boundaries a little. And sometimes this stretching becomes aggressively pathological for the system.

In many synagogues, for example, the president of the congregation sits on the pulpit beside the rabbi and makes the announcements regarding future synagogue activities. At a prescribed point in the service, worship ceases for a moment, and the president rises to say some ritualistic things about what will happen next week. Actually, it is often hard for the assembled congregants to take in what the president is saying, since the announcements tend to sound like a long jumble of names, places, dates, and times. The remarks may even be unnecessary for the very promotional purposes they are said to serve, since a list of the activities usually appears in bulletins or newsletters. Why then does the president insist on giving them?

The president's remarks accomplish an unstated agenda. For one thing, they signal the president's status. For another, they give credit to the other regulars who have organized things, conferring social status also on them. If the regulars listen carefully, it is not to find out what is going on, since they already know that, but to make sure the activity they are personally organizing is noted. The watchers ignore the entire announcement ritual, since they don't plan on coming to anything anyway.

But a pathological president may decide to convert the ritual into an opportunity to give a sermon. Standing at the lectern, she may drone on and on about the importance of the events, even quoting scripture or sacred lore gleaned as a child in some Sunday school class long ago. People now become restless, and week after week dread the interminable delay caused by the president, who has stretched the boundaries of this ritual role too far. Since the regulars know when the president's time to speak will come, they begin looking at each other with knowing glances during the prayer preceding the announcements, and even find their anger spilling over into the praying time afterward. This is a case of malignant pathology—a single individual imposes her own need on the ritual script and makes worship moments hard to attain.

Another example is a particular regular who has attended mass for years and even now, more than twenty years later, never accepted the changes introduced after Vatican II. He cannot comprehend why English should have replaced Latin, why the priest should have turned around to face the congregation, why involvement of lay people should be encouraged, why new music and even dancing now find their way into worship. As long as he limits his complaints to situations outside the worship experience, the man is benign. But suppose he feels obliged to grouse noisily from his seat during the celebration of the mass. He then interferes with the worship of those sitting around him. He may even disrupt the entire proceeding by drawing attention to himself rather than to the ritual action.

Most regulars will not be malignantly pathological. But some may, since, as regulars, they feel comfortable questioning accepted practice. If they do challenge the system, they may prove difficult to deal with, since their regular status makes them relatively immune to the normal self-regulatory mechanism (such as ushers) built into the system. They will argue that it is they who appoint the ushers to start with, and that they are the congregation's elected leaders to whom even the pastor (whom they believe they "hired") should answer. They may also be major donors and valuable workers who are essential to the smooth functioning of the church or synagogue. Pathological regulars who disturb worship communication are therefore a serious challenge to the system.

The third circle—the one we skipped over—contains the *movers*. In terms of involvement, they are somewhere between the watchers and the regulars, but they are usually in the process of moving toward one of these two extremes. They may be relative newcomers who began attending as watchers, but who now wish to break into the inner circle of regulars. So they attend things, get to know the regulars, volunteer for committee assignments, or get appointed to minor offices. They may also be moving in the opposite direction. As new people take over leadership positions, old people leave them. There is never a complete turnover, of course, and the network of regulars may even be a closed system. Despite its rhetoric inviting new members to become more active, the regulars may tacitly veto new additions to their ranks, preferring to rotate power and position among themselves every year or so. But there are always some people who find their psychological commitment to the church or synagogue waning and discover they are spending more time elsewhere, such as working for the local hospital or the Red Cross.

There may also be people whose movement away from the circle of regulars was forced upon them. People moving toward regular status will not usually display pathological symptoms, since that would work against their ultimate goal of acceptance within the circle of regulars. People who have chosen to move away from power will also rarely disturb the status quo, since they don't care enough to bother. But people forced to abandon their regular status against their will almost invariably become pathological to the system.

The reasons they may have been forced out are legion. Like the man who can't stand the change in the mass, they may be the Old Guard bent on maintaining the old-time religion. Like the longwinded president who speaks too long, they may be regulars who bend too many rules and angered enough other regulars that they are removed. Whatever the reason, they will probably be the center of a cluster of other worshipers who share their attitude or who consider them personal friends. So they are usually not loners, but representatives of rival groups in the system. They represent alternative group identities not so far beyond the pale that the system has already censored them out—like the man virtually at war with the worship decisions of Vatican II, who is nonetheless clearly and proudly Catholic. Because he embodies a lifetime of the way things used to be done, he presents a genuine option to the system as it stands.

> **It is the group of increasingly marginalized regulars, the people who resent being moved away from the center of power, which most often generates malignant pathological behavior, especially at times of change, when the rules are not taken for granted by almost everyone. Unless the group as a whole can reach compromises with the subgroups led by marginal regulars, or so successfully define itself that these would-be regulars give up and leave, the worship service will degenerate into an outright battle. Worship always provides a self-definition of the group at prayer. If the group is fraught with antagonism, the portrait provided by the worship service will show it.**

A final source of malignant pathology is the first circle, the *professionals*. By vesting people with the right to lead the worship ritual, we give them considerable leeway to determine what the worshiping community does. Professionals are not completely free to decide how worship should proceed. Usually they can be hired and fired, or at least removed by recourse to some higher authority. Usually, too, as professionals, they have studied the boundaries governing worship, both in their religious tradition and in their own particular church or synagogue. But that very learning permits them to rationalize that what they do is religiously valid and desirable. Moreover, as we saw before, religious professionals are often viewed as parental figures who, by definition, know what is right. As good professionals trained to know how to do things, aware of the many licit options, and anxious to create worship moments, these professionals are potential sources of novelty rooted in the best possible motives. But however well intentioned, innovations can, at times, fail and become pathological.

Again the list of possibilities is endless: the music director who refuses to let people sing songs that would become positive symbols in the worshipers; the preacher who thinks everyone comes only to listen to the sermon, and who expands it endlessly but cuts back on prayers; the choir that sings for fifteen minutes, oblivious to the fact that the congregation has been standing for a quarter of an hour and cannot think about anything except sitting down. Like any other individual, each professional has his or her own personal needs that may get unduly foisted on the worshiping group to the point of disrupting the worship ritual and destroying any possibility that worship will occur.

In all these cases then—regulars who change the rules, disgruntled movers, and professionals who misuse their power—we get individuals who allow their own needs to encroach on successful public prayer. We label that kind of system breakdown as worship pathology.

Worship Dysfunction: The Case of the Black Box   ◉

There is a second kind of breakdown that is even more serious. It is also more pervasive. Hard to spot in the first place, it is very difficult to correct. In worship pathology, there is at least an identifiable culprit, some particular person in the group who is poisoning the system. In *worship dysfunction*, there is no such malignant cell at all. The system just fails to function.

The mechanical analogy is usually called "the case of the black box." Picture a machine encased in an opaque box. The mechanical parts are not available to you for examination. All you know is that the machine does not do what it should. If you could see inside it, you might discover some particular part that is not functioning properly. But since you cannot do that, you have to treat the box as a whole and apply corrective pressure somewhere outside it, hoping that in some way you can get the correction to spread throughout the box until it starts behaving the way it should. Worship systems are often like black boxes: As far as we can see, everyone seems to be doing everything right, but worship doesn't happen.

Most of my examples so far are such cases of worship dysfunction. In the case of the Scout Sabbath, for example, there is no recognizable person at fault. The same is true of the Saturday morning bar or bat mitzvah syndrome. A church service built around a famous preacher may be another such case. Here the congregation is mobbed by tourists who come only to hear the great speaker. They sit through the accompanying liturgy to do that, but never seriously consider praying. The same may be true also of a mass devoted more to showcasing music than to using the music to move people to prayer—a modern-jazz mass, for instance, where the jazz, not the mass, is what people come for. In each of these cases, the worship system is in a state of dysfunction, since by definition, an outside observer would have to say that what happened was a successful celebration of scouting, family celebration, or entertainment, but not of public prayer.

In each case, however, the people involved may not be able to recognize that there is a problem. They come together to honor the scouts, to hear a famous preacher, or to enjoy some jazz—and that is precisely what happens. So the concept of dysfunction must be amended slightly.

 Systems are dysfunctional only from the viewpoint of our definition of their function.

This is very important, for it indicates the difference between mechanical black boxes and human ones. If, for example, your toaster breaks and burns every piece of bread, you would correctly observe that the toaster is in a state of dysfunction. We distinguish now between people standing outside the toaster waiting for edible toast, and the mechanical parts of the toaster. The people—those outside the system in question—unanimously agree that the toaster is dysfunctioning. That's because they can all agree that the purpose of toasters is to make toast, not charcoal. From the hypothetical perspective of the toaster parts, though, the toaster system is functioning with admirable perfection. Every time bread goes in, out it pops, perfectly burned. As a system for burning bread, the toaster is completely reliable. It never fails. If the toaster parts could talk, they would argue that the problem lies with the people observing it, who project unreal expectations on the toaster. It is not a toaster in the first place, they would say, but a burner. As a burner, it is functional and without peer. The people would then respond that if it were a burner, it should have been advertised in the store as such. No one with such a toaster would hesitate to get it fixed and convert it from a burner to a toaster. The point is this:

> ❀ **Dysfunctional systems often function very well at doing things that we do not claim we want them to do. They are dysfunctional only from the perspective of our own arbitrary definition of what they are supposed to do.**

The worship system may be functioning quite well, then, at something other than worship. The difference between it and the toaster, however, is first, that with the toaster, everyone agrees on what functional toasters are supposed to do, while the people observing worship systems may differ on what proper worship is. And secondly, even if we could decide what worship is, we would still be left with a system in which the internal parts are not mechanical components but other people—and people are not arbitrarily tampered with.

The example of the school system that cannot teach reading is useful here. If we define the school as a system that is supposed to teach reading, then the system is an obvious failure. No teacher or principal is deliberately sabotaging the teaching of reading, however, so we have no obvious case of pathology. This is system dysfunction. Predictably, the school board and PTA become frustrated at a general systemic problem and scapegoat something: the curriculum, perhaps, or the reading teacher. That is, they assume all breakdowns are pathological, so they work hard at finding a cell that can be blamed.

What nobody notices, however, is that the dysfunctional school system is doing other things remarkably well. Take the PTA, for instance. It socializes newcomers into the community, partly through its fundraisers that attract the energy of new and old parents. Critics complain that no matter how much money is raised, the kids still cannot read. But the fundraisers continue year after year, because their function is not so much to inject creative reading programs into the curriculum, but to let parents meet each other, work together, and network socially. The PTA serves political ends too; it is a stepping stone to running the school board, which, in turn, is just a step below town office. The PTA may be an absolute failure at bettering education— and thus be as dysfunctional as the school itself in that regard—yet it may function smoothly and effectively at its unacknowledged agenda. Even if it could be proved that, for over a century, the PTA has not helped children read better, its members would never vote it out of business. They would simply say, "We have to try harder."

We can now state a law of systems, a corollary, and a lesson about change:

> ❖ Law: Most systems are mostly efficient most of the time. If they seem to be inefficient, we are probably not looking at what they do efficiently.

> Corollary: Every human system has two agendas. One is stated publicly. The other is not. In the functioning of organizations, the unstated agenda takes priority.

Lesson: Whether they know it or not, the leaders of institutions got where they are because they learned to appreciate whatever it is that the institution is doing effectively. Despite the need to perform the official agenda more efficiently, they will resist any change that threatens the successful performance of the unofficial agenda.

In our example, the PTA states publicly that it exists to help children read. In fact, its existence is tied to the town's social and political systems. Only with respect to the official goal is the PTA dysfunctional. With regard to what it actually does, it functions beautifully.

The only way to get the PTA to change is to get its leaders to recognize that its stated goal is failing, while its unstated goals are succeeding. The next step is to recognize that scapegoating rather than correcting dysfunctional systems will only exacerbate a longstanding failure to achieve the stated goal. The leaders of the PTA may then discover that other school subsystems are also doing the wrong things right, but the right things wrong. Individuals in those subsystems must be won over to the cause of examining the system as whole. Eventually, we would have the equivalent of the parts of our black box examining the box from within and seeing the mixed messages and the faulty communication. And slowly, very slowly, the school system might heave with change brought about from within, change in which no one is scapegoated—and Janie and Johnnie might learn to read.

The worship system requires that kind of prolonged system correction. Here, too, although the system is failing at its stated agenda of public prayer, it is successfully accomplishing other things. It provides a social network for the regulars and a place to meet and greet each other. It awards status to those who work hard. It recognizes scouting. It just doesn't provide worship moments. Unlike the example of the public school system, however, the people in the worship system are not convinced that the stated goal of public prayer even exists, or that it should. The ability to read is an observable phenomenon that everyone recognizes as existing in some people and desirable for all others.

◉ **Worship dysfunction has been going on for so long that people are not even sure they can or should pray. So changing the worship system to facilitate worship will require, first and foremost, the recognition that worship moments are desirable and possible. When it comes to worship, people are so culturally deprived they don't even know what to look for.**

The absence of genuine worship in many North American churches and synagogues leaves unsatisfied the genuine spiritual need for public prayer. But to improve the situation, those who lead prayer need greater insight into what makes it work. Such insight can correct their own ineffective management of the rites they are supposed to lead. They may even find that many of their own ingrained habits are pathological to worship, in at least a benign way. But even after we have worked at correcting our own pathologies, we still will have the problem of handling worship dysfunction. How does a system get an unbiased self-portrait so that it can replace endless and useless scapegoating with a genuine overhaul of itself and achieve a new beginning?

These are the issues we take up in the rest of this book. The subtitle for the rest of the chapters might be, "Correcting the System: Making Worship Work Again."

Ritual Check List ◉

Words and Concepts You Should Know

- **Metacommunication** is communication about communication; it tells people how to read what we are saying. When metacommunication conflicts with communication, people find themselves in a double bind—unable to obey either form of communication without disobeying the other.

- **Some worship problems arise** from pathological members of the worship group, who inflict their own ideas on the group as a whole.

- **In every worshiping community,** there are professionals, regulars, movers, and watchers.

- **Pathology** is most apt to arise among disenfranchised regulars who have been relegated to movers. These people attract others who are discontented. They argue about worship because worship is the ritual arena where group identity is played out. Worship problems are usually communal problems involving group identity.

- **Pathology** may also arise from the professionals who use their knowledge and power to accomplish what they need at the expense of the rest of the worshiping group.

- **Most pathology is censored out by group pressure,** so it remains benign. If it spreads to infect the system as a whole, it is considered malignant. Other group members will attempt to remove a pathological member, to save the group.

- **More subtle and more deep-seated worship problems** arise from systemic dysfunction: cases where there is no malignant cell, but where the system does not function well.

- **Systems are dysfunctional** only from the perspective of our own arbitrary definition of what they are supposed to do.

- **Law:** Most systems are mostly efficient most of the time. If they seem to be inefficient, we are probably not looking at what they do efficiently.

- **Corollary:** Every human system has two agendas. One is stated publicly. The other is not. In the functioning of organizations, the unstated agenda takes priority.

- **Lesson:** Whether they know it or not, the leaders of institutions got where they are because they learned to appreciate whatever it is that the institution is doing effectively. Despite the need to perform the official agenda more efficiently, they will resist any change that threatens the successful performance of the unofficial agenda.

- **Worship dysfunction** has been going on for so long that people are not even sure what prayer is, and people have become so culturally deprived that they don't even know what to look for.

Conversation Points for Making Worship Work

1 ▪ We have all experienced uncertain communications and even double binds that occur when we are caught in the middle between communications and metacommunications. If you have a worship care group, go around the room where you are meeting, and ask people to talk about times when someone said something to them, but they were not certain what the person meant. Does anyone have any instances of double binds?

2 ▪ Take your worship care group into the room where worship is usually held. Have everyone sit where they usually sit during worship. Ask them why they sit there, and how comfortable they feel with the service, the environment, the rules of prayer. Are they watchers? Regulars? Movers? Professionals? Meet one week later, after everyone has had a chance to attend another Sabbath worship service, for which they had been instructed beforehand to look for watchers. Have them report back on how watchers could be spotted, what they did, what seemed to make them uncomfortable. Discuss how watchers can be made to feel more at home.

3 ▪ Visit another church or synagogue, preferably one where the worship is completely unfamiliar to you. Report back on what it was like being a watcher. Where did you sit? Were there moments of special discomfort? Why? Did anyone try to help you out or put you at ease? Were they successful?

five

The Presence of God at Worship

The most obvious approach to the problem of prayer is to consider it an issue of faith. If only we moderns could believe in God with the fervor of those who came before us, goes the argument, we would have no difficulty with our worship.

In favor of this approach is its evident simplicity. But it is just another way to scapegoat worshipers. Nothing will frustrate

 Our inability to believe is the result, not the cause, of worship failure.

people's hopes for prayer more than being told that their persistent failure to find liturgical satisfaction is their own fault. Charging worshipers with the admonition, "If only you had faith," is like saying to children with failing grades, "If only you had brains."

Scapegoating worshipers may conveniently salve the conscience of frustrated clergy who have trouble facing up to their inability to direct meaningful worship, but it only aggravates an already malfunctioning worship system. It also hastens the drift away from public worship toward such alternative public ritualizing as sports, politics, or pseudoreligious cults. The proper retort to those who advocate solving worship problems by haranguing worshipers to pull themselves up from the morass of their disbelief by their own spiritual bootstraps is H. L. Mencken's acerbic observation: "For every human problem, there is one solution that is simple, neat, and wrong." Assuming that we could pray if only we believed is simple and neat; it is also colossally wrong.

People find faith in many ways. The old adage that there are no atheists in foxholes expresses the truism that some people turn to God as a last resort when they realize how close they are to death. Other people find faith in exactly the opposite situation: not in moments of existential panic, but in flashes of eternity when nothing seems more certain than the radiant joy of life—a glimpse of the sunset over the Grand Canyon, or the moment of a child's miraculous birth. The foxhole syndrome and the Grand Canyon syndrome are cases of extreme experiences calling forth faith from deep within us, faith we did not know we had.

No one can seriously deny the catalytic effect that foxholes and Grand Canyons have on detecting faith buried deep within us. The problem is that these extreme instances of faith discovery rarely prove lasting. Lots of people say they have known the presence of God at one or more peak moments in their lives, but they never come to worship services because they doubt they can find the Grand Canyon in their liturgies. If we depend on foxholes, baby births, and setting suns to fill our churches and synagogues, we are in deep trouble.

A more sophisticated argument on the origins of faith comes from psychologists in the field of faith development. Erik Erikson has plotted the human life cycle as a succession of stages, each with its own opportunity for expanding human potential. Old age brings integrity and wisdom, says Erikson, but the first step on the long road leading to that final stage is infancy, which is when we learn the value of trust and faith. Some people may be more open to faith experiences because of their early childhood. One can hardly blame them if they are not.

Other theorists point out that faith is not a single monolithic thing that we either have or we don't. Instead, it is a complex phenomenon that grows through time. The foxhole syndrome in which faith in a supreme deity is evoked by fear of imminent punishment ranks very low on the scale of the kinds of faith mature men and women attain. Faith is attainable in many ways, and faith need not be stagnant. Healthy ritual can help faith grow.

> ▩ **Ritual is not the result of faith, but one of its causes— that is why we need good rituals. Ritual's power lies in its artistic capacity to present an alternative world where time and space unfold in structured ways that indicate pattern, plan, and purpose. Faith derives from trusting that the universe in which we live is meaningful and ordered, as opposed to being random, chaotic, and accidental.**

We need to see more fully how the experience of ritualized order leads to faith in general. Then we have to ask how we come to identify the object of our faith as God.

Stage One: Patterns and Metapatterns ▩

Faith is the belief in an eventual outcome of events despite the absence of empirical demonstration that such an outcome is probable. Suppose I drop a ten-pound weight from a ten-story window and insist that I have faith it will hit the ground. That is not faith, you will protest, but a conclusion fairly drawn from prior experience. Of course, it is theoretically possible that what has always happened will not happen this time, that maybe the law of gravity will be suspended just this once. In a way, then, as much as they are different, scientific prediction and faith in providence are at least on the same continuum: To some extent, we operate with faith every time we take a step. But we normally reserve the word "faith" for the confidence we have in what could not be predicted by scientific evidence. Faith in God implies the belief that God is *real*, even though science cannot demonstrate any cogent empirical grounds for believing it.

But faith is not *altogether* different from scientific knowledge. Science builds upon the patterns that it finds in nature. An unsophisticated way of detecting pattern is trial and error; our primitive cave-dwelling ancestors were no scientists, but they too would have predicted the fall of the ten-pound weight from a high building. Science replaces trial and error with finely tuned hypotheses that it expresses in mathematical formulations. When some of Einstein's theoretical predictions were finally demonstrated empirically, he is said to have reacted unemotionally: Since the mathematics worked out, he had already *known* he was right. So scientific knowledge depends on the discovery of order, either firsthand (we observe the same thing happening over and over again) or mathematically (we work out an equation that predicts the pattern in question, whether it has yet been observed or not).

Faith does not work with equations, but it also comes from the experience of pattern, whereby we come to believe that some things can be counted on. Faith is challenged when the unexplainable occurs: Why *should* good people suffer? But long-term faith may answer that there must be some ultimate order somewhere. That is God's answer to Job. Job is a perfectly just man who loses everything. When he wonders aloud about the apparent absence of moral pattern, God asks him, "Were you there when I created the universe?" Job is an anomaly, because his suffering is so extreme that he stands out as completely unpredictable. But science too faces anomalies, situations in nature that are completely unexpected and unexplainable according to what we know about the state of nature. Both religion and science are alike in that they respond to their anomalies by insisting that there is some overall pattern nonetheless, even if we cannot figure out what it is yet.

The Half-Baked Cake

As a child, I used to watch my mother stir together the recipe ingredients for my favorite cake. I would make a wry face at the gooey mess in the mixer bowl, convinced that the unappealing batter could never metamorphose into a delicious cake. My mother told me once that she recalled watching her mother bake, and thinking the same thing. Now she wanted to pass on my grandmother's advice to me—an old Yiddish proverb: "A fool shouldn't observe work that is only half done." I doubt that my mother knew she was teaching me faith at the time, but she was.

In that sense, it is less the miracle of the unusual—the foxhole and the Grand Canyon—that endows us with lasting faith as much as it is the miracle of the everyday, just as it is the recognition of nature's daily regularity that generates scientific principles. But there is an important difference between the patterning of experience that leads to religious faith and the patterning of experience that promotes science: Scientific patterns need not embody value; they simply exist as observable phenomena. Hypothetically, at least, we can imagine a world created by a malicious demon in which the laws of nature are a cruel hoax to frustrate good people who hold out pathetically for the possibility of a better world. Scientific confidence would still be possible in that world; religious faith would not. Faith emerges not out of the patterns alone, but from the trust that those patterns are beneficial in the end. Psychologist Gregory Bateson helps us here by differentiating among different levels of pattern.

Take any simple animal, a crab, for example, and note the similarity between the left side of its body and the right, or between its right front side, where a front leg protrudes, and the right back side, where a rear leg is found. The first case (left and right are the same) is called *bilateral symmetry;* the second (front and back are similar) is *serial homology.* Both, however, are alike in that they are patterns that hold between two different parts of the same animal. Bateson calls this *first order patterning.*

Now compare the crab with a lobster. What was true of the crab seems also to be true of the lobster. Lobsters are also bilaterally symmetrical, and they too exhibit similarities between their front and rear appendages. So a double pattern exists between the lobster and the crab: They both exhibit the same sets of relationships between left and right, and front and back. When two species demonstrate similar patterns this way, it is called *phylogenetic homology*. But phylogenetic homology is one step up from serial homology and bilateral symmetry since it is a pattern that holds between two patterns. If serial homology is a comparison of an animal's parts, phylogenetic homology is a comparison of those comparisons. Bateson calls this higher step in the chain of patterns *second order patterning*.

Another example of second order patterning begins with the similarity between a horse and a human. Horses and humans both have bilateral symmetry and serial homology. We can therefore compare the fact that horses are like humans to the similar fact that crabs are like lobsters. That is to say, we are now making a comparison (horses:humans :: crabs:lobsters) of the comparison (crabs: lobsters) of the comparisons (crabs: left and right sides are similar; front and back appendages are similar). Bateson calls this a *third order patterning*.

The point of it all is that when we talk about patterns, we are not always discussing the same thing. Patterns exist in an ascending order of increasing abstraction. Any fool can observe first order patterns just by holding a crab and noting its symmetry. The idea that the crab might be like the lobster is more difficult to conceptualize, since each animal is sufficiently unlike the other that it might not occur to us to see how they are the same. But it is relatively easy to hold a crab in one hand and a lobster in the other and observe the second order pattern that unites them both. By the time we get to third order patterns, however, we are hardly in the realm of empirical evidence at all, since we are comparing not the animals themselves, but the similarity of relationships between the animals. I can see a horse and I can see a human and I might even see the similarity between horses and humans. But surely I do not literally see the similarity between that similarity and another one, namely, the similarity between crabs and lobsters. The similarity of similarities is something I understand or deduce from the evidence, not something I actually see in the same way that I see the evidence itself.

Theoretically, we can go even farther—into the realm of *fourth order patterning*, where the patterns of patterns of patterns are held together in still one more pattern. At that point, we are so far removed from the evidence that it becomes virtually impossible even to picture what we are talking about. Here we enter the realm of faith. Religious believers hold to the proposition that the cosmos is a masterwork where somehow, despite death and disaster, it all makes sense. To the inevitability of human mortality, for example, Christianity teaches that Jesus overcame death on our behalf, and Judaism (even prior to Jesus' day) preached resurrection of the dead and reward and punishment in a world to come.

My favorite image in this regard is the Jewish tradition that imputes to Elijah the prophet the secrets of what I call the *metapatterns* of the universe. When medieval rabbinic scholastics found equally compelling logics leading to mutually incompatible positions, the two sides to a debate suspended their discussion but retained their respective stands. Holding the ultimate solution in abeyance, they are said to have announced, "Elijah will harmonize conflicting conclusions." My word "harmonize" is instructive here. It is an artistic term that expresses our faith that facts must cohere in the long run, just as musical notes should flow together melodiously or colors on a painting should blend together pleasingly. Things *must* be so, we hold, even in the face of the most mind-boggling evidence to the contrary. We may not see the metapattern that connects all the lower level patterning around us, not yet anyway, but Jews and Christians have been raised to take it on faith that such a plan exists.

> ❀ **A common first step toward a lasting faith in God, then, is a far cry from momentary peak events like Grand Canyon sunsets. It is the discovery, instead, of elementary patterns and then of second-level patterns and so on until we have a momentous vision of the top of the ladder, the existence of a metapattern linking all the patterns.**

The world now makes sense: It coheres, totally and absolutely; it forms a balanced whole with everything in relationship to everything else. Not only is it coherent, it is also comprehensive, since it assumes not just an island of order here or there, but everywhere and at all times, completely beyond the possibility of experiential confirmation.

In their essence, all ritual means pattern, affirming resolution, completion, and continuity. Rites of passage, for example, affirm continuity despite the obvious discontinuity of generational turnover and the wrenching metamorphosis of our stage-by-stage development from birth to death. Similarly, in political ritual, supporters of competing presidential nominees in the Democratic Party may threaten temporarily to tear apart their party at its preelection national convention, but veteran pols know that, in the end, everyone will come together as the band strikes up "Happy Days Are Here Again." Then, in January, no matter how bitterly contested the election the previous November turns out to have been, at the ritualistic swearing-in ceremony the new president will call for unity and take the oath of office as the president of *all* the people.

Another example of ritual's power to portray how everything fits together nicely in the long run is *rituals of reversal* that let the underdog experience what it is like to be on top for a while. There are also *rituals of conflict resolution* in which internal strains are played out in a ritual script that decreases the odds that they will fester until they eventually disrupt society. And if revolutionary social change does occur, it brings its own rituals that justify the revolution as the next logical step in the unfolding of a larger pattern called human history.

❁ At least as important as its content, then, is ritual's essential form: the ordered and inexorable unfolding of a script. Rituals work best if the script is seen as ancient and timeless. This often includes words we've heard before and songs we know and love. Even unbelievers may leave a religious ritual feeling (if not yet believing) that there is a divine plan. But this will occur only if the ritual that they leave has been such a successful micro-

cosm of ultimate order that it swept them up in the beauty of wholeness.

It was from the form as much as the content of the universe that Einstein drew his faith in the absolute necessity of an ultimately comprehensive pattern. Against the opposition of many of his colleagues who made up the elite echelon of the scientific community, he dedicated his later years to positing a grand field theory that would have united all the phenomena of the universe in a master synthesis of patterning. He never accepted the claim of quantum mechanics that the subatomic world works according to probability rather than by absolute mechanistic necessity. He said that God doesn't play dice with the universe.

But Einstein did not believe in God. I said before that this chapter would explore the relationship between ritual and faith. Our first step has been the discovery of how it is that the experience of ritualized order leads to faith in general. Now we have to ask how we learn to identify the object of that faith as God.

From Faith in General to Faith in God 🕮

According to the foxhole theory of faith, finding God is easy. Revelation comes quickly if your life flashes before your eyes. So too with Grand Canyon sunsets: Who can doubt God's reality in a blaze of incomparable glory? In truth, however, even there, if you are not ready to recognize God's presence, you'll miss it. According to a Jewish folktale, a rabbi is asked where God is found. He replies, "Wherever people let God in." I take that tale not as a moralistic scolding that people who don't know God are responsible for putting up defenses against God's entering their lives, but as a commentary on the fact that even people who want to know God may fail if they have not been taught to recognize the divine presence even when it knocks on their door. In that sense they miss the opportunity to let God in.

Popular religious literature and the media have stereotyped the experience called "knowing God," so that it is assumed that God appears only in sunsets and foxholes, the very, very grand and the very, very frightening. When people have religious experiences that fit into neither of these categories, it never occurs to them to think they are experiencing God's presence. What we need is a generic conceptualization of the ways people identify God, one that is applicable to all times and places. That will enable us to avoid limiting God's presence in general to any particular cultural manifestation of it. Freed from the mistaken notion that how God appears in one era is how God must appear in another, we can look afresh and see where God is most likely to be found for us. That insight will have major implications for our worship policy. To name but two:

> **If God is no longer found predominantly in the realm of the magnificent, we need to take a new look at the centrality of magnificent music in religious services. If God is to be identified in the presence of human caring and love, we may have to rethink sanctuary seating plans that impose separation and anonymity on people.**

The key to finding God in American worship is located in the word "community."

Built for Community

Some years ago, I gave a speech at the old convention center in downtown Minneapolis. As I entered the building, I marveled at its stately quality. Sitting majestically on a full square block of land just beyond the downtown tourist hub, the center seemed to symbolize the full depth of local tradition that makes the Twin Cities unique. Appropriately enough, an inscription chiseled into the granite on the building's upper facade read, "Built for Community." Yet the building was slated for destruction, its place to be taken by a bigger, "better" structure. Would the new one also be dedicated to community, I wondered, or would its inscription read, "Bigger and Better"?

The fate of the Minneapolis convention center is a sad symptom of a cultural conflict being played out in synagogue and church worship as the twenty-first century dawns. On one hand, there is the view that the most meaningful human experiences are located in the warmth of human relationship; if God is experienced anywhere, it is in caring loving communities. So worship should strive to replicate patterns of loving care. It should break down the formal distinctions of social distance that divide people from each other. Openness and trust, as well as human bonding across class, race, age, and gender, rank high on the list of signs of spiritual being. In stark contrast are traditional European models of religious worship, primarily those associated with cathedral architecture and high culture. This form of spirituality is deeply individualistic, not communal. It assumes that people go to pray to escape the fetters of social life and to commune directly with a God who is beyond human society. God is seen as mighty, transcendent, and far from the madding crowd. Advocates of this approach point out that the alternative community model typified the countercultural revolution of the 1960s and 1970s, and that we are beyond all that now. Community building may indeed be a worthy goal, they say, but it is hardly the search for God, since God is present only in the grand and the beautiful. What we need, they add, is lofty music, sweeping drama, and high culture of impeccable artistic taste.

Is that true? Or can God be present also (as Elijah learned) "in the still, small voice"? Is God really available only in the stratosphere? Or have we been so conditioned to think in those terms that we miss the presence of God elsewhere? Is God present beyond us? Or among us? Or both? How, that is, do we in our time find God in prayer?

Finding God in Prayer   ❀

Before answering these questions, let us examine some personal testimony about knowing God, from other people in history, in the hope that we can find a pattern that is common to the way everyone discovers the divine in their worship. We can then apply that pattern to ourselves and see how we are the same as those who came before us, as well as how we are simultaneously different.

In the 1890s, a German scholar named Philipp Bloch discovered an eleventh-century document that described Jews who believed that by fasting for a stipulated number of days, and then by muttering prayers with their heads between their knees, they would catch a glimpse of God in supreme glory, surrounded by angels saying the words of praise we know so well from our own liturgies, "Holy, holy, holy, is the Lord of hosts."

The religious community in which Bloch lived—nineteenth-century German Jewish intellectuals—ascribed to a trust in rationalism that was far removed from the sort of mystical contemplation of God suggested by Bloch's discovery. Its members had, in fact, already accepted the faulty presumption that classical rabbinic Judaism must have opposed mysticism. They therefore faced this newfound discovery with a certain ambivalence. While the find was obviously important to scholars, it was the very antithesis of the staid rationalistic experience typical of enlightened synagogues then. Bloch himself found it difficult to imagine that the worshipers whose practice he had unearthed were typical of what he assumed was the essential Jewish spirit inherited from the past. So he concluded that the mystics he was studying had been marginal to mainstream Jewish tradition. He said they had flourished some time after the formative influences of rabbinic Judaism had been laid, and that they had lived in "distant regions of the East," meaning some place influenced by "mystery cults" and the mystical "excesses" that scholars of the time vaguely lumped together as "orientalism." By implication, these people were a "special case" that was irrelevant to modern life.

Nevertheless, Bloch painted a fascinating picture of worshipers whose prayers were marked not by their content, but by their form, a form that exhibited a certain rhythmic regularity, like an eastern mantra. What mattered most was not what the words meant, but how they sounded. Its language was excessively lengthy, composed chiefly of chains of synonyms in apposition to each other and selected only for their poetic value. The total cognitive message, such as it was, could be captured in one simple sentence: "Praise God." Worshipers were caught up in the rhythmic flow of the words, which, together with the sensation brought on by fasting and the blood rushing to their head as a consequence of being upside down, invoked a state of trance: They hoped thereby to lose their sense of standing on the earth and, if you like, to "trip" through heaven to see God.

We now know that these worshipers were not marginal to ancient Jewish spirituality. They are sometimes called the Chariot Mystics because of their assumption that God inhabited a chariot in the distant heavens, driving the chariot across the sky the way the sun appears to move from east to west. Chariot mysticism was central to the age that gave us the nascent church and the rabbinic tradition at the same time. Bloch was wrong on his proposed date and place of their activity. We now date these mystics as early as the second century, and we place them in the very heart of Palestine itself.

We should also look more carefully at the word "mystic" that has been used to describe them. It sounds at first like an innocent description, but "mystic" is really neither innocent nor descriptive. In the nineteenth century, pinning the label "mystic" on someone stigmatized them. Bloch's selection of the term functioned the same way his faulty date and place for them did: It distanced them from his contemporaries. Even today, when our appreciation of the variety of authentic religious experience has increased dramatically, calling people mystics evokes a suspicious sense that they are, at the very least, not entirely normal like the rest of us. Find people who are really religious, and you say, "Ah, yes . . . well, they are mystics"—which is equivalent to saying, "I'm not like that, and do not intend to be." My unofficial translation of "mystic" is "off the wall," meaning "all right for them, but not for us." By calling our great spiritual ancestors mystics, we imply that theirs was an interesting sect for its time, but you wouldn't want to join it.

But do you think *they* knew they were mystics? Did they belong to a National Association of Mystical Worshipers, pay dues to a mystics' guild, or go to mystics' conventions? Just to ask these silly questions is to answer them. These so-called mystics were just the Rabbis, the same ones known to us in imperfect fashion from early rabbinic literature that is nothing if not rationally conceived and arranged. Like anyone else in any other time, they had families, held jobs, and lived a rational existence; they also gave us the logical system of Jewish law that stands even now at Judaism's core. Yet when they prayed, they temporarily stepped out of their daily routine, hoping to stand, like the angels, face-to-face with the Holy One of Blessing, and lose themselves in uninhibited praise of the God of light. Then they would return to their tasks in this world.

Another example is the apostle Paul. Paul's letters to churches in the first century are the epitome of logic and reason. Yet Paul owed his very apostleship to the mystical vision that he had on the road to Damascus.

It is misleading to believe that either people are mystics or they are not. In truth, there is only a mystical temperament, available to all men and women at all times. Not that the mystical temperament is universally expressed the same way, any more than the universal human potential for music results in just one kind of melody. The forms change, even though the human expression in general does not. So I am not arguing that we should emulate the specific *forms* of worship that I have described so far. We need to discover *our own* mystical forms of prayer that will achieve the same spiritual goal as the people who knew God in other eras. Toward that end I must now introduce three technical terms into our discussion.

First, *cultural backdrop*, which is akin to the backdrop of a play— the balcony for the balcony scene from *Romeo and Juliet*, for example. Backdrop is the context that allows actors to play their roles. As Shakespeare recognized, "All the world's a stage, and all the men and women merely players." Backdrop is necessary for the roles we play in real life no less than for those contrived by playwrights. The whole point of backdrop, however, is that it does not draw attention to itself. It remains unnoticed while the drama is being played out on the stage. If you doubt that, imagine that your best friend is playing Juliet, and she asks how you enjoyed the performance. Can you imagine responding, "I liked it. The balcony was beautiful!"? Yet without the balcony as a backdrop, there could be no balcony scene. Our lives depend on the unconscious setting, or backdrop, offered by our culture. But we generally take it so much for granted that we are hardly even aware of what that backdrop is, unless experts such as social critics draw it to our attention.

In the first two centuries of our era, the cultural backdrop of what was then called Palestine was Hellenism. Among other things, this philosophy divided the universe into two warring forces, light and darkness. God as light became a dominant image in the so-called mystery cults, as well as in Christianity and Judaism. None of these escaped the influence of Hellenism as a common cultural backdrop. (All religions were, so to speak, actors on the same cultural stage.) For example, Jesus was regularly portrayed as light, a dominant liturgical metaphor in Christian liturgy even to this day. Paul saw the risen Jesus "in a light from heaven that flashed around him." And Judaism features a Saturday evening prayer (called *Havdalah*) that distinguishes light from darkness.

Now we understand why the early synagogue worshipers whom we have described sound so strange to us. They believed in a universe with the earth at the center, but with concentric circles of light around it, the outermost circles being the heavens, which God, the source of light, inhabited. The worshipers' goal, toward which the trancelike state contributed, was temporarily to break loose from the limitations imposed by their earthbound conditions—a mixture of light (or soul) and darkness (or body)—so as to travel to the regions of pure light, for which the soul had an affinity anyway. There they would join the angels, who, unlike humans, were composed of nothing but light, and glorify the God of light. My point is that as strange as that may sound to us, it was perfectly consistent in a culture where the dichotomy of light versus darkness was taken for granted.

Consider now just the image of God enthroned in light, surrounded by lightlike beings called angels who, dazzled by God's brightness, do nothing but utter praise after praise of God. We have no trouble recognizing that image too. It has survived for centuries. Now imagine your lifetime experience with religion as if it were a video tape. It would be composed of a series of frames that pass rapidly through the camera to give us the illusion of motion. Suppose, now, you collapse all the frames and assemble a master frame that expresses all your experiences with God. That hypothetical single frame goes by the second of my three technical terms, *master image*. The master image we have been describing here—God enthroned in light—is typical of the cultural backdrop of Hellenism.

But a master image must be congruent with the cultural backdrop it expresses. Other cultures at other times have therefore developed their own master images. Again, the analogy of a play is useful. The master image of *Romeo and Juliet* (the picture you would expect to see on a *Playbill*, or the one you think of first as typifying the play's content) is the balcony scene; the reason it fits so well, however, is not that there is something innately striking about balconies. Its success as a master image of the play is partly because the physical distance between Juliet on the balcony and Romeo in the garden is symbolic of the play as a whole, whose theme, after all, is the gulf between the two warring families to which Romeo and Juliet belong. Similarly, though our abundant familiarity with the image of God as light being adored by angels of light might make us think otherwise, there is nothing inherently necessary about it either. Its popularity in the formative era of Judaism and Christianity was due to its success at evoking a dominant cultural theme of light, which everyone took for granted at the time. It became permanently encoded in the classical liturgies of the two faiths and persists to this day, even though it can hardly be said to have the same power for us as it did for people in its original Hellenistic context.

Finally, I come to my last technical term: *synecdochal* (pronounced sin-EK d'k'l) *vocabulary*. We normally think of vocabulary as words, but it is a lot more than that. Vocabulary is any way we convey a message. Shaking hands, nodding formally, and kissing passionately are all different vocabulary items—ways to send messages about relationships when we greet people. So vocabulary can be soundless movement and gesture. Vocabulary includes objects too. For Christians, the prime religious item may be a cross; for Jews, it may be a Torah scroll. If you combine movements and gestures with objects, you get more complex ritual actions: raising the cup of sacramental wine, carrying the Torah, and so on. Through gesture, action, and object, we say as much as we do with words; sometimes we say more.

Vocabulary can be further divided into those instances in which a word, gesture, object, or action wholly contains the message, and cases where it merely hints at the message in some agreed-upon fashion. If, for example, I say, "This is a good book to read," you may duly note the advice and read the book. But that is all there is to it. Imagine, however, climbing in the Himalayas to find a guru, whom you ask, "Tell me the secret of life, O Holy One." The guru produces a worn object from beneath a cloak, and says, "Read this. It is The Book." Here we have a common noun "book," being used not to identify a simple object, but to point beyond that object to something further. The same applies to the word "cross" for Christians, and "Torah" for Jews. Words, gestures, and objects can point beyond themselves to a reality that vocabulary cannot really describe, but only suggest. As we saw in chapter 2, sometimes what is pointed to is so deeply rooted in our psyche that it cannot be defined; then we get vocabulary that we call symbolic.

There is, however, a medium position too: vocabulary that is synecdochal. Synecdoche (pronounced sin-EK-d'-kee) is a literary term meaning the use of a part to refer to the whole. Suppose I say, "The pen is mightier than the sword." It is highly unlikely that I have such depth of attachment to pens or to swords that either word is really a symbol. On the other hand, by "pen" I don't mean just a pen, but the act of writing, by which, further, I have in mind literature and the human spirit. Similarly, the word "sword" here is not just a sword, but an image suggesting violence and war. What I really mean to say is that, in the long run, spirit is more powerful that brute force. In the medium-range usage, a word points beyond its most literal meaning, but not so deeply that it has no single specific referent at all. Synecdochal vocabulary means words, gestures, and things that point beyond themselves to greater wholes that cannot fully be captured in speech.

We will be looking more deeply at language in a later chapter, but for now we can add to what we noted in chapter 2 (on symbols) by observing three different uses of liturgical language.

1 ▪ *Signifying function:* A word signifies when it stands for a particular literal, concrete referent.

2 ▪ *Synecdochal function:* A word "synecdochizes" (to coin a verb) when it goes beyond itself to suggest a greater whole that cannot fully be captured in speech, and this can only be hinted at.

3 ▪ *Symbolizing function:* A word symbolizes when it goes beyond any single particular referent at all, including any conceivable whole of which the sign value referent is a part. It functions primarily to evoke depth of commitment.

Liturgy relies on all three uses, but the one that particularly interests us here is synecdoche.

❂ Synecdochal vocabulary consists of words, objects, actions, and gestures that suggest a whole greater than themselves; liturgy provides synecdochal vocabulary to suggest a particular master image. Trained by our cultural context to recognize the reality of God in that image, we use synecdochal language to invoke God's presence in our worship.

We can observe this system working in the concrete instance of the Chariot Mystics. Let us picture some third-century Jews praying in the ancient synagogue of Beth Alpha near the Sea of Galilee. If you go there, you can still see its remnants, a brilliant floor mosaic, one section of which displays God as the sun surrounded by the zodiac signs designating the heavens. The cultural backdrop of the time is Hellenism, and the master image is God arrayed in radiant glory. For synecdochal vocabulary, worshipers depended on things such as body posture, words as mantras, and the mosaic floor's light imagery. For example, they recited their poems of praise, culminating in the words from Isaiah's vision, "Holy, holy, holy," as they simultaneously looked at their synagogue mosaics that displayed God as master of the sun. This would have led them to the reality of God's commanding presence in the radiant heavens, which they would have experienced as a mystical journey beyond their earthbound selves.

> ▦ **How are we aware of God in prayer? Through synecdochal vocabulary of our time that best suggests the reality of a master image that itself best reflects the cultural backdrop in which we stand.**

It would never occur to us to fast for three days to induce a vision, but that is only because our cultural backdrop is different from that of ancient Palestine. Our master image is no longer a God of light circling the globe in the farthest heaven; and the synecdochal vocabulary that worked so well then will fail now. But the model of worship as cultural backdrop, master image, and synecdochal vocabulary holds for Christian as for Jew, and in all ages, even though the particular content of each of these items changes.

My second example, much closer to home, is nineteenth- and early twentieth-century western Europe, especially Germany. A famous book by theologian Rudolf Otto, *The Idea of the Holy*, describes worship then. Otto observed that prayer in his day meant to be aware of the radical gulf between ourselves and the ineffable Deity who evoked absolute awe. Otto's God is utterly transcendent. Otto accurately described the churches and synagogues that many of us know from our youth. They were influenced by the upper-class western

European spirit. You didn't walk into them and talk, or smile and say, "Hi, there." You entered them aware of your human weakness relative to God and waiting for the God of awe to appear. Why was that kind of worship typical of Germany?

To answer that, we can begin with Germany's cultural backdrop, which was not Hellenism with its overriding concern with light versus darkness. Instead, the cultural theme was one of order: There was a place for everything and everything stayed in its place. This reflected a German penchant for arranging, classifying, and organizing people, places, and things. Such a system emphasized the importance of putting *people* too in their respective categories. Class consciousness—the social distance, if you like—that separated one class from another told people their place: You knew who you were by who you were not.

The image of God as an awesome, distant Being was therefore not something at which Otto arrived out of the theological blue. It was an extrapolation from the exaggerated social distance that marked human relationships in German society. Social classes retained their distinctiveness by erecting impenetrable barriers between themselves and others. Formal titles and strict dress codes, for example, militated against easy social mingling across class lines. Paralleling the space separating one social class from another was a veritable social chasm that separated all social classes—all people, in general—from God. Thus was born the master image of God as transcendent, of God as the ultimately distant Being.

◉ So successful was this redefinition of God in terms of wider European society that many of us still take it for granted, as if the master image of God were not just image but God's very being. A transcendent deity is really just another imperfect way of imaging the Divine, favored by one society in one particular time and place. But our liturgy was reconstructed on that image only a century ago. It was then transmitted that way to us, as if it were inevitable that only by celebrating God's regal distance from us could worship successfully invoke God's presence.

We all know very well the synecdochal vocabulary that European, and then American, worship developed to invoke transcendence: grand churches, the glorification of baroque architecture, music piped from a hidden choir singing so well that parishioners didn't dare join in, and enhanced social distance between the officiating minister and the people in the pews. To be sure, this was no invention of the nineteenth century alone; it had been building for some time. But we emerged from the nineteenth century with architecture that pointed to God in the distance and with masterful choirs singing four-part harmony composed in a key marked, Angels Only.

It is fascinating to speculate on whether the people who prayed in those lavish structures, sitting formally through endless services without participating, were mystics. Surely Jews and Christians who thought of themselves as the epitome of rationality would have denied that allegation. But should we believe them? No less than the worshipers in antiquity described above, they too emerged with a sense that God was present in their prayers. They differed only in how God's presence was conceived, and therefore how God's presence was known. If, by definition, "mystical" means "oddly (and irrationally) religious," then they were not mystics. But if mystical refers only to the tendency within all of us to find God in our own way, then they were as mystical as their predecessors who celebrated God's light-giving capacity by fasting and joining the bands of praising angels in the heavens surrounding the earth.

A God of Intimacy　　❖

After this brief stopover in Europe, we arrive back home in America, with the debate over the relative significance of community. The threefold way of looking at worship works here as well. What is the cultural backdrop of America, if not just the opposite of Europe? Europeans understood the grand art of Monet's *Water Lilies*, while we have Andy

Warhol's *Campbell's Soup Cans*. Our music has changed too. America has given us jazz—the people music of African-American spirituals—and Pete Seeger's folk idiom. We've been raised on the folk guitar, not the organ; on Copland's *Rodeo*, not Handel's *Messiah*. From 1901 to almost the end of his life in 1934, Sir Edward Elgar composed five marches that he called collectively *Pomp and Circumstance*. His goal was to rescue the splendor of Great Britain's glorious tradition from the homogenizing impact of modernity. In 1942, only eight years after Elgar died, the American Aaron Copland wrote his own musical tribute to the best that humanity had to offer, but called it *Fanfare for the Common Man* (emphasis added).

Copland loved America precisely because its cultural backdrop tried to eradicate European class distinctions. In America, we work hard to obliterate social distance: We use first names; address envelopes without care for titles; build public schools and universities where every American is invited—ideally—to attend; and jettison the dress codes that have traditionally marked off one class from another. Since we now live in a cultural backdrop of theoretical equality, our master image can hardly feature a God of transcendence. It is difficult for us to imagine God as endlessly distant from us; instead, we think more easily of God being immanently present among us. And our synecdochal vocabulary will be words, gestures, actions, and objects that bring God into our midst. Walt Whitman captured the American religious ethos when he wrote, "God comes a loving bedfellow and sleeps at my side all night and close on the peep of the day."

Synecdochal vocabulary for American worship, therefore, must point to intimacy, not distance. That is the point of "community," a term we use for the people from whom we anticipate love, friendship, and care. Far from deprecating worship that celebrates community, we should appreciate it as a mode of prayer where God is likely to be present among us.

In the last few decades we have been concerned about the destruction of community. The century began with an abundance of communities that came about naturally, such as native farming communities or enclaves of immigrants from tiny towns in Europe. In these communities (as in Garrison Keillor's fictional town of Lake Wobegon, for example), people grew up, married, and grew old together. But urbanization brought people to huge metropolises, where they gave up their ethnic enclaves. For a while, they lived together in neighborhoods and kept up ties with extended family members, who remembered what it was like to be related to a common set of ancestors and blessed with a common memory. In the 1950s, we moved out farther still to suburbs, where we soon lost track even of our neighbors and learned to race in cars on endless thruways to impersonal destinations. People who once sat on front porches hailing friends and passersby now build backyard decks to protect their privacy from strangers. Extended families have disappeared, and even the nuclear family is in trouble. Most observers would agree that if there is one crying need in our time, it is for us to know one another again, to rebuild neighborhoods, to know a place where we can greet one another in all the intimacy that America promises—and that is where the church and synagogue come in.

We live in what can be described as a limited liability community. By that I mean we join organizations and hold them responsible, or liable, for a limited number of duties that we maintain on an invisible list in our minds. If the health club does not maintain its exercise equipment, I will quit. If the PTA fails to make good on audio-visual equipment for my child's school, I will withhold my dues. Our lives have become a series of interlocking limited liability associations, which we join with specific ends in mind. But where is the place we do not join, the place where we just belong, like the natural community, the neighborhood, or the family, marked by the potential for total liability, where we simply care for one another? That place is—or should be—our churches and synagogues.

People complain that churches and synagogues are often too impersonal. One woman captured the sentiment in a phrase that haunts me still: "The Baptist church on the corner is so big, we call it

'Fort Baptist.'" What she didn't say is that across the road was "Fort Catholic," and that "Fort Jewish" was right next door. The staff within the forts are so busy that it has taken some time for them to become aware that people hardly come any more. But those who have assimilated that bitter truth argue now that we must renovate the forts to create community. But the question remains: Is community mere "groupieness," or does it theologically resonate with the presence of God? Is community mere sociology, or is it ecclesiology, a question of the nature of the church (for Christians), the Jewish People (for Jews), and, therefore, the locus of the presence of God?

I do not mean to say that God is known *only* in the intimacy of community. Sometimes we do still have a sense of God's presence in the magisterial grandeur of a cathedral. But because the cultural backdrop has shifted away from an emphasis on social distance, it is increasingly unlikely that we can recognize God anymore as distant and transcendent. Instead, it is in the intimacy of a caring community that God will most likely be located. What we still need most is to learn how to develop worship where such a community is a reality.

I should be clearer about the nature of community that I have in mind here. Educator Parker Palmer distinguishes three kinds of community: therapeutic, civic, and marketing. Therapeutic communities, such as the many 12-step or self-help groups, feature a shared intimacy where love and support can blossom into healing. Civic community is the democratic model of small-town life, where too much intimacy is avoided. Equality is demonstrated by equal rights before the law, the process of free speech, and the right to vote on matters that affect the common good. A marketing community is organized around economic principles of maximizing profit, effectiveness, and a bottom line.

Of the three, the only one where God is distinctly not going to be found is the marketing community. Yet that is exactly what the synagogue or church as limited liability community has become. The board meets to determine efficiency, which is defined as capturing the market share of worshipers, parishioners, or members. The rabbi, priest, or pastor is the CEO, and is responsible to the board for effective management technique and for marketing and packaging the product: religious services, for which people pay annual fees called membership dues, tithes, or weekly donations.

The civic community and the therapeutic community, by contrast, are places where God may indeed be found, but in different ways. The civic enterprise is outer-directed: Members belong to help achieve the good for each and every member. This is the arena of social justice; it is where God enters as the God of justice. The therapeutic community is inner-directed: Members belong to find wholeness and healing; here God enters as the God of love.

A spiritual community of worshipers, which is what I argue for here, combines the love of therapeutic healing and the justice of civic concern. But it must be more. Palmer notes, for instance, that educational communities also need to be more. Unlike therapeutic communities, classrooms exist to discover truth, and as much as truth is discoverable best in an atmosphere of love, not fear, the search for truth is not essentially organized around the need for individual healing. But neither truth is something on which the majority vote rules, so even though classrooms require justice, they can hardly be equated with civic communities either. So too with the worshiping community in search of God. Though requiring love and justice, it must combine some third feature also. What is the elusive third feature necessary for a community intent on love and on justice to become also a community of prayer?

The answer should be found in the notion of prayer. Earlier, we said that a worship system has both a horizontal and a vertical axis. Insofar as the worship community seeks out healing and justice for its members, it attends to the horizontal axis only. What makes it a community of prayer is precisely its intention to seek out God, to evoke the divine presence within it as it goes about its rituals of worship. The problem here is that the very term "vertical" suggests the old-fashioned notion of distant transcendence, which is precisely the least likely place where God will be found in American society. We need, somehow, to rescue the word "transcendence" from "distance."

The remarkable feature of the Grand Canyon sunset as people define it is that even though it is grand, it is not distant. On the contrary: People who find God in nature report an overwhelming sense of being drawn into the wholeness of being or of feeling part of the natural beauty that they are observing. Members of a worshiping community seek love and justice for each other; the community is fully engaged in achieving therapeutic healing and civic welfare. But the community soon discovers the presence of God in these goals, for the reality of the Divine becomes patent in the acts of healing and of justice that motivate the group whenever it meets. Eventually, the group becomes aware also of how much every member is part of a grander whole that only God can see and know. When worship suggests the eternal templates of a religious vision, and when worshipers identify with those templates as part of their lives, they become aware of God's transcendent reality.

> **American worship insists on knowing God's presence intimately through the miracle of healing, interpersonally in individual acts of justice, and transcendentally in the marvel of the patterns, the patterns of patterns, and the ever increasing metapatterned complexity of which even the tiniest cell is an intrinsic part. The God who was enthroned in glorious light for worshipers of the second century and the God who resided in transcendent distance for nineteenth- and early twentieth-century Europeans we find today in the threefold worshiping community of healing, justice, and pattern.**

In later chapters, we shall see that we are bringing into being our own newly favored synecdochal vocabulary as well: music that people can sing; humble, everyday language, rather than elegant linguistic dinosaurs; and spatial designs to connect, not separate, the people in the pews. The key is the breakdown of distance and the rediscovery of connectedness. I have no trouble at all seeing here our rediscovery of God's presence.

I began this chapter by talking about ritual's role in presenting the reality of cosmic design to worshipers. Out of the discovery of pattern in prayer (the microcosm), worshipers extrapolate the competence to posit pattern in the universe (the macrocosm). From the celebration of ritualized patterns that cohere endlessly and are repeated regularly, we internalize expectations that even the chaos of life may be only a small part of a larger pattern. We learn to have the faith that prohibits our giving up on life in the middle of its inconsistencies.

Whether our faith stops at faith in the patterns of the universe or goes on to become faith in God as well depends largely on what we mean by "God," what evidence of God we expect to find, and whether we would recognize God sufficiently to "let God in." If God is seen by us as we imagined in our childhood, we may not find in our prayers clear and ample demonstration of God's reality. Similarly if we look only for the grand triumphant fingerprints that a mighty distant God might leave behind, we may be making the error of looking for God in today's world through eyeglasses that became blurred with age almost a century ago. But God is not on that account absent. We need only change our eyeglasses.

Ritual Check List ❀

Words and Concepts You Should Know

- **Our inability to believe is the result**—not the cause—of worship failure.

- **Both science and faith arise from the experience of pattern.** Scientific patterns need not embody value; they simply exist as observable phenomena. Faith emerges not out of the patterns alone, but from the trust that those patterns are beneficial in the end.

- **Patterns build on one another** in an ascending order of increasing abstraction, eventually creating a metapatterned universe.

- **Even unbelievers may leave a religious ritual** feeling that there is a divine plan, if the ritual has been a successful microcosm of ultimate order, and if they were swept up in the beauty of wholeness.

- **Successful worship requires cultural backdrop,** a master image of God, and synecdochal vocabulary. Cultural backdrop is the assumptions of culture that we take for granted, but without which, everything we do would appear foolish. Master image is the way our cultural backdrop encourages us to think about God. Synecdochal vocabulary is words, gestures, and things that suggest the reality of God beyond themselves by using a part to refer to a larger whole.

- **European culture bequeathed us the master image of God** as an awesome, distant Being, but the American cultural backdrop has broken down social distance. Its worship should seek to reveal God in community.

- **Of the many kinds of communities,** a marketing community is least likely to know God. Yet synagogues and churches have become marketing communities.

- **A worshiping community** combines the benefits of a therapeutic community (love and healing) with a civic community (justice and goodness). It connects both of those with the reality of God as seen in the metapatterned universe.

- **American worship** insists on knowing God's presence intimately through the miracle of healing, interpersonally in individual acts of justice, and transcendentally in the marvel of the patterns, the patterns of patterns, and the ever increasing metapatterned complexity of which even the tiniest cell is an intrinsic part.

- **God can be transcendent without being distant.** To know God, we must create worship that replaces distance with connectedness.

Conversation Points for Making Worship Work

1 ▪ If you have a worship care group in your church or synagogue, discuss the cultural backdrop of our time. Everyone knows something about our age. To what extent is my description of the American cultural backdrop typical of the stories that group members have to tell? How many people have extended families or neighborhoods they can count on? Ask people if they belong to a small group to whose members they would go for support (some version of a therapeutic community). Does the synagogue or church fill that role? Why? Why not? Does it fill that role for the majority or even a large minority of the members?

2 ▪ Ask people in the group about their concept of God. If they say they do not believe in God, ask what concept they have rejected. As people describe the God in whom they do believe, see if any of the concepts mentioned satisfies any of the nonbelievers. Ask people if they have ever had any experiences that they would describe as a sign of the presence of God. If so, what are they? Sometimes belief in God is the difficult part; experience of God is easier.

3 ▪ Did any of the experiences of God that people mentioned while discussing Conversation Point 2 come during public prayer services? If not, where did they occur, and why did they *not* come from synagogue or church worship?

six

The Script of Prayer: Words Spoken

"Does God really need so much praise?" asks one person. "I just cannot believe what the prayers say," says another. And yet another asks, "Why do we repeat those old-fashioned things, not prayers that are relevant today?"

As I have engaged people in honest discussion of their worship over the years, these comments characterize the most common objections I have received. Quite clearly, most people think that prayer is about words. Worship regulars will have memorized favorite prayers and become adept at the congregational responses. Watchers may be unable to follow all the details of what is going on, but they manage to read through the liturgical text in their hands and get some quick idea of what the service is all about. No wonder people confuse praying with reading, as if the liturgy were a theological treatise. They leave services either admiring or dismissing what the prayers said, the way they leave a class in philosophy or psychology as a disciple or a critic of Plato's *Republic* or Jungian archetypes.

In part, they are right. Most prayer does use a text, after all, and prayer books come packaged like philosophy and psychology books. You can, indeed, read them, and they do, in fact, say something that we are expected to take seriously. But literary texts are more than inert words on paper. They were written by someone, at some time, and are intended to be read by someone else at some other time. All texts are messages. They may be telegrams, diaries, newspaper editorials, or even prayers, but whatever form they take, the meaning they provide goes beyond their literal content. Prayers are a specific genre of communication. More precisely, as we shall see, they are a combination of several genres of communication. They invite us to ask the same questions of them that we might of any conversation:

- What does the text say?
- How does it say it?
- What does it mean?
- How does it get said?

These questions do not exhaust the criteria for analyzing texts, but they do help us think about our worship texts in a useful way. As an example of what I mean, consider the opening gambit of the standard American greeting ritual: You meet someone on the street and recite the prescribed ritual text, "Good morning. How are you?"

First we ask, "What does the text say?" This is equivalent to what people normally consider the text's *content*, which at first glance seems self-evident, merely a matter of quoting the words verbatim, "Good morning. How are you?" It would be unlikely that anyone would pay much attention to it beyond that.

There was a time in the study of linguistics, however, when what the text says was thought to depend on the history of the words used to make it up. So early linguists ferreted out how the words were used in the past and then listed all their meanings from whenever people started saying them until now. In studying the phrase, "good morning," for example, they would have discovered that the English word "morning" goes back at least to the thirteenth century, when it was used only for the period of time before daybreak, and was spelled in a variety of ways, including "morwnynge" and "morwene." Around 1400, the King Arthur legends give us the example of "gode morwene." By Shakespeare's time it had become "good morning," but the word "good" had not yet become firmly attached to the specific titles of the day's arbitrary divisions. So along with "good morning," "good evening," and "good afternoon," Shakespeare has his characters say (in general), "Good time of day to you." Even the most simple taken-for-granted text has a history, and for a period of time, at least, there were linguists who thought that only its history could reveal what the text really said.

We now know that the history of a text is relatively unimportant in understanding what a text says. Spoken language is used by people who generally have no idea how words once got used, but who are experts at how words ought to be used in their own time.

So we can next ask, "How does a text say what it says?" Closely tied to the *what* of a text's content is the *how* of its means of presentation. If the first question was part of classical linguistics, the second was studied by classical philosophy and then literature, usually in the form of logic or rhetoric. You may have studied Aristotelian syllogisms or the rhetorical devices of, say, Lincoln's *Gettysburg Address*, as typical ways that texts argue their case. The key word is "argue." Here too an older, limited understanding of language once governed the way texts were studied. Philosophers thought that any text that had any sense to it worked by means of argumentation: The "necessarily true" forms of argument were "logical"; and the false but sometimes convincing brands of reason were just "clever rhetoric." The issue boiled down to the idea that texts should somehow claim to reflect a state of being.

How a text says something was therefore equivalent to its capacity to reproduce a true state of affairs. In the case of "good morning," if it was evening instead of morning, or if it was raining—so that the day was hardly good—the greeting would be judged untrue. Words were believed to be like pictures. They reflect reality and are true or false.

For a long time, this single-minded view of language was taken for granted. But eventually it became clear that language does things other than just reflect reality. Imagine a scenario where I say, "Good morning," on a rainy afternoon. I then recognize my mistake, and add,

"Oh, it's afternoon already. Sorry. I meant to say, 'Good afternoon'— and come to think of it, it's not really very good, is it?" Imagine too that you get so annoyed by my confused response that you cry out, "Good grief!"

What possible picture of reality can "Good grief!" convey? Grief can never be good, not the way a morning or afternoon can be. Obviously, "good grief" says what it does in a way that is different from how "good morning" gets its point across.

Since the early 1900s, we have seen two breakthroughs in the study of language, one in linguistics and the other in philosophy. The results are that our first two questions about texts can be answered more broadly now. The linguistic breakthrough was a series of lectures at the University of Geneva from 1906 to 1911, in which Ferdinand de Saussure portrayed language as a living, dynamic system that is very much alive in every speaker's present but unrelated to how the same or similar words were used in the past. (You were perfectly able to say, "Good morning," for instance, even before you read the paragraph above on the history of "gode morwene." Knowing how the phrase was used once upon a time will probably have no impact on how you use it in the future.) Saussure concluded that linguistics should study the way words are strung together in the present by ordinary speakers of a language. The history of the text's usage is irrelevant to what a text says. Instead, the *what* of the text's message is inherently connected to *how* a text is said. The two questions of *what* and of *how* are so closely tied together that they may even be one question.

At about the same time that Saussure was lecturing in Geneva, another European, Ludwig Wittgenstein, was preparing to take over his father's steel business in Vienna. In order to learn the business thoroughly, he was sent to England to observe the steel factories of Birmingham. While there, however, he gravitated to the study of philosophy and visited Bertrand Russell at Cambridge. When World War I broke out, he returned home to fight for the Austrian army. While holed up in the trenches, he worked out the first draft of a philosophical system that would summarize better than any other work the view of language as "pictures of reality."

Wittgenstein's genius was incredible. Even as most of Europe's great thinkers were adopting his philosophy as the final word on how language works, he was leaving it behind altogether, convinced that his work was all wrong. Only after several years of teaching mathematics, working as a gardener, and becoming an accomplished self-taught architect, did he return to the study of language, with a view toward correcting his earlier view. He no longer assumed that the only sensible way to use language is to develop word-pictures that reflect reality.

He compared the use of language to playing a game. Just as many different games are possible with the same pieces, so many different functions are possible with the same words. And just as it would be foolish to judge a chess move by the rules of checkers, so it would be invalid to judge the phrase "good grief" by the rules applicable to "good morning," or for that matter, to other word combinations in which the adjective "good" is used (like "My sister is a good sport" or "A good movie is hard to find"). We use language in different language games, so before we can pass judgment on whether a given sentence is appropriate, we have to know what the particular game and its rules are.

The end result of the "later Wittgenstein," as his second philosophy of language became known, is that philosophers no longer expect that the texts we use will always give us pictures about reality. Word-pictures are only one of language's uses, and not the most important one at that. Like Saussure, Wittgenstein saw that the content of a text is not separable from its form. The *what* of a text's message is part and parcel of the *how*, the rules of the game in which it is being said.

> ◉ **Meaning comes not just from text, but from context. The question of what a text says must be asked along with the question of how it says it. The history of what a text meant once upon a time has no necessary relationship to what it means now. And the text's content depends on the rules of the language game in which the text passes**

from message sender (speaker or writer, usually) to message receiver (hearer or reader).

These lessons about language are now embraced almost everywhere, except the study of liturgy. We can hardly blame ordinary worshipers for not knowing them, but the failure of clergy to do so has resulted in two terrible consequences.

When people ask what a prayer text says, they still expect to receive a lecture on its history, as if what it meant in the past determines what it must mean today. What the texts meant to the people who wrote them is not unimportant, but prayers that meant one thing to our ancestors can mean something different to us. There is something inherent in human nature that makes us constantly seek out meaning, and we do that by continually reinterpreting everything we encounter, do, say, and hear.

An even more disastrous consequence is that worshipers insist on treating all the sentences in their prayer books as if they were part of one single language game called "theological truth," whose sole function, they assume, is to offer portraits of reality with which they are expected to agree. As long as people persist in thinking that liturgy is just theology, a liturgical language game consisting of saying out loud various sentences whose content they should be willing to affirm as true, they will be bitterly disappointed by prayer. They will find many sentences meaningless or boring; and they will feel guilty because they do not literally believe everything they say. If they are "guilty" of anything, however, it will be that they are applying the wrong criterion to prayer—like treating "good grief" as if it were just a variation of "good morning"—and their "punishment" will consist of the fact that their prayer will always be found wanting.

A new approach to the language of prayer begins with abandoning the simplistic twofold questioning that characterized earlier attitudes. Prayer cannot be studied in terms of its objective content (on the one hand) and the way that content is argued (on the other hand). So we turn to the latter two questions on our list, subtle but important variations on the first two questions we looked at. Instead of asking, "What does a text say?" we can ask, "What does it mean?" And instead of asking, "How does it say it?" we can ask, "How does it get said?" The all-important difference here is the emphasis on the interaction between the text and its readers, who come to it with different ideas of what they should be doing with it. They can study it (like geometry), proclaim it (like a political manifesto), sing it (like a love song), read it (like a novel), argue it (like a legal brief), or pray it (our liturgy).

Words never say anything on their own. Readers always interpret them. So instead of asking what the text says in and of itself, we have to ask what the text means to the reader who reads it. Similarly, instead of asking how the text itself says something, we have to ask how that something gets said in the first place—that is, what are the rules of the language game that result in the liturgical equivalents of "good grief" rather than "good morning"?

These latter questions go together. The question is not how prayer texts somehow conspire independently to give us a theologically accurate picture of reality, but how worship is a unique human activity in which words are used in special ways to do special things. What are those ways, and what are those things?

> ❀ **If we can avoid the self-defeating notion that our prayers are pictures of reality that demand intellectual assent, we will have gone a long way toward making it possible to say them meaningfully, even if we do not believe them to be literally true.**

If our words of prayer are not photographic representations of truth, then what are they?

Constituting a Present: Words That Perform ❀

Perhaps the most popular treatment of liturgical language relies on what philosophers call performatives. The term goes back to 1955, when a philosopher named John Austin gave a series of lectures at Harvard University. He had been nursing the idea ever since 1939, and now that he made it public, it was quickly adopted as a very interesting way to think about language.

The essence of Austin's groundbreaking idea is to be found in the title of the book into which his lectures were transcribed: *How to Do Things with Words*. By this he meant that words do not just report things that exist independently of the reports. That was the old way of thinking, as if words described an independent thing called reality and were true if they got the picture right but false if they did not.

Austin's idea, instead, was that words can actually bring reality into being; they accomplish something; they are powerful tools that establish a state of being, rather than just report on it. Once we get the idea of what he is talking about, we can think of many instances when liturgical or ritual language (especially) doesn't just describe. It *performs*. Here are the examples Austin offers:

- "I do!" said during a marriage ceremony and meaning, "I do take this woman/man to be my lawfully wedded wife/husband."
- "I name this ship the Queen Elizabeth," said while smashing a bottle against a ship.
- "I give and bequeath my watch to my brother," said in a will.
- "I bet you ten dollars it will rain tomorrow," said while shaking hands on a wager.

Can saying it make it so?" asks Austin of his own examples. It certainly can, he answers, as long as certain conditions are fulfilled:

- The people involved must recognize a conventional procedure that includes conventional language said by conventional people.
- The people saying the performatives must be appropriate and must follow the rules of the convention; they have to mean what they say.

If, for example, the owner of a liquor store takes a bottle of wine off his shelf and smashes it over the hull of my boat without my permission, and then declares, "I name you the New Yorker," his statement doesn't count, even though there is nothing wrong with the actual words he said. It's not that what he said is "wrong"; it is just "no good."

Similarly, even if I did name my ship the New Yorker, but did it with a sly smile on my face and admitted afterward that I didn't really mean it, you might express doubt about the boat's name. You might ask, "Is it really called that?" Here too the performative doesn't work, even though the right person said it under the right set of circumstances. The question again is not so much whether what I said was true, as whether what I said counted.

If a five-year-old child says, "I bet you a year's allowance," or if I say, "I give and bequeath to my brother the Brooklyn Bridge," these performatives do not count; that is, they don't perform what they were supposed to perform. In the first case, we don't hold children accountable for foolish vows; in the second, I cannot give away what I do not own. Austin calls such unsuccessful attempts at using language *infelicities*. John Searle, another philosopher who has studied the matter, calls them just *defective*. He differentiates between *brute facts* that we suppose exist somewhere in nature (whether or not they really do) and *institutional facts* that come about because we have all agreed to recognize them under certain conventional circumstances. Marriage, bets, bequests, and namings are institutional facts whose success depends not on words alone but on words in action, which is the process of saying certain things in certain contexts. These are technically known as *speech-acts*.

Worship is frequently composed of performative language. Nearly every rite of passage brings an institutional fact into existence, and nearly every worship service features some statement in which people say things to establish a fact about themselves, a fact that did not exist before they said it. Here are some instances of what I mean, this time taken from the 1978 *Lutheran Book of Worship:*

- "I baptize you in the name of the Father and of the Son and of the Holy Spirit."

- "I give you this ring as a sign of my love and faithfulness."
- "We commend to almighty God our brother/sister and we commit his/her body to the ground: earth to earth, ashes to ashes, dust to dust."

If we look carefully, we see that the explicit performatives are used at precisely that part of the ritual script that corresponds to the ritual moment. They accompany the ritual actions that mark the rite's taking place, and they serve to instruct us on how we are supposed to understand the physical actions being undertaken at the time.

- In baptism, the rite calls for water to be poured on the candidate's head, at which time the performative explains how we are to understand the water being poured. Baptism officially occurs at that very moment.

- In a wedding, the bride and groom exchange rings and tell us that this is no simple barter of goods, but something that "I give . . . as a sign of my love and faithfulness." At that moment, the marriage happens.

- Similarly, at the moment that a body is being buried, the accompanying performative statement tells us how to "read" what is occurring before our eyes. Instead of just filling in a hole in the ground, or dispensing with some human remains, an institutional fact of Christian burial is accomplished.

In each case, a ritual moment happens only because it gets performed with language in the right way. In addition, a lengthier ritual script leads up to the transformative moment and then leads away from it as well. If the script is followed with care, we leave the baptism, wedding, or funeral with the feeling that this liturgy worked out. People do not ask whether the state of affairs portrayed is true: "Is she really baptized?" "Are they really married?" "Is he really buried?" These questions are patently irrelevant. It is against the rules to object in retrospect that you don't believe in baptism, don't accept marriage covenants, or won't go along with Christian burial. Baptism, marriage, and burial are institutional facts that become true by virtue of an implicit agreement that if the appropriate ritual is said in an appropriate way by the appropriate person, they will automatically come into being.

Worship assumes the mutual acceptance of certain institutional facts and the way these facts come into being. It requires in advance that all involved accept the existence of the institutional world that is about to unfold before their eyes. They must give themselves over as willing partners to the words and actions that will bring that world about. They implicitly commit themselves to be part of a universe where water sprinkled on heads means that people are baptized, where an exchange of rings means that people are married, and where bodies covered with earth means that they are commended to God for everlasting rest.

> **Baptism, matrimony, and burial are institutional states of being. They are artistic constructions of physical states that we decide in advance to recognize. Institutional states are born as liturgical words are said. Performatives thus establish an alternative world of reality.**

Recollecting the Past: Words As Stories ◉

The alternative world presented in worship encompasses the past as well. By analogy, consider what happens when we read a novel. As we get further and further into the story, the characters become real for us. We interpret their behavior on any given page in the light of previous events from earlier chapters until, like living friends and neighbors, they develop evolving biographies. They owe their depth of character to the way their present arises out of their past and builds a foundation for a future.

In *A Tale of Two Cities*, for example, Charles Dickens portrays the reign of terror that gripped the French Revolution. His unlikely hero is Sydney Carton, who lays down his life to save another man from the guillotine. The book begins with an unforgettable line: "It was the best of times, it was the worst of times." For the rest of the book, we get a painstaking analysis of the worst of times. But at the end, we see the best of times too, as Carton's self-sacrifice is memorialized forever in his final words, "It is a far, far better thing that I do, than I have ever done; it is a far, far better rest that I go to, than I have ever known." The reason we appreciate his final testimony is that through some four hundred pages, we have gotten to know Sydney Carton, and we have entered the universe of Madame Defarge and her knitting, of the upper-class English gentry, and of the miseries of French prisons. We recall Carton, who was described earlier as "the idlest and most unpromising of men," and we ponder whether the Sydney Carton who chooses the guillotine is the same Sydney Carton who knew nothing more noble than a life of dissolute luxury. That is the great irony behind Carton's final lines. Without that, those lines would lose their appeal. It is only Dickens's genius as a storyteller that permits us finally to see Carton's inner nobility and to realize that he is the symbol of the best of times to which the very first line in the book alerted us.

So too with the lines of liturgy, which we recite not as solitary individuals saying them for the first time, but as the latest links in the chain of a faith community that has said these things for centuries. They are the community's lines, not just our own. The chief character in the liturgical story that we repeat whenever we meet for worship is the entire Christian church or the entire Jewish People—not just now, but forever. To their role as performatives (establishing a present), then, we can now add a second function of liturgical language: establishing a past.

❀ **The words of worship are artistic constructs. They fill in the background of the community through which we descend; they describe the heroes or martyrs whose memory we hold dear as if they are our own extended family; they remind us of our story, the events of our corporate life as a people or church, without which we would not be here praying as we do.**

For example, the *Lutheran Book of Worship* says, "In many and various ways, God spoke to his people of old by the prophets. But now, in these last days, he has spoken to us by his son." And Reform Jews read how God "did wonders for us in the Land of Egypt, miracles and marvels in the land of Pharaoh." Whether God spoke to his people of old by the prophets or did wonders for us in Egypt is no more demonstrable as a fact than is the institutional fact that a child is baptized, a ring is given as a sign of love and faithfulness, or an aged grandparent is commended to almighty God. In the case of marriage, all we see is rings changing hands. We agree in advance, however, that the exchange will count as something called marriage. So too in worship, we cannot see the history that formed us into the Jewish People or the Christian Church. But we can reenact or recollect that history, making it our own.

> ▦ **Each worship service is a rereading of a sacred script and the establishment of a new sacred reality, a world that did not exist until we willed it to, one that we establish anew with every sacred performance. Part of the script rehearses history as we choose to see it, the people of the past as we care to recollect them, and a selective perception of the events that made us what we are.**

Looking to the Future: Words As Hope, Commitment, Inspiration ▦

Worship establishes a present and links us to a past. But it also has an impact on our future. The story we establish as our own has consequences for what we will become, not just for what we were. For analogies, look again at literature. Even in fiction, characters once established are not free to do whatever they wish. Their characters and accumulated experience determine, to some extent, what they will do. Madame Defarge is described by Dickens as a woman absolutely consumed with the will for revenge:

There were many women at that time, upon whom the time laid a dreadfully disfiguring hand; but there was not one among them more to be dreaded than this ruthless woman. . . . The troubled time would have heaved her up under any circumstances. But imbued from her childhood with a brooding sense of wrong, and an inveterate hatred of a class, opportunity had developed her into a tigress. She was absolutely without pity. If she had ever had the virtue in her, it had quite gone out of her.

Now at the end of the tale, Madame Defarge has the power to save the innocent prisoner awaiting the guillotine. But she cannot, for the simple reason that even her creator, Dickens, is not free any more to do with her as he wishes. She is the opposite of Carton; she cannot use her "strong and fearless character," her "shrewd sense and readiness," or her "great determination" for anything but revenge. She cannot change her nature any more than history's real avengers can. Her character is cast and cannot be capriciously remade to demonstrate the best of times. She epitomizes the worst, for even at the end, Dickens writes, "It was nothing to her that an innocent man was to die for the sins of his forefathers. She saw, not him, but them. It was nothing to her that his wife was to be made a widow, and his daughter an orphan." True to character, her last orders on the day preceding the guillotining are, "Take you my knitting, and have it ready for me in my usual seat." Fictitious character that she is, she must nonetheless act in character, molding each future action as a natural outgrowth of her past.

In the world that we weave through our prayers, we too formulate a character that is our own. We become Christians or Jews of such and such a stamp by virtue of the story that we say is ours. To invoke prophetic vision is at the same time to implicate ourselves as believers in all that flows from that vision. To begin the story and then to take it all the way up to the present is also to expect it to end, and not just in any way, but according to the cues for ending that were established along the way. As a work of art, the constructed world of reality that our liturgy gives us must be both comprehensive and coherent. By "comprehensive," I mean that the story told in worship does not end abruptly in the middle, without the realization of the dramatic fore-shadowing given us earlier in the text. By "coherent," I mean that it must be consistent, as consistent as Defarge, who knits by the guillotine until the end.

> ▣ So worship is filled with anticipations of the future: hope, promise, commitment, and inspiration. These are the still unwritten chapters of our tale as Christian Church or Jewish People. They are the future that we dare to assume because our tale is comprehensive and because it is coherent throughout.

Sometimes the lines of worship that anticipate the future are evident:

- "God bless you and keep you."
- "God have mercy on you."
- "Next year in Jerusalem."
- "Lord, may this eucharist take away our sins."
- "Peace be with you." "And also with you."

The wishing form of prayer is explicit in the way we respond to it. Normally we answer prayers with *Amen*, meaning, "May it be so." Jewish prayer sometimes ends also with *Ken yehi ratson*, "May this be God's will." So, too, Christian prayer gives us, "Thy kingdom come, thy [God's] will be done," "Hear us, good Lord" (from the Lutheran intercessions), or "God our creator, hear our prayer and bless us" (from the equivalent rubric in the Reform Jewish service for the Sabbath) amount also to expressions of hope. Sometimes, then, the anticipations are clear: wishing that God fulfill our requests, or explicit statements that "We hope and pray . . ."

But sometimes the hoping aspect of our prayers is only implicit in a statement that we make entirely on faith. Knowing that our story commits us so intensely to a single conceivable outcome at the end of time, we state what has yet to be the case, and we are convinced that it *will* indeed some day be the case. "On that day," goes the conclusion to Jewish worship service, "our God shall be one and God's name shall be one." It is not so much a question of "Do we really believe it?" as "How can we really be so bold as to say it?" We dare say it because we have internalized our story of the world in such a way that no other ending could possibly follow. So we say it as hope, as anticipation, as commitment to the story's integrity, and as exhortation to ourselves to take the story seriously in our perception of our lives. Similarly, we recite creeds that inspire us and commands that exhort us, until in the end, the fullness of the liturgical vision becomes so plain that it cannot be denied. We are committed to this sacred way of perceiving reality, and we leave worship with a sense that the world is shaped differently than it was when we entered. Saying has indeed made it so.

By no means have I exhausted the many uses of language in prayer. But I have tried to show that the ways we use language during worship are many, and that they should not be judged by the rules governing the game of scientific description. All along I have reiterated my theme of worship as an art form, and art as the means by which we create alternative realities, transforming emptiness and chaos into meaning and pattern. As soon as this simple lesson is grasped, many other word-oriented worship exercises fit into place too: the sermon (or homily), for example, which does not so much teach us a set of objective facts that we did not know before as it lets us see things we have always known—but in a new light, with new artistic models, stories, and hopes for improvement.

The Church with a Window

New York's midtown area houses a Lutheran church that is part of a modern high-rise office and shopping mall. Visitors are invited to look outside the church through a sanctuary window that could have been colored in with a stained-glass biblical scene, but was left transparent instead. The view leads onto the street, where homeless people shuffle back and forth amid the wealth of New York's East Side. The point of it all is to see the outside with the vision of the inside, to grasp the message of worship and then to apply it. Before coming to pray, we might have passed the poor without noticing them. But now, after praying the words of the prophets and committing ourselves to justice and charity, the world outside is seen in a new light. We leave with the sense that we are called to end poverty: How can we do otherwise and still remain true to the story of our prayers?

All good art works just that way to establish alternative realities. When I was younger, I used to go to the Museum of Modern Art, where I would sit in front of Picasso's monumental *Guernica*, its visual message of the terrors of war displayed like a wraparound screen in a room dominated by its sheer size and conception. When the museum returned the work to Spain, its rightful owner, I sympathized with the decision, but was upset that I couldn't take my children to sit before *Guernica* any more.

Instead, my children chose to watch *M*A*S*H* reruns so frequently that they knew in advance how each episode would end. "Don't miss this one, Dad," they would say. "This is the one where. . . ." The fact that I had memorized the visual script of *Guernica*, so to speak, did not dissuade me from coming to see it again and again; just as they, having memorized the dramatic script of *M*A*S*H*, still sat through its reruns night after night. What *Guernica* was for me, *M*A*S*H* became for my children. Both are works of art that establish alternative worlds in which war is unthinkable.

What differentiates *Guernica* and *M*A*S*H* from worship is this: However compelling the alternative worlds of Picasso and Hawkeye may be, they are not our story. They invite us to share the insights of their author-artists, but we remain mere visitors in their worlds. I am not a "Guernican" or a "Mashie" in the same way that I am a Jew. Religious worship, by contrast, is never fully worship until those of us who pray go through the script of prayer and make it our own. I do not playact at being a Jew, or just recite in a detached way the stories, recollections, and promise of my Jewish prayers. Nor do I pretend that my life-cycle ceremonies transform people's lives. In my world, they really do.

Think, then, of prayer as being on a spectrum of literature going from private and silent reading to public and audible performance (see Fig. 6.1). Novels go at the far left end. Poetry is found a little farther to the right. Drama is much closer to the right end, and finally, public prayer goes at the far right.

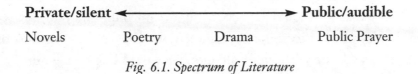

Private/silent ◄————————————► **Public/audible**

Novels   Poetry   Drama   Public Prayer

Fig. 6.1. Spectrum of Literature

The left-hand side is what we consider personal and therefore silent reading. What novels we read are our own business. We enjoy them in our leisure time, curled up on a sofa or before bedtime. Poetry is a little closer to public performance. No one, in fact, would be surprised to see us reading poetry out loud; hearing the poem is part of the point. Drama is altogether public. We might read the script of a play, but we are far more apt to see it performed. No one can claim to be an expert in, say, modern American drama, without ever seeing (or at least trying to see) the work of Tennessee Williams or Arthur Miller.

Finally, we get to liturgy. Prayer, too, is drama. Those of us who say its words are sacred actors. The drama even comes with actions, built in by the collective playwright called the Christian Church or the Jewish People: Stand here, sit there, bow at this point. And we wear special garb, like the costumes called for in any other drama. It is participatory drama, to be sure, but drama nonetheless. Yet, on the private/public spectrum, it belongs even farther to the right than ordinary theater because this is *our* drama, not somebody else's. The lines are our lines, and the characters we play are ourselves. When the actress playing Lady Macbeth is done with her performance, she takes off her costume, washes off her makeup, and goes home, not as Lady Macbeth but as the real person she is. She is not allowed to murder someone on the way home and claim justification because she really *is* Macbeth's wife, and murder is what she does. But if worship works, I leave the script of my sacred drama only after I have internalized its every claim. I go home with no dichotomy between my real self and my worshiping self. I really am what I pray: the liturgical vision of the world becomes my own. The history I recall is mine, calling me to a future that is mine as well.

We are blessed with freedom of choice, so there is no inherent necessity that we should act according to an ironbound plot devised on the day of our birth; but if, some day, we are able to look back on our lives with the wisdom of old age, we would like to see our lives not as an accumulation of disjointed experiences strung loosely together through time, but as a coherent whole, with the seeds of the future planted at every successive moment of the present. The words of prayer locate us in a continuum between a sacred past that we identify as our own and a vision of a future that we hope to realize as the logical outcome of the story of our lives.

"But It Doesn't Always Work That Way"

That is how worship ought to work. Regularly going through a sacred script, week in and week out, should commit us to a world that the script brings into being: a world of transformed identity, stories and history, promise and hope. None of these are so much objective things that liturgy reflects as they are institutional facts that worship establishes.

At least, public prayer is supposed to work that way. The problem is that it often doesn't. People think that the failure is due to the fact that the words of prayers say things that worshipers cannot believe. The truth is just the reverse. It is not true that worship is banal because its words are sterile; it is true that the words sound sterile because the worship is banal. When worship is well conducted, the words come alive as the story of who we are, whence we come, and where we are going. When worship is poorly conducted, the words fall flat and we have trouble taking them seriously. The fault lies less in the words than in the conduct of the worship.

❋ **If public prayer is a drama, the script should at least be performed in such a way that we cannot doubt its script.**

Clergy who are charged with leading worship usually overlook two especially dramatic elements of services: music and space. Even the people professionally charged with the service music often fail to see it as an inherent part of worship. They may decide on the music without ever discussing the liturgy as a whole with the rest of the clergy team. The situation with regard to worship space is even worse, because at least there are clergy charged with music, whereas in most synagogues and churches, no one at all is in charge of space. Imagine a Broadway musical in which the music has almost nothing to do with the plot, where there is no director, and where no one worries about where the actors stand, whether the audience can hear the melodies, and how the actors on the stage connect with the people in the seats. That is what bad worship is like.

Before turning to the liturgical demands of music and space, however, we can say one more thing about words. I said before that the validity of the words of prayer depends on the quality of the worship in which the words are recited. Even the best liturgical script falls flat, for instance, when the minister drones on in a monotone and the cantor sings seemingly unrelated music to a sprinkling of tired people who are sitting here and there in a dismally lit sanctuary, and feeling, therefore, unconnected both to what is happening and to each other. Nonetheless, when words do not work, the fault may also lie in the way they are couched in the prayer book. Where they are said in a foreign language (Hebrew, for Jews; Latin, for Catholics) it doesn't much matter how well the script is written. Worshipers are taught to appreciate the words without knowing exactly what they mean. It is enough to have some general idea about the theme of any given prayer, or, sometimes, not even to bother knowing that. Prayers may be chanted or even used as a mantra; we appeal to tradition, or to nostalgia, or to obligation, or even to ordinary habit to get worshipers to appreciate why we are saying things that they do not even dimly understand.

In most churches and synagogues, however, at least some prayers are in English, and for many worshipers, most prayers are. English is practically the sole language of worship or Protestants, the dominant language for Reform Jews, and the norm (since Vatican II) for Catholics. The problem then becomes that we can get away with saying almost anything only if people do not know what it means. We can even manage to do so, to some extent, if we provide English translations on a facing page or in an accompanying book, like the old Catholic *Missal.* But the minute we ask them to say the English, they will insist that they speak their lines with integrity. They know full well that this is supposed to be *their* drama, not someone else's. They know they cannot playact and still call this prayer.

To be sure, the explanations given above as to how prayer language functions can go a long way to overcoming people's hesitation. If they know that what looks like an objective statement of scientific fact is really a statement of hope or a recollection of a sacred story, they may be able to say what is otherwise unsayable. But good liturgy should go further than that. People who create prayer books are obligated to provide a text that is easily interpreted as functioning in one of the ways that I have specified, rather than a text that appears to be nothing but scientific facts that you either accept or reject. If we force people to approach their prayers only with scientific models in mind, they will almost surely reject what the prayers say.

How, then, should prayer books be composed? What guidance exists for people who write their own prayers and add them to already created services? A lot could be said on this subject, obviously, but a single all-important guideline will suffice here: The magic word is *poetry*.

In 1967, literary critic E. D. Hirsch Jr. suggested that the way a text is printed influences the way a reader reads it. His test case was drawn from a debate in the British press, where readers had argued the question of whether "prose can become poetry through typographic rearrangement." The example in question was a piece of prose that was as unpoetic as anyone could imagine:

> When a Chinese calligrapher "copies" the work of an old master, it is not a forged facsimile, but an interpretation, as personal within stylistic limits as a Samuel or Landowska performance of a Bach partita.

This unremarkable piece of prose had been reframed "poetically":

> *When a Chinese calligrapher "copies"*
> *The work of an old master, it is not*
> *A forged facsimile, but an interpretation,*
> *As personal within stylistic limits*
> *as a Samuel or Landowska performance*
> *Of a Bach partita.*

Now whether the second version counts as poetry, I leave for poets to determine. The question in my mind was whether readers would approach it as poetry and treat it differently than they did the prose version. To answer that question, I tried a simple experiment in my classroom. I typed both versions of "The Calligrapher" on separate sheets of paper; then I gathered students around a conference table and handed each of them one of the two at random, instructing them, "Look at what I give you and decide what it is. Do not look at each other's sheets, however, because you may not all have the same thing." I gave people some time to read the text, and when I saw that they were ready, I asked them to explain to the rest of the class what they had been given. In addition, I timed how long it took the various people to read their sheet and then to turn it over, content that they had determined what it was.

In general, the people with the prose read their sheet quickly, decided it was some unimportant statement about an arcane subject in which they had no interest, then turned over their page and waited for new instructions. When it came time for them to identify their text, they dismissed it as some dull, uninteresting statement about a calligrapher.

The people with the poetry, however, usually took longer examining their text. They were not so quick to turn it over. Since it looked like poetry, they assumed that there must be some poetic depth to it, possibly some wisdom from Chinese literature that must have something to do with what they were studying, even if they were not sure what it was.

The difference between the way we approach prose versus poetry is profound. With prose, we automatically categorize what we read as either fiction or nonfiction. Since prayer is presumably not just fiction, we decide in advance that any prose prayer must be nonfiction. But our model for judging nonfiction is invariably drawn from the language game of science. Whether it be the morning newspaper or the latest nonfiction best-seller, we read nonfiction prose with only one criterion in mind: is it true or false? The problem, as we saw, is that scientifically speaking, most prayers are neither true nor false. They cannot be judged by their truth value alone. They are not meant to be a simple verbal picture of reality. They link us to our past, establish institutional facts for our present, or help us to dream, to hope, and to aspire. All of that ambiguity is missed in simple prose statements that strike the average reader as either profoundly true or absurdly false— or, sometimes (as with the prose version of "The Calligrapher") not even interesting enough to warrant the time it would take to find out.

Poetic statements, however, capture the possibility that a text might mean more than it seems at first glance to say. That is why the people who received the poetic version took longer to analyze it, and why they were more likely to think that it was really about some Chinese wisdom, or at least that it had something to say to them, even if at first, it seemed not to. We are trained from early childhood not to expect to understand poetry right away; we know poetry works by suggestion, or by literary devices like metaphor, rather than simply describing the world the way scientific prose does. A prayer written across the page in obvious prose patterns is likely to be dismissed as untrue or prosaic, while the same thing arranged poetically will prove engaging enough to convince readers that they should wrestle with it for underlying meaning beyond its obvious "truth" contents.

Most prayer books, however, insist on presenting prayers in paragraphs of prose, as if their content *must only* express age-old theological truths. Truth does matter and content does count. But form counts also. Religious truths are rarely so straightforward that they can be captured in a set of declarative sentences. While we may be stuck with the prayer books that our church or synagogue provides, we can at least lobby for poetry that evokes the genuine depths of religious sentiment; and if our services have room for additional readings that we choose on our own, or if we are composing our own worship for special occasions, we should make sure that we choose or write prayers with language that allows the liturgy to work the way it should.

Ritual Check List ❀

Words and Concepts You Should Know

- **The question of what a text says** must be asked along with the question of how it says it. The history of what a text once meant has no necessary relationship to what it means now. Its meaning depends on the rules of the language game in which the message passes from message sender (speaker or writer, usually) to message receiver (hearer or reader).

- **In the language game called science,** sentences are supposed to provide accurate pictures of reality; they are expected to describe brute facts. Words are always true or false, depending on how accurate the description is. Sometimes prayers have to be judged that way, but not always, and not even usually.

- **If we are careful not to judge prayers** by the wrong language game, we can say them meaningfully, even if we do not believe them to be literally true.

- **Sometimes, the words of prayer are performatives.** Rather than reflect the brute facts that already exist, they create a new kind of reality, as when we say, "I pronounce you husband and wife." The new kind of reality created by language is an institutional fact.

- **Institutional facts are artistic constructions of reality.** They are as real as brute facts. In bringing them about, performatives establish an alternative world of reality: a state of being, for instance, with marriage, families, constitutions, and courts, a world where people can promise, hope, and have expectations. Through public prayer, a community determines the alternative world of reality in which it wants to live.

- **Sometimes the words of prayer** *look to our past.* They fill in the background of the community through which we claim descent. They provide a chain of heroes or martyrs—our extended family members, really—whose memory we hold dear and who link us to the events of our corporate life that, as a People or Church, we accept as our own.

- **Each worship service is a rereading of a sacred script.** It recollects history as we choose to see it, the people of the past as we care to remember them, and the events of our people that made us what we are and that will determine what we choose to become.

- **Sometimes, the words of prayer** *look to our future.* They fill us with anticipation, express our hopes, commit us to certain actions, inspire us to act differently, and serve as promises of where we want to go and what we want to do.

- **"Prayer can do all these things** because it is a *participatory sacred drama* in which those of us who say the words are sacred actors. The drama even comes with costumes and actions, built in by the collective playwright called the Christian Church or the Jewish People.

Conversation Points for Making Worship Work ❀

1 ▪ Go through a single service in your prayer book and decide which prayers give you "scientific difficulty." Now try to see them not as scientific statements, but as one of the other language games described here. Can you successfully say them as part of a sacred story, perhaps, or as a form of anticipation, hope, or wish for what may some day come about?

2 ▪ If public prayer is a drama, the script should at least be written well and then performed in such a way that we cannot doubt the institutional facts, sacred history, and anticipated future that it portrays. Think of the way an average Sabbath service is performed. Is it fully participatory, or do people tune in and out?

3 ▪ One problem with our prayers is that because they are presented to us not as poetry but as prose, we judge them as if they are scientific descriptions of brute facts. The same thing said poetically might capture the possibility that a text means more than it seems to say at first glance. That is because we are trained from early childhood to expect poetry to work by suggestion rather than to describe the world the way scientific prose does. A prayer written as prose is likely to be dismissed as untrue or prosaic, while the same thing written as poetry will encourage the reader to wrestle with it for underlying meaning beyond its obvious "truth" contents.

   Find a prayer in your book of worship that has been written as prose. Now rewrite it as poetry by rearranging the lines. For instance, the paragraph above might begin this way:

One problem with our prayers
is that because they are presented to us
not as poetry but as prose,
we judge them as if
they are scientific descriptions
of brute facts.

Now see if you can further rewrite difficult prayers so that they begin to work for you. Change the words around until they scan more or less the way poetry does. You may even want to change some of the words to get the right emotional tone and nuance. For example:

A problem with prayer
is that it is presented
as poetry, not prose.
We expect it to be science,
and without much thought,
we cavalierly dismiss it
as simply false.

seven

The Script of Prayer: Words Sung

Music plays different roles in different religions, but it is especially important for traditions that feature fixed public liturgies. It covers many styles, however, even within Jewish and Christian worship. Just consider the variety of music we have called sacred.

The ancient Jerusalem Temple in the time of the Rabbis and of Jesus and Paul featured levitical choirs and a veritable orchestra of instruments: woodwinds, percussion, brass, and strings. The Temple was not unusual in that regard, since the pagan sacrificial systems of the time were likewise outfitted in musical splendor.

Probably in reaction to that pagan musical style, the early church and synagogue looked less favorably on instrumentation. Singing, however, continued, and eventually Judaism and Christianity developed their own chanting traditions. In Christian worship, the predilection to sing the liturgy became central to monastic worship, and eventually, churches were built with large choir sections where monks performed their liturgical hours through song.

The Reformation newly emphasized the centrality of the Bible and declared public prayer to be the obligation of all the laity. Lutheran worship developed a repertoire of hymns for congregational singing, and Calvin wanted to limit the music to biblical texts.

In the nineteenth century, Jewish worship went through its own "reformation." It came in the wake of Napoleon's sweep across Europe, as Jews were finally freed from medieval ghettos and allowed to enter "cultured" European society. Jewish music now moved in two directions, one in eastern Europe and the other in western Europe.

In eastern Europe, which Napoleon never conquered, worship in traditionalistic congregations proceeded in a style unconcerned with modern western aesthetics. Jews here elaborated on their centuries-old cantorial solo mode. The cantor (*chazzan*, in Hebrew) specialized in a finely crafted and intricately executed liturgical performance that was rooted in fixed musical sequences that had been memorized over many years of oral instruction. When people speak of Jewish liturgical music, they usually mean this specialized cantorial style that reached new heights in artistic sophistication by the nineteenth century.

Theologically speaking, this cantorial style depended on a prayer leader who was viewed as the congregation's spiritual representative to God. The Hebrew title for the prayer leader, *sh'liakh tsibbur*, literally, "the agent of the congregation," aptly expresses this rabbinic ideal. He was charged with singing much of the liturgy on the people's behalf, frequently repeating it after the people had prayed it first. Prayer in the traditional eastern European synagogues oscillated back and forth between the noisy sound of people praying, usually out loud but not at the same pace, and the cantor delivering a heartfelt solo elaboration on a traditional melodic sequence. Judaism never delegated liturgical celebration to the prerogative of a special class of clerics, as occurred in the medieval church. But it also never developed the monastic tradition of unison singing.

Sephardi Jews (Jews who found refuge in the Muslim Mediterranean when they were expelled from Spain in 1492) never adopted the eastern European emphasis on cantorial solo performance. Instead, they did most of the singing communally, using an enormous variety of melodic modes depending on the holiday in question and the part of the liturgy being sung.

Back in western Europe, meanwhile, Jews whom Napoleon freed from the ghettos tried to reform their worship by making it sound more like the enlightened aesthetic preference of the churches around them. Jewish reform of the nineteenth century differed from the Christian Reformation three hundred years earlier, since Jews, who had never had a strong unison singing tradition among their clerics, never developed the parallel phenomenon of congregational hymns among their laity. Instead, Judaism created a mutation in the art form that it did have: the cantorial solo. Old synagogue favorites were recast to fit the aesthetic demands of modern western art standards. This nineteenth century Jewish Reform music began in Vienna and migrated toward the urban capitals of enlightenment culture, such as Berlin and Hamburg.

In Poland, however, Chasidic Judaism had developed yet a further musical mutation: a tradition of wordless melodies called *niggunim* (pronounced nee-goo-NEEM). These were usually based on native folk tunes that were not necessarily Jewish. They could be sung slowly at first, and then faster and faster to produce a group ecstatic state.

I haven't even mentioned the musical chanting tradition of the eastern church; or the Mantuan court tradition of Salamone Rossi, whose seventeenth-century Jewish music sounds distinctly *not* like synagogue liturgy to most of us today; or the liturgical use of "Hatikvah," which comes from the same folk melody that Smetana used when he composed *The Moldau*, but now, as the national anthem of the State of Israel, has been set to lyrics that express "the hope of two thousand years, to be a free people in our land, the land of Zion and Jerusalem"; or Christian folk-rock services, with strains of Bob Dylan, heard ubiquitously in coffeehouse masses in the 1960s; or a revival of chant and meditation in a style of worship called Taize.

❀ **The most significant characteristic of Jewish and Christian music is its remarkable diversity. We have known chants and modern art songs, solos and hymns, biblical lyrics and melodies with no words at all, instruments**

and bans on instruments. It is difficult to find a single common denominator to the music that, at one time or another, we have called sacred.

What Makes Music Sacred? ❁

What is it, then, that makes music sacred? People generally imagine it
must be something in the music itself, by which they mean the sound
that they associate with church or synagogue as opposed to the sounds
of bars, dance halls, discos, and the stage. A little thought, however, will
demonstrate how subjective any single criterion for sacred music is. It
seems hard to imagine that sacredness inheres in certain musical styles,
but not in others, since, for example, African-American spirituals
sound nothing like Bach chorales, the traditional chanting of Moroc-
can Jewry is a far cry from measured Gregorian tones, and none of
these sounds much like Verdi, Brahms, or Mozart, who, in turn, don't
have much in common with each other. If we think of "Hatikvah" once
again, it might fairly be argued that, no matter what Jews think, the
melody is just a poor variation of a theme from *The Moldau*, so the song
is not sacred. But try telling that to Jews for whom "Hatikvah" expresses their fondest religious aspirations.

Only the Choir Sings This One?

At a service celebrating rabbinic ordination and cantorial
investiture, a student-composed service called for "Hatikvah" as
the final hymn. Before it was sung, a seminary official
announced that the choir alone would sing it. The congregation
was to sit quietly and not sing along. The official had been hor-
rified that the students had selected "Hatikvah," which he did
not consider a sacred song at all, but merely a national anthem.
The student-composed liturgical script mandated it, however,
and he was stuck with it. He solved his problem by relegating it
to the choir, which was to sing it in a reasonably "spiritual"

arrangement: slowly, artistically, and with organ accompaniment. The three thousand people present, however, with the front rows of students and faculty leading the way, saw "Hatikvah" as sacred and refused to be silent. As the anticipation of yet another generation's rabbis and cantors being consecrated to their life work merged with the Jewish People's hope of centuries, they broke out in song, several bars ahead of the choir in the loft. The moment was not memorable for its liturgical synchrony. But it demonstrated that songs do not come prepackaged as sacred or profane; their sacredness depends on something other than purely musical considerations.

"Hatikvah," then, is a song that has become sacred to some people despite the fact that neither the folk melody on which it is based nor the version that became *The Moldau* was ever thought of that way. If we now look at the opposite phenomenon—songs that have been considered sacred from the day they were composed—we arrive at the same conclusion: Sacredness cannot lie in the music itself.

No one would deny that Ernest Bloch's *Sacred Service* and Verdi's *Four Sacred Pieces* are sacred. Their composers proclaimed that fact in the titles themselves. Before Bloch started to compose his service, he even secluded himself, as in religious retreat, so he could come to artistic terms with the sacred material that he would integrate into his masterwork. But it seems hard to imagine that what prompted their titles is the sacredness of the musical sound itself rather than the purpose that the music was expected to serve. Palestrina could compose a madrigal today but a motet tomorrow, the former for use in a profane setting and the latter in a sacred one. Are the two *sounds* so different that one is obviously sacred and the other not?

An obvious alternative might be that the Bloch and Verdi pieces are sacred because of their lyrics, which are sacred texts. That seems true enough, but it can hardly serve as a defining quality of sacred music, since, in that case, any music would be sacred as long as the words were sacred, and the whole problem with which we began was the sense that sometimes the same sacred lyrics are put to music that we consider purely secular. I once heard the Friday night prayer that celebrates the holiness of the Sabbath (the *Kiddush*) sung to the tune of "La Marseillaise," for instance. Would we, by analogy, find it acceptable to have the Christian *Sanctus* or the Jewish *K'dushah* sung to the nationalist strains of "My Country 'Tis of Thee," or to the former Soviet Union's "International," or, even worse, to "Deutschland, Deutschland, über Alles" (a song featured by the Nazis)?

I mention national anthems particularly because they usually began as sacred hymns themselves. The melody of "Deutschland, Deutschland, über Alles" is still sung as a hymn in many churches. It was not invented by the Third Reich. It was composed in 1797 by Haydn, and was later adopted as the anthem for the Austrian empire, entitled "Gott erhalte, Gott beschütze, unsern Kaiser, unser Land" ("God Keep and Protect our Kaiser and Our Land"). Even "My Country 'Tis of Thee" is just America's version of the more religiously sounding "God Save the King/Queen," the national anthem of Great Britain. But the British title retains the song's original connection to religion, since it is a petition for divine protection of a monarch who was believed to rule by divine right. Most anthems were sacred songs when they began. But are they sacred still? Their melodies haven't changed, so melody alone cannot be the hallmark of sacred music.

So, sacred songs like "God Save the King/Queen" can become secular national anthems. And national anthems like "Hatikvah" can sometimes become sacred. But other secular songs can probably never become sacred: Could we sing a *Sanctus* or the *Sh'ma* to the Beatles' hit, "She Loves You (Yeah Yeah Yeah)"? Obviously not! There must be some independent standards to judge the music itself. That puts us back where we started, demanding some musical criterion for sacred, but unable to settle on one that is true for all accepted pieces of sacred music.

At least, people say, we have a right to demand *good* music during worship. If we do not know what makes music sacred, we do know what makes it good. The argument here seems to be that, as the loftiest of human activities, worship demands music of impeccable taste. Otherwise, we would not be taking seriously its claims to speak to God. Let us agree, for the sake of argument, that we could reach consensus on what is good music—a doubtful hypothesis, I think, but worth granting for a moment anyway. Imagine it to be the work of such composers as Bach, Beethoven, and Brahms. We still have the problem that many religious traditions—Orthodox Judaism and most ethnic churches, to name two—would probably not pass the test of good music, yet their music is obviously sacred. Apparently, by this narrow definition of "good," not all sacred music is good. But it is equally true that by the same definition, not all good music is sacred (Beethoven's fifth symphony, say, or the "Toreador Song" in *Carmen*). And though it is taken for granted here, it is by no means self-evident that God has the same taste in music that philharmonic subscription holders do.

Suppose, however, we expand our definition and say that good music is whatever any given culture says it is: Bach and Beethoven in the classical tradition of the west, but other things in, say, Japanese Shinto or Haitian Voodoo. We can say that, at the very least, we should adopt the principle that we ought to offer to God only our finest creative accomplishments, so that even though not all good music is sacred, all sacred music must be good, according to the local definition of good. That would apply to genuinely ethnic musical preferences as well as ancient or medieval chanting modes. It would also provide us with a mandate to do for our time and place what others have done for theirs: to create new music according to the highest aesthetic criteria available.

Unfortunately, that won't do either. The biggest problem is that even music that everyone agrees is both good and sacred often turns out not to facilitate worship. What shall we do with Aaron Copland's *In the Beginning*, Leonard Bernstein's *Kaddish*, or even Bach's *Mass in B Minor*? All three are certainly sacred, and Bach's Mass may even have been used for worship once, but I can't imagine using any of them for that purpose now. Bernstein's *Chichester Psalms* contains a gorgeous rendition of Psalm 23 that might be plundered for use as a solo in modern worship, but the rest of the work—much as I love it—will never win wide appeal as a liturgical favorite. By contrast, the great liturgical favorites of all time do not always pass musical muster with connoisseurs of musical taste, which, of course, is the problem we started with in the first place!

> ⊛ **Not only can we not agree on what makes music sacred, but even if we could, it would not follow that all sacred music is good music, and even if that were true, not all sacred (and, therefore, good) music is applicable to worship. Here, as elsewhere, worship seems stubbornly intent on advancing its own criteria for what is desirable.**

To be sure, even the best liturgical music has its limits. If the words are downright offensive, for instance, the music cannot launder their message. Texts that are perceived as sexist, racist, religiously triumphalist, or otherwise immoral will not work as public prayer, even when they are delivered with the most welcome melodies. Professional singers sometimes miss this reality. Trained all their lives to appreciate music, they may underestimate the extent to which even the most beloved tune will be heard discordantly if its lyrics are offensive. If a song has sexist lyrics, for instance, they should either change the words or omit the song, rather than sing it for its musical appeal, and alienate sensitive worshipers.

But music can overcome other problems that we have with words. As the words of most popular songs demonstrate, we expect more from language when it is spoken than when it is sung. Words put to music may be quite banal on their own, but with the right musical setting, they soar to heights of suggestiveness. Think of Broadway musicals and movies, which have given us such classics as, "When you walk through a storm, hold your head up high," "Somewhere over the rainbow," and "Tomorrow, tomorrow, I love you, tomorrow—you're only a day away." Here are lyrics that no one would just say. When they are sung, however, they set people to crying and become the language of hope to millions of theater goers.

Prayers are very much like the lyrics of musicals. They often say apparently simple things that come out sounding banal if they are rendered in ordinary prose. Many old prayers, especially, retain the language of antiquity that means little or nothing to average worshipers who may even question whether they believe what they say. Prayers in languages other than English (Hebrew, for instance, for Jews) can be even worse, because most people have no idea what they mean, and therefore they all sound the same. Music rescues such prayers from their apparent ordinariness. Once set to music, people look forward to them. They associate them with the feeling tone of the music in which they are set. Liturgy that is hard to read may more easily be sung.

Since music has such power, it is not surprising to find that attitudes toward it run very deep. When people debate the musical merit of their worship, they resort to the sort of unbending absolutism that we rarely encounter elsewhere. Remembering what we said earlier (chapter 2) about symbols, we can explain this forensic heat. We said there that unlike signs, symbols are things to which we are attracted or from which we are repelled so strongly that we cannot even explain why. Music digs down deeply in our psyche; the old standbys of our youth echo in the chambers of our soul long after their sound waves have dissipated into space. The music we love is a symbol for us. People may support their taste in liturgical music by claiming that it is sacred and good, whereas the music that other people advocate is neither. But as we saw, it is unlikely that they can prove either point, much less demonstrate why (even if they are right) that has anything to do with the case, since lots of music that is both sacred and good is absolutely ruinous in worship. The real reason they like the music they do is that it symbolizes positively.

In the face of such a raging issue, it is no surprise to find rabbis, priests, and pastors abdicating musical responsibility and delegating it entirely to musical specialists who may have little understanding of worship, but who presumably know good music in the same way that theologians know a good doctrine when they see one. This does not always solve the problem. Musicians, after all, have their own musical tastes: musical sounds that symbolize to them no less than music of a different sort may symbolize to others. The truth is, according to the canons of western composition, there is such a thing as good music. Musicians have learned to recognize it, appreciate it, play it, love it, and often, live it. Music is a demanding taskmaster. People who aspire to excel at it would often rather starve than give up their ambition to sing at the Met or play in the philharmonic. Asking musicians to select music for worship *solely* on the basis of its musical quality is tantamount to asking philosophers to write prayers purely on the basis of the logical strength of a chain of reasoning. But in some worship settings that is exactly what happens, with disastrous consequences.

> ▧ **Musical expertise should certainly not be bypassed when it comes to selecting the music for public prayer, but musical quality as defined by musical elites is not the sole, nor even the most important, factor to be considered. Insistence on good music often comes at the expense of the very liturgical moments that are the whole point of the liturgy that the music is supposed to serve.**

As long as we persist in imagining that sacred music means "music that is sacred" in the same way that soft ice cream is "ice cream that is soft," we will get nowhere. "Soft" is the name we give to the consistency of an ice cream compound that corresponds to a certain molecular or chemical makeup of the ice cream, whereas "sacred" bears no relationship to any particular quality inherent in the arrangement of sharps, rests, and eighth notes. If we want to know what criteria to apply to the music of our worship, we have to start the discussion all over again.

Music As Performative

The idea of performatives is a useful way to start thinking more productively about the worship music that we choose. We saw before that the study of language, too, is befuddled by the simplistic notion that words must be judged only by the extent to which they verbally mirror some objective state of affairs called truth. Prayer, we decided, is not always a specialized kind of text that reflects theological truths; it may be an act of speaking in which words accomplish something (the way "this meeting is adjourned" actually adjourns a meeting). The spoken word of prayer does more than mirror an independent reality existing outside ourselves; it *performs*. We can apply that same insight to music. The music of prayer also does more than convey independent truths or ideas; it, too, *performs*.

> **If we want to know what sacred music is, we have to ask first what sacred acts are, since sacred music is not music that is sacred, but music that performs sacred acts. Reviewing the diversity of sacred music in the Jewish and Christian traditions demonstrates that, in every case, music is considered sacred not on account of what it is, but on account of what it *does*.**

Sometimes, sacred music expresses texts that are considered sacred in such a way that the meaning of those texts is enhanced. That is the case with Bloch's *Sacred Service* and Verdi's *Four Sacred Pieces*. The Chasidic *niggun*, however, deliberately has no text, but is sacred because it is used to attain a sacred state of bliss in the context of Chasidic worship practice. Haydn's "God Keep and Protect our Kaiser" and Great Britain's "God Save the King/Queen" were sacred when they were dedicated to rulers who were presumed to enjoy divine rights, and were sung by their subjects to acknowledge religiously what God had willed. "Hatikvah" may or may not be a sacred song, depending on whether it is sung by secular Israelis before a soccer match or by

Jews affirming an age-old religious vision of a holy land rebuilt after two thousand years. Copland's *In the Beginning* is sacred because it expresses the sacred text of Genesis, and Bernstein's *Kaddish* is sacred because it expresses a Jewish prayer. Yet neither Copland's nor Bernstein's piece is liturgical. They both do something religious, but what they do religiously is something other than make prayer happen.

Music is performative. From their respective religious traditions composers learn the goals of religious life, such as expressing a sacred text, giving thanks, inducing awe, and attaining a trance. They create music to accomplish those goals.

> ◉ **To the extent that music performs successfully in a sacred cause, it is sacred music. To the extent that the cause is worship, it is liturgical sacred music. The type of worship that the music is intended to facilitate depends on the tradition in question.**

We can now return to the question of how good sacred music must be: Must the music of worship be good by specifically musical standards? For centuries now, the elite of Europe and North America have argued that it must. The assumption seems to have been that artistically excellent music moves us to a higher form of religious consciousness than do lower forms of music. It has even been argued that lower forms of music produce lower levels of morality. The search for an uplifting musical idiom was the motivating theory behind the nineteenth-century conversion of medieval Jewish chants into artistically acceptable western art songs. And the same process can be seen as recently as our own day.

The Composer Remained Unconvinced

A worship service was planned to honor a young composer who had used his considerable talents to write folk music for his church. The service music contained a simple but effective song that he had composed years earlier when he had been just a teenager. But it had been rearranged with sophisticated harmonic structure and set for the organ, at a tempo of only about half the speed of the original, which experts had deemed too raucous for "real" worship. The rearrangement was unquestionably better music, but it failed miserably as worship. Musical critics commented on the miracle that had transformed a simple melody into a sophisticated musical event. Worshipers who knew the old setting, however, were disappointed. "Better get used to it," they were told, since the melody had been refurbished and recast to last forever. It was now worthy of prayer and would raise the assembled congregation to levels unattainable by the composition in its original state.

The composer remained unconvinced.

Who was right: the critics or the composer? At issue first is whether liturgical music ought to last forever. It is widely assumed that it should, but why should it? Presumably, God deserves the best music we have to offer, and things that are our best are lasting. Lurking behind this argument is the assumption that the music of prayer is an offering to God, like the sacrifices of the Temple that once stood in Jerusalem. We say that we also offer our words to God. But do we? And even if we do, is our God really the kind of demagogic potentate who demands only the best, even if the best defeats the general purpose of rendering us worshipful? The theology of prayer as sacrifice is well attested in Jewish and Christian sources, so theologians will have to work out the extent to which we still ought to conceive of it that way. But even if the traditional theologians are right, their insistence on lasting music is replete with problems.

First, the preference for lasting is culturally biased. A form of Buddhist art, for instance, deliberately avoids producing what is lasting; it specializes in beautiful sand sculpture that takes months to fashion and then is blown away as a reminder of the transience of what our senses perceive as real. True, Jews and Christians are not Buddhists, but it still is not clear why we so readily assume that religion demands that which is lasting.

Second, we should ask, "Lasting for whom?"

Not My Favorites

When some colleagues and I taught worship for chaplains in the United States Navy, I dropped in on a class that was designed to expand the Navy's musical repertoire. A traditionalistic Episcopal priest objected, "What's wrong with the old-time favorites?" An African-American pastor standing next to him retorted, "They're not *my* old-time favorites."

The western musical repertoire sounds lasting only to people who hail from the grand European tradition. Jews who adopted art music for their worship were adapting themselves to that tradition. Yet the music they adopted has proved to be anything but lasting. Liturgically, at least, we hear less and less of it. The same can be said of the great classics in Christian worship. The question is not whether Bach and Mozart are lasting. They clearly are, at least for westerners. The question is whether just because they are lasting they should be used in worship, and the answer is that if we insist only on lasting music in public prayer, then for many people, public prayer may not last.

By comparison, it is worth recalling a famous debate that occurred among architects when modern architecture was coming into being. In 1895, Viennese architect Otto Wagner published a book called *Modern Architecture*, in which he argued that buildings should be designed as just the opposite of the neo-Gothic, Baroque, and Rococo architecture that dominated the main boulevard circling the inner city of Vienna. In opposition to the official architectural establishment, Wagner and his colleagues formed a school of thought that championed function over arbitrary form. Before long, Wagner's notion was expanded into the philosophy of what is known as the Bauhaus school, often recalled crisply in the curt motto of one of its ideologues, Mies van der Rohe, "Less is more." Decades later, American architect Robert Venturi expressed the artistic conflict beautifully when he parodied Mies van der Rohe. In response to "Less is more," he retorted, "Less is a bore."

This debate on architecture is aptly applied to liturgical music.

Assuming that music that is not lasting is "less" than music that passes the test of time, is the music that is "less" really "more" or is it "a bore"? From a purely musical perspective, the music that people prefer for their worship often doesn't have the highest possible artistic merit. But worshipers who are moved to pray by it would probably judge that "less is more." Musicians with trained ears and heightened sophistication to music at its best would say that "less is a bore." They are both right. Musical purists undoubtedly find much of what passes for liturgical music boring. For them it fails in its function. But for most people, musically exciting compositions, though "more" in terms of music, are not necessarily "more" in terms of worship.

✸ **Texts we sing should be judged along with texts we say solely on the degree to which they facilitate worship, for sacred music is music that performs in a sacred way, and worship is one such performance.**

How Music Performs in Worship ✸

In the last chapter, we saw some ways in which spoken texts perform in worship: They create a present, establish a shared past, and commit us to an anticipated future. Music performs too, but somewhat differently.

Music As Support System for Words

The most obvious function of sacred music is its ability to be a support system for the lyrics of prayers. The assumption seems to be that the whole purpose of music is to enhance the verbal message of the text. It is common, therefore, to provide composers with a liturgical text, which they are commissioned to set to music. They try to outfit the text in question with an appropriately expressive sound. To some extent, music does function that way, but most people misunderstand precisely how it does so.

Music does not refer to a state of affairs the way words do. That is the problem with advanced program music like Berlioz's *Symphonie Fantastique*, Beethoven's *Pastoral Symphony*, or Tchaikovsky's *Romeo and Juliet*. Program music is "about something." It may even try to imitate a sound of whatever it is that it is about—like the cannon fire in Tchaikovsky's *1812 Overture*. But more often, program music is more subtle than that.

Aaron Copland Explains

There are two kinds of descriptive music. The first comes under the heading of literal description. A composer wishes to recreate the sound of bells in the night. He therefore writes certain chords . . . which actually sound like bells in the night. Something real is being imitated realistically. . . . The music has no other *raison d'être* than mere imitation at that point.

The other type of descriptive music is less literal and more poetic. No attempt is made to describe a particular scene or event; nevertheless, some outward circumstance arouses certain emotions in the composer that he wishes to communicate to the listener. It may be clouds or the sea or an airplane, but the point is that instead of literal imitation, one gets a musicopoetic transcription of a phenomenon as reflected in the composer's mind. That constitutes a higher form of program music. The bleating of sheep will always be the bleating of sheep, but a cloud portrayed in music allows the imagination more freedom. (From Aaron Copland, *What to Listen for in Music*, reprinted by permission of the Aaron Copland Fund for Music, Inc., copyright owner.)

Composers of advanced program music often have to indicate in words what their composition is about. Tchaikovsky wrote *Romeo and Juliet*, for example, which we can enjoy simply as music. But we have to know the story in order to recognize that the piece is a musical version of the Shakespearean drama. The first theme, for instance, symbolizes the fight between the Capulets and the Montagues. So, to say that sacred music must primarily express the text of a given prayer presupposes that everyone knows the prayer and that its musical expression works in a subtle way beyond direct description, like the clouds in Copland's example, and not the sheep. That may happen sometimes, but imagining that the function of sacred music is only, or even mostly, to express sacred text is as limiting as imagining that symphonic music must always, or even primarily, be programmatic. Surely music goes beyond this narrow definition of function.

There is also a second objection to the usual justification of sacred music as primarily expressive of a prayer's text. This objection is not musical, but textual, for if this simplistic definition of music underestimates the power of music, it also underestimates the scope of words. As we saw above, liturgical sentences are rarely just descriptions of things. They perform, in the sense that they bring into being certain states of affairs, or they recollect, or they express hope, or they commit us to a vision. It is not wrong to think of music as a support for the text, but insofar as music supports it, what it supports is the text's *function*, not its literal *meaning*.

Take the "Song of the Sea" (*Mi Khamokha*), a liturgical staple in Jewish worship that recollects the parting of the Red Sea for the Israelites crossing to escape from Egypt. The music doesn't actually picture every word of the text that celebrates the crossing. The real question to be asked is what the text *does*, not what it *pictures*. If its performative task is recalling the crossing, for example, the music might be soft and melodic, evocative of fond recollection, rather than a stirring rendition of a sea parting its waves. If the text functions as a promise of God's salvation yet to come, the music might express hope or confidence in the future, perhaps by making use of a traditional motif that expresses the Jewish historical past or borrowing directly from the cantillation traditionally associated with the "Song of the Sea" in the Bible. A competent composer knows that the music should do what the text does, but not necessarily mean every word that the text literally says.

The main performative function of music does not depend on the words of the text. Only a word-centered culture like ours would reduce all the arts to alternative expressions of verbal messages. Music has its own way of speaking to us. We have to consider, therefore, the ways in which music in our worship operates purely as music.

Music As the Structuring of Time

More than most media, music speaks to us because of what we associate with it. We hear a sound, think back, and remember that this same set of tones comes to us every year at this time. On New Year's Eve, for example, people of my generation (who remember bandleader Guy Lombardo) hear "Auld Lang Syne." It is played now by a different band in a different key and different tempo, but we know what it is and we think, "Ah, a new year!" Christmas carols tell Christians it is Christmas again. *Shabbat* songs inform Jews that the Sabbath is here, just as the *Adir Hu* melody tells them it is Passover and the familiar strains of *Kol Nidre* (whose Aramaic text they do not even understand) announces that it is Yom Kippur.

Liturgical traditions come with such melodic reminders of the calendar because an important function of sacred music is the structuring of annual time. For Christians, it establishes the requisite appreciation for Advent or for Lent, and for Jews, the High Holidays, Passover, or Purim. Most contemporary worshipers have only a foggy understanding of their musical traditions, however. Compared to our ancestors, who lived in an oral society and depended on what they heard rather than what they read, we are culturally disadvantaged when it comes to recognizing musical cues. Nonetheless, we depend on some songs to tell us what time of year it is and how we should be feeling inside as we prepare to welcome one holiday rather than another.

That is one reason why people resist musical innovation. If they had a large repertoire of songs to mark the time of year, they wouldn't mind omitting one of them and introducing another. But having only a meager set of melodies with which they associate any given sacred occasion, they can be counted on to react with downright hostility if the cantor or music director tampers with it.

Music As Communal Bonding

If music binds us to our common past because it evokes the temporal associations that we share, it bonds us to other hearers in our present as well. We listen to the same symphony and experience its tensions and resolutions together, so that, even in a concert hall so dark we cannot see each other, we emerge as a group.

Ross Speck and Carolyn Attneave are psychotherapists who apply systems thinking to therapy. Their description of a jazz session indicates what I mean when I say that music bonds even strangers together in a common appreciation of the flow of time.

The Network Effect

In Preservation Hall in New Orleans, old black men from the early Dixieland era improvise and invent jazz nightly. The audience of habitués and tourists begins the evening relatively unrelated to one another, at separate tables and in couples or small groups. Under the mystical, religious, tribal, hypnotic, musical spell they become closely knitted together. They sit tightly pressed. The small group boundaries dissolve. They clap, sway, beat out rhythms, and move their bodies in a united complex response. The group mood is a euphoric high, and the conventional bonds dissolve. New relationships melt away the conventional barriers of status, generation, territory, and sex. Young middle-class white women, black street people, elderly spinsters, and hippie youths recognize a mutuality and express it in gesture, contact, and words. This lasts until the musicians give out and the people depart. Many leave in groups they might never have contemplated before they came. For those brief hours they have become involved with one another and with humanity in general in new ways, with new feelings, new relationships, and new bonds. However briefly, they have been a part of a social network. They have experienced the network effect.

To be sure, not every characteristic of a jazz session applies to worship. We saw in chapter 1 that some rituals (like a presidential nomination) do produce a euphoric high, others (like a funeral) produce a cathartic low, and still others (like seeing friends daily for lunch) produce no intense emotional peak at all. It all depends on the nature of the ritual moment, which is defined by the script of the particular ritual. But every one of these group rituals, regardless of the emotional intensity of their desired moments, must at least unify the participants around some commonly conceived scripted requirement, and the jazz session demonstrates one such example beautifully. The people entered the room as lone individuals or (at best) small groups of two or three. But as the music put them in sync with one another, they found their individuality merging into a common sense of shared experience—like several flashlight beams splaying at random around a ceiling until they eventually land together superimposed in one brilliant burst of light. As Speck and Attneave put it, they experienced being "involved with one another and with humanity in general."

Good liturgical leaders use music to establish a rhythm to their worship, so that everyone progresses together through the liturgy. The tradition in many African-American churches, for example, is to move together, beating time, swaying, clapping, or singing. A whole room filled with the sound of a resounding hymn has the same affect. Sometimes the effect is to fasten everyone's attention on a particular event being celebrated in the liturgy; or it may establish a shared emotion or even just a sense of sharing the experience of a common melody with common associations for everyone present.

> ❋ **Music works, as mere words do not, to convert individuals into a group where they can experience together the message of the alternative world being established in their prayers.**

Music As Emotion

Without doubt, people get emotional about music in ways that they do not when they hear mere words. Philosophers have long recognized music's unique ability to move us, sometimes to tears (of sorrow or of joy), sometimes to revolutionary zeal (there is a reason armies march to battle to the strains of drums and bugle), sometimes to more complex emotional states we never even knew we could realize.

Why music should possess this unique capacity to stir our emotions is not clear. Does it come from something inherent in musical structures? Is music's power universal, or does it depend on cultural training? In part, music's emotional strength certainly seems related to what it is—music—and therefore to whatever elements constitute music as its own art form. In part, too, it derives from the fact that music recalls the past to memory. We saw that symbolizing depends on just that uniquely human propensity to remember, and that symbols, by definition, are those items about which we feel most strongly even without rational reasons to justify those feelings. So in addition to whatever inherent technical quality music has to stir our feelings, we should not pass lightly over the fact that the sounds we hear today attain meaning because we once heard them somewhere else: in our youth perhaps, as a lullaby sung while we rested in our mother's lap; or on Christmas Eve or *Kol Nidre* night; or in peer groups where, as teenagers, we discovered our first glimpse of independent adulthood.

So the emotions that music prompts are really two kinds. First, there are compositions that evoke emotion for technical reasons that composers may understand or not, but which they surely set into motion by the insight that constitutes their claim to musical genius. I don't suppose every human being on the face of the earth is automatically moved in the same way by, say, Beethoven's *Violin Concerto*, but in the western world, at least, where ears are trained to hear the same potential sets of sounds the same way, very many people are. And parallels must surely exist in other cultures. Thus, when people trained to appreciate the art of music for its own sake say they want only the finest music in their sacred repertoire of sound, it is because they know the incomparably sublime sense that grips them when they hear good compositions, and they are understandably frustrated if other worshipers who lack musical sophistication do not experience the same thing.

Emotions well up too when we experience time as structured. I began this book by noting how we human beings cannot bear the thought of senseless anarchy. We like to pattern our lives in terms of recurrent events, from the memory of things that happened long before we were born (religious fasts and feasts) to the recollection of episodes drawn from our biographies (birthday parties, fiftieth wedding anniversaries). True, great music has its own inherent musical structures that somehow speak to us; but ordinary music, too, sometimes *symbolizes*, in that it draws on its evocative power to bring to mind our past, to remind us of the cyclical passing of the years and thus of the moments that mattered once and (through musical recapitulation) matter still. This is the second kind of emotionality stirred by music, all music, but sacred music too, so that sometimes it is not great music we are after in our sacred services, but just music that symbolizes for us: the Christmas carol of our youth or the strains of *Kol Nidre*, without which it would seem that Christmas or Yom Kippur does not even arrive.

Music As the Knowledge of God

Musicians the world over testify to the innate spiritual power of music. We should not be surprised, therefore, to find that music used in worship invokes a certain sense of the presence of God. We saw, however (in chapter 5), that God is known in more than one way. Different kinds of music establish different modes of openness to the many sides of God.

Cantor Benjie-Ellen Schiller of the Hebrew Union College in New York, illustrates four different ways of knowing God, each of which demands a different musical type along with a matching bodily posture. These are (1) music of majesty, (2) music of meditation, (3) music of meeting, and (4) music of memory.

Music of majesty corresponds to most of the lavish repertoire of the western art tradition. It is the full-bodied music of a magnificent pipe organ filling a cathedral and thrilling the people who throng there. It conjures up the posture of standing erect, arms outstretched to heaven in exaltation. Think of the final movement of Beethoven's ninth symphony, most settings of the *Gloria*, a Christmas carol like "Hark! the Herald Angels Sing," most synagogue versions of the *Sh'ma*, and the final strains of *Kol Nidre*, or the *Great Alenu*, which is the version sung on Rosh Hashanah as the cantor and rabbi prostrate themselves before the ark in recognition of God's rulership.

Most of this music arrived with the Enlightenment and the certainty that God would be present as a distant and majestic ruler. Church music was composed especially to acknowledge God's transcendence and glory. Jewish cantors and composers copied church style by making old synagogue favorites sound the way church music did— not by aping Christian melodies, but by setting and performing Jewish music to evoke the same emotions. Reform Judaism especially developed a rich and varied repertoire of this music of majesty, which proclaimed the presence of a mighty God who rules the universe in grandeur.

Music of meditation is just the opposite. It suggests the bodily posture by which we bow our head, close our eyes, and focus inward rather than outward. Typical of this music of meditation might be a soft, gentle version of "The First Noel," which announces for Christians, "Born is the King of Israel," but does so with the accent on Jesus' just being born: It evokes the tender image of a mother and child, not the grandeur of a potentate ruling from a throne on high. Jewish examples may be found after the silent prayer—the familiar settings in Reform worship to *May the words . . .* or (in Hebrew) *Yihyu l'ratson*. Prayers of healing are usually composed in this meditative mode. Even on occasions where majesty is the order of the day, a full service will probably include some meditative moments, as a sort of musical downtime, so to speak, an opportunity to know God as Elijah did, not in the whirlwind but in the still, small voice within us.

The most significant innovation of our time has been *music of meeting*, the music that invites the stance of reaching out to one another, holding hands, or otherwise connecting with God not on high or even within, but through the miracle of community. Most of us have years of experience with majesty and at least some experience with meditation. But only recently have we discovered that God may be known through meeting. Martin Buber foretold that possibility when he wrote his masterpiece *I And Thou*, which quickly made an impact not only within the Jewish community for whom he had written it, but in Christian circles as well. *I and Thou* was published in 1923. Buber was well ahead of his time, but he saw that the days of knowing God only as the majestic deity were numbered. "All real living is meeting," he wrote. For him, we know God best the way we know a friend: immediately, directly, unmediated. The English title, *I and Thou*, is misleading, because the old English word "thou" is so distant and formal. Buber's native language, German, has two forms of address, the formal *Sie* and the familiar *du*. Buber deliberately entitled his book *Ich und Du*, meaning, "I and You, God, You whom I know the way I know a dear old friend, the way I know a family member, someone near and dear to me." God is the eternal friend whom we engage in dialogue.

Buber went even farther than acknowledging God's immediate presence to us as a friend. He held also that God can be known even when we engage other people in the mutuality of being present to and for each other. Music of meeting, then, connects us horizontally with others. It is the way we know God's presence among us because we are no longer alone, but intertwined with others around us.

Music of meeting naturally invites group singing, a sure sign that we are not alone. It may suggest bodily contact, eyes meeting, or a hand stretched forth to clasp our own. But traditional worship in church and synagogue has favored formality. Seen primarily as a way to sing praise to a sovereign deity (music of majesty), it favored formality, which is precisely the opposite of the way we greet a good friend. Our traditional musical repertoires are therefore especially lacking in music of meeting. Yet since, in our time, we are apt to know God best precisely through intimacy, music of majesty and music of meditation are not enough. We desperately need music of meeting if we are to know God in our time. We need music that is singable and cantors who encourage congregational participation.

 The single greatest need for worship is to connect individuals in community, that they may know the mystery of genuine meeting, and thereby the presence of God among us. Our single greatest lack is music of meeting. Musical experts within each faith who truly know their art will consciously and conscientiously develop a rich repertoire of music of meeting; they will teach these melodies and sing them, even if they are not as sophisticated as the accumulated repertoire of tradition. Without the ambiance of meeting, regularly satisfying worship will not occur, because the certainty of God among us will be wanting.

A final way of knowing God is through the miracle of connecting ourselves backward through time. Toward that end, worship requires *music of memory*. Every tradition has such favorites. These too are not necessarily the highest form of musical idiom, but they are songs that echo through history reminding us of the community that came before us. We find it meaningful to know that they too celebrated with the same words and music that we still use. It is as if time had collapsed us all into a single magical moment when the entire congregation of the faithful, or the whole Jewish community at Sinai, stood together. This music of memory evokes no particular body posture, but it does suggest that our eyes turn backward in search of our past. We may listen reverently or sing with all our might, depending on the song. Music of memory may simultaneously be music of majesty, meditation, or meeting. But we sing it because it is traditional. It evokes the miracle by which our faith began, the incredible satisfaction that comes from knowing that we didn't make it all up just yesterday. Connected through time, we are ready to believe that God, who transcends time, is real.

How does God's presence become real to us in public prayer? That is the question that should determine

which of the four kinds of music we select at any particular point in the liturgy. The liturgy has its own flow in this regard. Given the structure and shape of the service, should worshipers acknowledge God's majesty? Should they turn inward to know God in meditation? Should they connect as a community to know that God is among us? Or should they recollect the miracle of a community that goes back through time and will be here tomorrow just as it is today?

Both Sound and Sense   ◉

In the previous chapter, while dealing with the texts we say, I introduced the name of Ludwig Wittgenstein, an extraordinary genius of our century. Now, in concluding the chapter on the texts we sing, I want to invoke the insight of a second creative intellect, the French anthropologist Claude Lévi-Strauss. Lévi-Strauss had a lifelong fascination with ritual, and saw the compelling relationship between speech and song in the life of the spirit. When he wrote his four-volume magnum opus *Science of Mythology*, he labeled its chapters as if they were sequential parts of a musical score: The introduction was called "Overture," and the conclusion—more than sixteen hundred pages later!—he named "Finale."

In the "Finale," Lévi-Strauss turned to myth and music, which he compared to mathematics. All three, he said, are part of the human need to structure the universe in meaningful ways. Mathematics is pure structure, just an assemblage of random Xs and Ys joined by arbitrary signs signaling functions like addition or subtraction, multiplication or division. The brain must work mathematically as it forces the data of consciousness into logical categories without which we would be overwhelmed by pure chaos—the anomie and entropy that people fear most. But human beings are not pure brains that share logical structures the way computers share program instructions. So the structures by which we organize reality must be communicable from person to person, generation to generation.

Lévi-Strauss saw two such means of communication in ritual: pure sound that is heard without any cognitive content, and pure content that is heard without any differentiation in sound. *Pure sound* is music; *pure sense*, which is what Lévi-Strauss called pure cognitive content, is myth. By "myth" he meant more than some vague recollection of Greek or Norse stories of heroes. He had in mind the universal practice of telling tales about the world: as diverse as the myth of the chickadee's origin, which he found among Native Americans, and the myth of Oedipus that we inherit from the Greeks. Myths are like our spoken texts in prayer: They are pure sense in that they provide cognitive content and depend on the meaning of their words to get their point across. At the other extreme is our repertoire of music, pure sound that depends on the arrangement of notes to communicate its message.

Human beings require both sound and sense to complete their understanding of reality. We are neither pure sense nor pure sound users. We need both scripts that say and scores that sound. Fully satisfying rituals come about when we successfully unite the two. That seems to me to be the essence of how ritual works: the combination of sense and sound, our two primary human channels for communicating to one another the patterned structuring of experience.

It is rare, therefore, for religious ritual to feature texts that are rendered as if they were pure readings. Instead, we develop chants, traditional singsong ways of reciting them, so the pure sense of the text moves toward the satisfying middle ground where sense and sound come together. If a prayer leader reads prayers that worshipers expect to be sung, the congregation is invariably disappointed: It is as if the prayer wasn't really "said." Of course it was "said," but "saying" prayer is unlike any other "saying." It cannot be judged the way we judge other reading events. It must be judged for what it is—worship, the ritual recitation of a text, where sense must eventually be joined with sound in an exercise of imposing structure on chaos.

Similarly, it is rare to find pure music in ritual. We have pure instrumental music here and there, but it does not predominate. As we saw in the first function of sacred music discussed above, most church or synagogue composers attest that their art lies in interpreting the sense behind a sacred text or teaching, not arranging pure musical notation in such a way that music as pure sound occurs. They write musical interpretations *of something*, of "Ave Maria," perhaps, or of Psalm 150, or of the *K'dushah*. Here too, then, the pure form of the communication is sacrificed as the pure sound is outfitted with words.

> ⊛ **In ritual, the pure sense of the spoken text attracts the sound of chanting, and the pure sound of musical notation is given lyrics that make sense. At its best, ritual is the experience of pattern. In content and form it imposes order, creating what we called an alternative world. That world is expressed through a text that is both spoken and sung. Together, sense and sound create a universe that did not exist beforehand.**

Ritual Check List   ⊛

Words and Concepts You Should Know

- **There is no common denominator** to the music that we call sacred.
- **Not all sacred music is good music,** and not all good music is sacred music. Some music is both sacred and good, but it does not facilitate good worship.
- **Music symbolizes** (see chapter 2). That is why successful worship depends on music more than on any other factor.
- **If we want to know what sacred music is,** we first have to ask what sacred acts are, since sacred music is not music that is sacred, but music that performs sacred acts. Music is sacred not on account of what it is, but on account of what it does.
- **To the extent that music performs successfully in a sacred**

cause, it is sacred music. To the extent that the cause is worship, it is liturgical sacred music.

- **Texts we sing should be judged along with texts we say** simply and solely on the degree to which they facilitate worship, for sacred music is music that performs in a sacred way, and worship is one such performance.

- **The music of worship does five things,** and should be chosen according to what we want it to do at any specific point in the flow of the service: It enhances the message of the words, evokes associations of the flow of time in the sacred calendar, bonds together the worshiping community, stirs our emotions, and helps us know the presence of God.

- **The single greatest need for worship** is to connect individuals in community, so they may know the mystery of genuine meeting and, thereby, the presence of God among us. Our single greatest lack is music of meeting. Musical experts within each faith who truly know their art will consciously and conscientiously develop a rich repertoire of music of meeting. They will teach these melodies and sing them, even if they are not as sophisticated as the accumulated repertoire of tradition. Without the ambiance of meeting, satisfying worship will not regularly occur, because the certainty of God among us will be wanting.

Conversation Points for Making Worship Work ❋

1 ▪ Go back over the five functions of worship music. Then go through the music used at a recent worship service that you have attended and decide if the music accomplished what the structure of the service required.

2 ▪ Since music helps us know God in four ways, we need four kinds

of music: the music of majesty, the music of meditation, the music of meeting, and the music of memory. Go over a recent service and decide if the music was selected according to its potential in evoking the presence of God. Which of the four ways was chosen, and why? Would the service have been more evocative of the Divine if another type of music had been used?

3 ▪ Since music of meeting is hardest to accomplish and the most needed of all, decide if you have enough music of meeting at your worship services. Are people really singing it? If not, why not? Here is a check list of some questions that you should consider:

- Is the music being taught well?

- Do the people know the words?

- Do they have song sheets with the words in front of them?

- Is the music too hard for people to learn?

- Is the music sung in a key that ordinary singers find accessible?

- Is the space adequate—that is, do people hear each other in community or do their voices die out because the room is acoustically dead, or because people are sitting too far apart? If need be, ask an acoustical engineer to check out your room for you. You may even have to add an overhead microphone or two so people can hear each other. And the cantor may have to conquer the limitations of space—a concern we will take up in detail in the next chapter.

eight

Sacred Space: The Message of Design

We mistakenly take for granted the spaces that we occupy. We label one place as the living room and another as the den, for instance, as if their definitions were derived from a source higher than ourselves. The easy chair, we think, goes only here, for the simple reason that it has always gone here. We change our clothes with casual abandon, spending small fortunes to keep up with new styles. But rearranging the spaces in which we live goes distinctly against the grain. We relate to the spaces we occupy as if they had an objective life of their own, sometimes to the point that we allow ourselves to be overwhelmed by their arbitrary limitations that permit some activities and prohibit others. A useful starting point is a fuller appreciation of the way we allow space to determine our activity rather than the other way around.

Sometimes just naming our spaces one way rather than another predetermines what we do in them. Some years ago, my family added a room to our house, and we had to decide what to call it: a den or a study? If the former, we would install a television set and encourage family gatherings and conversations. If the latter, it would hold bookcases and a computer, with a working ambiance antipathetic to conversation.

How we decorate a room also matters. Everyone has had the experience of visiting a home where the "living" room is furnished in such a way that it is impossible to live in it. Sometimes the furniture is so formal that you feel uncomfortable just being there; or the chairs and sofa are arranged so that only four people can easily converse together, while everyone who arrives after must sit on the periphery of the room, where they can talk to each other but not to the people in the middle.

> ⊛ **What we label our spaces, how we interpret those labels, and how we then arrange the space to accord with those interpretations determine whether the spaces work for us, or whether we remain enslaved to them.**

Spatial Codes: "Build-Ups" or "Put-Downs"   ⊛

Spatial messages are never clearly articulated, but are deeply ingrained within us. We all have favored ways of treating backyards, kitchens, offices, and porches, or of deciding who gets access to what parts of our house and how they should behave there. We may not be able to articulate these beliefs, but let someone break a spatial taboo, and we recognize it quickly, for spatial boundaries signify our notions of what we hold dear. Several examples are worth considering:

- People in some cultures entertain guests in their kitchens, then are surprised to find that friends from other backgrounds resent being relegated to what they consider second-rate space.

- An award-winning television program set in Victorian England was called *Upstairs, Downstairs*, a spatial metaphor for the class structure of the era being portrayed. The servants lived upstairs; those they served lived downstairs. The butler, however, was allowed to roam freely downstairs, because he was a bridge figure: a servant, to be sure, but in charge of all the other servants and a trusted confidant of the master and his family.

- The two-tiered racial system of pre-civil-rights America was never more blatantly displayed than when the Supreme Court ruled that a New Orleans black man named Homer Plessy could not sit in a "whites only" section while traveling on the East Louisiana Railroad. That 1896 decision produced the official American doctrine of spatial access: "separate but equal." In the reversal of that position (the 1954 decision in *Brown v. the Board of Education of Topeka*), the Supreme Court ruled, in effect, that separate spaces are by nature not equal. They cannot be. Space is never neutral.

- America began to break loose from its racial straitjacket (a spatial image itself, by the way) when an African-American woman, Rosa Parks, refused to give up her seat—her space—and move to the back of the bus.

- Our cultural imagery is filled with spatial metaphors that set off who and what we are:

  > Go to the head of the class
  > Jockeying for position
  > Off in left field
  > Front runners, underdogs, top of the heap
  > Someone's right-hand man/woman
  > Moving up the ladder
  > Build someone up
  > Put someone down

Church and Synagogue Architecture: A Lesson in Space

Roman orgies differed widely from modern state dinners, and both of these have little in common with the seating arrangements on a synagogue pulpit, or the pecking order of dignitaries at a college graduation ceremony. But they are all alike in their symbolic monitoring of ritual space. Who gets to sit where tells more about the occasion than do all the speeches on the program. The watchers at worship (whom we described in chapter 3) know instinctively not to walk freely around the sanctuary during services or to sit in the front rows, where the regulars meet and greet each other. The language of space may be subtle, but no public event occurs without it.

Religions have their own vocabulary for and perceptions of the way their spaces should be treated. Take the word "sanctuary." For a long time, in medieval churches, communion was the prerogative of the clergy, who celebrated the liturgy privately; the people may have been present, at best, for the consecration of the bread and wine, not for partaking of them. The result was the gradual splitting off of the clergy from the laity into sharply divided classes, with the clergy occupying a separate room at one end of the church, and the laity inhabiting the main space. Laypeople could see the clergy through a door or over an intervening screen, but could not *enter* the clergy's space. The word "sanctuary," which was previously used to designate the area around the altar, now was used only for the separate room where the sacred elements were housed and where the sacralizing activity occurred. By contrast, Calvinist theology denied the sacrificial intent of the mass and emphasized the essential equality of all believers, so the Reformed Church took steps to reverse the separation implicit in a sanctuary reserved for ordained persons only, and redesigned churches in which the whole worshiping space—wherever the spoken liturgy could reach—became known as the sanctuary.

A similar development had already occurred in Judaism. The ancient Jerusalem temple boasted an area where the sacrifices occurred and ordinary people could not go. It was further subdivided into several discrete zones, each with its own degree of sanctity and accompanying rules of access. The most sacred was the Holy of Holies, which only the high priest could enter, and only once, on the most holy day of the year. By contrast, the synagogue, where worship with words superseded worship with sacrifice, designated the entire room where worship occurred as the place for public prayer, open to priests and nonpriests alike. To this day, Jews and Protestants call their entire worship space the sanctuary, whereas Catholics reserve the word for the area immediately around the altar.

We said above that ritual provides a microcosmic reflection of the religious pattern imposed on the universe, in that worship is a sacred drama whose script plays out the way the liturgical participants are led to see their world. More than just a stage for the ritual drama being enacted within it, the worship space becomes a paradigm for the way worshipers would like to see the world as a whole. Where, for example, a religion preaches huge class, or even racial, divisions, it will enact a liturgy where those divisions are evident in its use of space. If it sees the world as a hierarchy of forces spiraling upward to heaven, it will develop a ritual featuring hierarchies. If, on the other hand, it preaches radical equality, it will break down spatial privileges on its liturgical stage to signal that since all are equal here before God, all must be granted the same equality outside the church or synagogue walls as well.

The liturgical use of space presents a nonverbal argument for the imposition of our religious values on the society we inhabit. The argument is of necessity silent; but precisely for that reason it is beyond discussion, powerful in its very "givenness," something we take for granted, and more effective than any verbal rhetoric could be.

How do people recognize the spatial message of their worship? Sending African-Americans to the back of a bus must have been blatant enough, but in worship the message is less obvious. We pick up the clues without even knowing how. Here, the history of church architecture is instructive.

At first, Christianity was a rebellious faith that met in private households. The church was just a private home with a room large enough to house the worshipers.

After Constantine's momentous decision to support it, however, Christianity became an official imperial religion. It exchanged private

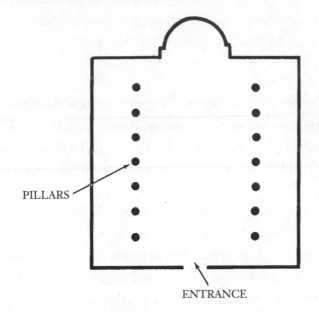

Fig. 8.1. Floor Plan of Basilica

household prayer for worship in basilicas (see Fig. 8.1), long halls supported by two weight-bearing rows of columns running from front to back.

As a veritable throne room, the basilica signaled the elevation of Christianity into the uppermost reaches of society. Its design focused attention on those in authority who sat at the front to address the subject people. The liturgy began with an imperial procession from the entrance in the rear to the throne area in the front, after which the liturgy told the tale of how regal splendor had replaced Christianity's simple home origins.

Sixteenth-century Europe saw progressive unfolding of the Protestant Reformation, and by the seventeenth century, the official Catholic reaction (the Counter-Reformation) had responded not only in word and doctrine, but in church design. Protestants, who reacted against the lavish Catholic iconography and who taught the doctrine of the priesthood of all believers, often opted for simple churches devoid of imagery and open to lay and clergy alike. Where preaching the word replaced the eucharist as the chief form of worship, churches began looking like lecture halls with a large, preacher's pulpit dominating the space. Among Quakers, however, the silent call of the Holy Spirit that was presumed to speak indiscriminately to all believers displaced the hierarchic idea of a preacher talking "down" to the masses. The result was simple meeting houses with no pulpit at all.

In response, Catholic churches reemphasized their lavish liturgy by designing a new kind of High Church space that was like an enormous theater, where the liturgy's message was delivered to the masses with the pomp not of a court, but of an operatic performance (see Fig. 8.2). Seated far away, but with an uninterrupted view of the proceedings (as if in a gallery at a great operatic spectacle), people observed what liturgical scholar J. G. Davies has called "a sort of heavenly grand opera." In this new baroque church style, artists like Bernini painted ceilings that emphasized the pre-Copernican cosmology for which the Counter-Reformation stood. Just by sitting in their seats, surrounded by the vast artistic panoply of baroque worship, those who came to pray felt first-hand the spatial impact of knowing that the earth was the center of the universe. Their seats were the earth, around

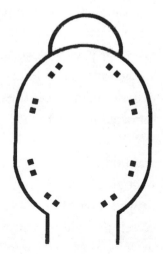

Fig. 8.2. Floor Plan of Baroque Church

which swirled the painted angels on the ceiling, and even the heavens themselves, with all their hosts. The spatial design left the assembled multitude with little doubt that, despite the claims by some that a new age had dawned, the truth, like God and the universe, was as unchanging as the great cosmic drama being played out before their eyes.

In each of these cases, we find a different church structure, rooted both in church tradition and in a particular historical era. In the fourth century, even a fool knew enough to recognize the basilica structure as a sign of imperial splendor; so the movement of the church liturgy from homes to basilicas translated into the message of the church supreme at last. The baroque grand-opera floor plan was similarly conditioned by the larger society in which the church resided; its affirmation of the cosmos depended on the fact that the particular class of men and women who attended worship was trained to appreciate the artistry of baroque art and music. The arts conspired to give the unified picture of the universe favored by the building design.

What is true of churches is true of synagogues. Jews, however, have often been barely tolerated or even downright persecuted by their Christian or Muslim host societies, so were not free to design synagogues fully expressive of Jewish identity. Also, without the considerable finances that the dominant religion enjoyed, Jews lacked the economic capability to build glorious structures that were designed to last forever. Nonetheless, their places of worship gave a message of their place in society, even against their will. Like contemporary storefront churches of minorities in America, the humble style of most European synagogues reflected precisely the marginal role that Jews played in European culture. There are exceptions, of course: great synagogues in Spain, for example, that testify to a Spanish golden age, and the many grand synagogues of modern Europe that are lost forever because Hitler destroyed them. For Jews as for Christians, then, the places we call sacred tell the tale of who we are, where we have come from, and where we believe we are going.

Beauty, Efficiency, and Tradition: Theme, Convention, and Style ❀

Creating sacred space is therefore more than an architectural chal-lenge. It requires a fine balance among three elements: structures that are beautiful, structures that work, and structures that incorporate enough tradition to make them readily recognizable as appropriately Christian or Jewish. To be sure, our places of worship sometimes delib-erately or inadvertently omit one or even two of these elements. Men-nonites, for instance, opted for efficiency but deliberately rejected traditional imagery and ostentatious beauty. A famous synagogue in the American Midwest was designed by an architect who understood beau-ty but not Jewish liturgy; his design is gorgeous, but it is ritually inef-fective. Chicago's Willow Creek Church pursues efficiency and advertises its independence through buildings that look very corpo-rate and distinctively "un-churchy."

One way to evaluate your synagogue or church space is to ask yourself how it balances beauty, efficiency, and tradition. A way to do that is to think of your building as a sacred edifice that proclaims the truths for which you stand. Richard S. Vosko, a consultant for wor-ship environment, insists, "Buildings are about people; they are not about space. The people's story is the truth they tell." How does a building tell a people's truth?

There is such a thing as artistic truth, as there is religious truth, but these are not the same as scientific truths. Science has established a means of testing its truths. If, for instance, I claim a truth that I have discovered in my laboratory, it passes for truth only if other scientists can replicate my experiment on their own. Neither religion nor art works that way. Religious truths, such as "It is a good thing to love your neighbor as yourself" or "God is just," cannot be proven true or false. Similarly, we can never prove the truths we glean from Michelangelo's Sistine Chapel paintings or the triumphant climax of Beethoven's ninth symphony. Yet religions and artistic traditions alike claim to say something about reality, and, therefore, to have truths that science cannot fathom.

It is helpful to think of these religious and artistic truths as *themes*. By that I mean eternal verities that a tradition never tires of reiterating in one way or another. A Christian theme is the timeless truth of being saved from sin and overcoming death. A Jewish theme is the paradigmatic truth of the human journey from slavery to freedom, or the ultimate redemption of all the world. I call them themes because their message is never exhausted by any simple statement. Different ways of alluding to them run throughout a religion's history. Christians and Jews may not accept every aspect of their themes literally, but that does not make them stop repeating them. They just think of different ways to express what they mean.

> ❂ **Themes are the eternal truths that lie behind the stories, images and metaphors that religions never tire of telling. They are beyond empirical demonstration. They are what the religion is all about.**

If scientists proved tomorrow that resurrection is impossible or that the Israelites had never been in Egypt, the truth value of the themes that lie behind the story of the resurrection of Christ or the exodus from Egypt would be unaffected. As long as we build our lives around the themes of our faiths, we remain true to the historic religions that preach them.

Because the themes are not scientific in nature, they cannot be forced into the straitjacket of algebraic equations, or the simple declarative prose of an eyewitness description of an accident scene. Religious themes are necessarily told artistically through poetry, song, dance, and architecture.

Over the course of time, artistic traditions develop conventionalized ways of expressing religious themes. Catholics and Episcopalians, for instance, expect churches with crosses and stained-glass windows. Lutherans may anticipate passion plays as well. The way the Christian themes are portrayed in these various media are *conventions:* They are the normal artistic ways that the church tells its truths to the faithful. A conventional way of painting St. Peter, for instance, is to provide him with a set of crossed keys, a sign that he received "the keys to the kingdom." The evangelist Mark is associated with a lion, Luke with an ox, and John with an eagle. Jesus is conventionally depicted on the cross, or kneeling at Gethsemane.

Jews have conventions too, but they do not have the centuries of endowed artistic production that Christian art has enjoyed. Jewish conventions are apt to appear informally: like religious-school textbook art displaying Moses with a patriarchal beard and a staff; or the kitsch statues and drawings of Chasidic rebbes on fire with religious enthusiasm. The parallel for Christians would be some of the portraits of Jesus that customarily hang on kitchen walls. Having a facial portrait is a conventional way to remember him, but different portraits bespeak different religious times and places: A 1941 version by Warner Salman made its way into millions of Christian homes, but by the 1970s, a more rugged form painted by Richard Hook had supplanted its popularity, especially among contemporary evangelicals.

Conventions operate officially and unofficially, and they come and go. They are not all equally old, but what makes them conventions is that they extend through at least several generations. Like strands on a rope, they intertwine through time, so they can best be illustrated by a vertical ropelike axis extending from our own day down to the dawn of a religion's origins (see Fig. 8.3). Every generation exists somewhere along that rope dangling through time. It inherits its ongoing artistic tradition, but chooses some strands of the rope over others, artistically framing anew the ones it selects for its own period.

If the vertical axis is a ropelike timeline charting the development of the conventions that tell a religion's timeless truths, the horizontal axis represents the particular point in time that a given generation inhabits. Second-century Christians, for example, share the horizontal axis "second century" with Jews and with pagans of the time.

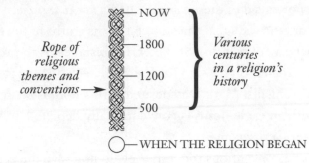

Fig. 8.3. Ongoing Religious Tradition Extending Through Time

Each group inhabits its own vertical axis of particularistic themes and conventions (see Fig. 8.4). The Christian rope is made of images of Jesus, whereas the Jewish rope features stories of rabbis and the pagan parallel was given over to the mythic tales of Hesiod and Homer. But no matter what their inherited themes and conventions may be, the fact that they share a common horizontal point in time means that they are all equally influenced by the artistic *styles* that are then in vogue. Christians in the second century regularly portrayed Jesus as the sun, and rabbinic midrash from the same era relayed tales of Rabbi Akiba in search of God, who was also displayed as the source of light. As we saw above (chapter 5), light was a ubiquitous sign of good and of eternity for pagans, Jews, and Christians in that era.

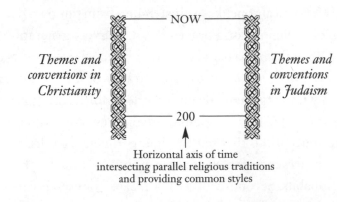

Fig. 8.4. Themes and Conventions in Judaism and Christianity.

❀ **Religious art is therefore a means of expressing (1) timeless *themes* through (2) traditional *conventions* that are modified by (3) contemporary *styles*. Religious artists apply contemporary styles to traditional conventions to express themes that tell timeless truths.**

Styles are drawn from general culture and then adopted by religions that feel at home in that culture. A religion kept out of the cultural mainstream will often unwittingly demonstrate its own marginality by passing over the style in question; while a religion that takes a prophetic stand against the culture in which it finds itself may deliberately avoid using the styles that symptomize everything it is struggling against.

Consider basilican and baroque architecture, for instance, both of them styles of their respective eras; they cut across religious lines. Basilican style was featured by pagan temples too, not just early Christian churches; and as long as Judaism was at home in the late Roman empire, it too built basilican synagogues, albeit on a much smaller scale. Since Judaism never became the official religion, it never had the need or the means to expand the basilican model into all the regal splendor that marked the Christian churches after Constantine. Baroque architecture too was common in theaters and palaces, as well as churches, but not in synagogues, which had become marginal to Catholic Europe, and not in the Protestant churches that rejected the style as Catholic and built oppositional churches without the lavish imagery associated with Catholic worship.

In any event, even when churches adopted current styles (like baroque), it applied these styles to its own conventions, in order to express its ancient themes in a new and contemporary way. Christians at worship recognized the messages because their experience in society at large prepared them to appreciate the language of space typical of their own culture at their own time and place.

Particularly in times of rapid social change worshipers find themselves locked in a conflict between current style and inherited convention. Like it or not, they are members of the society in which they live; but they inhabit religious traditions too, with inherited themes and the favored conventions by which those themes have been expressed. Worshipers must regularly negotiate a complicated interplay between the age in which the religion finds itself and the religion as it has been handed down through time. In the drama of worship, space is an artistic means of communicating traditional themes in the context of recognizable conventions, but according to the newly dominant style.

To be a member of any society and of any subgroup within that society means learning to recognize spatial cues, even though we cannot consciously describe what they are. We associate room size, seating arrangements, color schemes, lighting intensity, and all the subtle things that go into our perception of space with culturally conditioned meaning systems. The people trained as professional liturgical planners are steeped in the liturgical traditions that provide the traditional spatial code. They learn the rules of sanctuaries, pews, choir lofts, and pulpits, until they are able to arrange the space in accordance with all the canons of their glorious past. What they may not recognize, however, is that the rules in question were part of a code whose message, however valuable once upon a time, may now be lost on worshipers, or even be detrimental to worship in a new age. Seeing only the historically oriented traditional axis of interpretation, they may fail to appreciate the contemporary axis of their own age, the spatial language typical of the style that today's worshipers speak.

To put the matter bluntly: Five hundred years of basilican architecture generated a religious tradition rooted in basilican space. But eventually, people charged with arranging sacred space had to decide whether basilicas were inherently necessary for proper Christian prayer, or whether they were historical accidents that had evolved to provide a spatial message consistent with Christian ascendance in late antiquity, but whose continued use would be dysfunctional to Christian worship of a later period.

More immediate to our own time is the parallel question
the awe-inspiring transcendent spaces we have inherited from
nineteenth century and before. We saw above that transcendent stru
tures promote a message of a distant God. Should we retain then
without alteration? Or should we judge them negatively just as an earlier age negatively judged basilicas? Can we afford to emphasize the
nineteenth-century view of God as distant? Aren't we better off adopting a contemporary style that suggests a God whom we can know more
intimately? Rabbis of grand synagogue sanctuaries often speak glow-
ingly of the beauty of their worship environment without realizing that
although they read the message of their space as grandly transcendent
and spiritually uplifting, their congregants decode the same spatial
message in contemporary American terms that deny the very spirituality that the rabbis affirm.

I am not arguing for a wholesale destruction of the buildings we
have inherited. A hundred-year-old synagogue may be beautiful and
resonant with tradition. Only a fool trashes tradition and beauty for
efficiency. But alongside beauty we do need worship effectiveness, or
our worship spaces will become
beautiful museums to which no
one goes, except as a passive
observer for what the clergy as
curators keep carefully displayed
under glass.

Renovating space always means balancing these three things: beauty, effectiveness, and tradition; and the balancing is done by applying new styles to traditional conventions.

In our own time and place,
we have internalized a language of space that differs from imperial
Rome, European baroque, and nineteenth-century transcendence.
What is the code that Americans use to translate the meaning of the
design cues in our worship spaces?

The code is not the same for all Americans. Thus, to take but one
obvious example, Southern Baptists, Catholics, and Orthodox Jews will
see different messages inherent in the same spatial structures; so too
will old Irish and new Latino Catholics. Men and women also experience

e differently: Benches for kneeling may mean voluntary humility men who are high-powered executives, but suggest enforced humiliation for women who have been abused. But insofar as they are all acculturated into American society, they all tend to see the different spatial designs according to a common interpretive code that governs the way Americans relate to their spaces.

I have already said that theology should guide our decisions. Another way of putting it is to say that our decisions to retain or to alter our received spaces should depend on the kind of universe we want to display in the drama of our worship. But whatever we decide, we cannot avoid facing the fact that Americans will interpret spatial messages according to the American code. To direct worship without taking into consideration the way worshipers will perceive what we direct would be like sending messages in Morse code, even though we know the receivers at the other end no longer organize the dots and dashes the way we do. We have to ask how space is perceived in the dots and dashes of American perception, or we will always be in the position of holding worship in spaces that provide messages that other people decipher differently than we do.

The first step to an appreciation of space is the ability to see it, not just to accept it. A fresh look at any given worship space will reveal certain categories of appreciation.

How People See Space: Fixed, Semifixed, and Personally Negotiable

 Space is fixed, semi-fixed, or personally negotiable. *Fixed space* includes things like the shape of the perimeter, the built-in fixtures like the ark, the pipe organ, and the lighting—things that cannot be altered without structurally revising the entire nature of the area in question. Fixity comes about through design or accident; the design may be theologi-

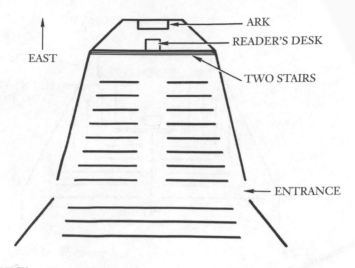

Fig. 8.5. Floor Plan of Hebrew Union College Sanctuary in New York.

(Jews in the western hemisphere have traditionally faced east in public prayer, the direction of Jerusalem. In this particular floor plan, the necessity to face east results in fixed space with a dysfunctional narrowing around the pulpit. It lacks thrust-stage effect that would allow the liturgy to be acted out in the midst of the congregation.)

cally sound—most synagogues face east, for example—or just structurally required—the doorway opens onto the street, say (see Fig. 8.5).

Semifixed space includes things that can more easily be altered by worshipers who want to change their space, but who, for financial or other reasons, cannot consider renovating the whole place. Many new churches and synagogues have semifixed movable chairs, for example, instead of fixed pews bolted into the floors. Some have large stagelike altar or pulpit areas that are fixed, but increasingly, they have begun adding semifixed additions that extend those fixed areas into the congregation (see Fig 8.6).

Finally, *personally negotiable space* is space that individuals establish as their own boundaries for individual movement. When fixed space limits us, we may try to modify the situation by semifixed alterations, like chairs instead of pews, or a reading desk in the middle of the congregation (see Fig 8.7). But innovative worship often requires more. It

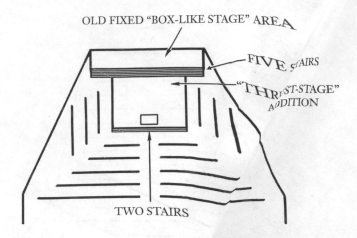

Fig. 8.6. *"Thrust-Stage" Semifixed Addition to Fixed Pulpit Space*

(The space folds back under the raised pulpit, where it can be stored if all the liturgical action is to take place from the high pulpit. On average days, it can be used as a secondary community focus in addition to the primary formal focus of the original fixed structure.)

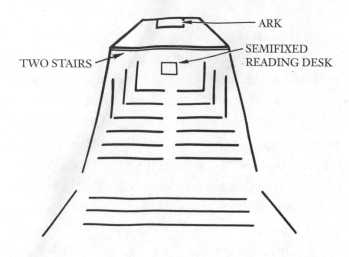

Fig. 8.7. *Hebrew Union College Sanctuary Showing Semifixed Reading Desk*

(Recognizing the impossibility of adding a thrust-stage in the narrow east end of the sanctuary, students customarily ignore the formal focus entirely and conduct worship from this movable pulpit, which can be repositioned on the fixed raised area for formal occasions.)

may require that we overcome fixity by crossing old boundaries, as when a preacher leaves the pulpit to draw closer to the congregation, or a cantor walks into the congregation to lead group singing.

If you are not going to renovate an old space completely, you can still overcome some of its inefficiencies by breaking the space down into degrees of fixity. What parts are fixed, and what does the fixing pattern lock in (or out)? What semifixed areas exist, and what alternatives can you take advantage of? How can you use your own freedom of movement to negotiate space personally to transcend the spatial limitations of structure?

Distance: Intimate, Personal, Social, and Public　❀

Territoriality is common to animal behavior everywhere. We do not like it when people step into our space, and (at the other extreme) we wonder why people we love appear so distant.

On Elevators, Barbecues, Offices, and Podiums

Compare an elevator with a backyard barbecue. When people first get into an elevator, they gravitate to its four different corners to establish an appropriate distance from strangers. If the elevator gets crowded, however, they have no choice but to squeeze closely together. Unless they all know each other— say, they all work in the same office—they manage it by staring straight ahead, avoiding conversation, and pretending that these people whose very body heat they can feel are not really there. The crowded elevator exemplifies *intimate space*, in this case, intimate space that is enforced on the people riding in it.

By contrast, an aerial photograph of a barbecue crowd would show the guests gathering into little clumps of conversationalists, with the members of the conversations being a little farther apart than in the crowded elevator, yet not so far apart as the distance from one corner to the other that elevator occu-

pants adopt if they are able to. The barbecue conversationalists automatically deploy themselves with *personal space* separating them. The ideal elevator distance, a little greater still, is
like the distance we use in our offices when we engage in business meetings with strangers: certainly not intimate, and not
even personal, but close enough to be *social space*. If the host at
the barbecue is our boss, she might come out to welcome us.
We would hardly expect her to appear behind a podium on the
balcony to give us a speech. But she might stand at social distance from us, with ourselves gathered around her, and from
there tell us how good it is to have the whole corporate team
assembled. The balcony talk would characterize a political
speaker who comes to address the crowd, and would be an
example of *public space*.

Anthropologist Edward T. Hall maintains that each of these spatial designs has a maximum and minimum range—a low and high
end—each of which we find appropriate for certain human relationships but not for others.

Space, Register, and Focus: Establishing Intimacy or Distance ◈

Applying this pattern of space to worship goes a long way toward
understanding why people sit where they do and how people in different parts of the congregation experience worship differently.

First, look at the space separating the people who read and direct
worship (the professionals) from the nearest pew (where only regulars
sit). In most churches and synagogues, even that distance is at the high
end of social and maybe even the low end of public space. Certainly it
is public for the majority of the worshipers, who sit well back from
the front row. That perception, however, is only partly explainable by
the real distance involved. It is also due to the way that the professionals use their voice and other verbal cues, which we can call *register*.

Table 8.1. Space Types and Human Activity

SPACE TYPE	RANGE	DISTANCE	TYPICAL ACTIVITY
Intimate	Low End	Touching	Lovemaking, wrestling
Intimate	High End	6"–18"	Intimate conversation
Personal	Low End	18"–2½'	Spouses or family members standing together
Personal	High End	2½'–4'	Normal friendly conversation, the way people who are never intimate stand together
Social	Low End	4'–7'	Impersonal business, counseling or therapy session
Social	High End	7'–12'	Formal business with the boss, who sits behind a desk farther away
Public	Low End	12'–25'	Different degrees of formal addresses
Public	High End	25' and up	

❊ Register is the degree of formality with which we speak. It is established by the words and phrases we choose to use, and by the way we speak those words. Conversation with friends is pursued with a very low register on both counts. We use simple words, often without proper sentences, and we speak in a relaxed way as well. Very high register would be the president's State of the Union Address: high, flowing rhetoric, delivered with formal style.

Attuned to a distant orientation, the pulpit speakers turn on what is called *formal style*. It characterized by a stilted manner and stylized speech patterns. As public distance increases, formal style becomes what has been called *frozen style*, which is perceived as the appropriate way to relate to strangers. Religious professionals, who are steeped in their traditions, often prefer transcendent architecture because it is traditional, and because they feel comfortable negotiating its spaces. The average worshiper in the pews, however, is more likely to identify it with frozen style and not feeling at home. Add the fact that the "public address" mode of prayer normally occurs in fixed space, where average worshipers (watchers, perhaps) are afraid to get too comfortable lest they break some social or religious taboo, and you have an environment that alienates people from each other.

Now look at an infant's baptism or a wedding liturgy. The baptism features a small gathering of people, many of whom know each other and have chosen to stand around the font at low-end intimate distance. The priest or minister knows better than to address the assembly from far away. The feeling tone is natural and warm. The wedding group, by contrast, may be large, but nonetheless, the ministering official may be moved by his or her familiarity with the couple and by the intimate nature of the occasion to speak directly to the bride and groom, who stand at high-end personal distance—some 2½ feet away. Thus the wedding address too will be warmer, devoid of the formal—let alone, frozen—style that would normally typify an event of such size. In other words, even in a formal setting, it is possible to break down a sense of alienation.

Much depends on whom the speaker selects as the focus for his or her remarks. When Romeo sees Juliet through her balcony window, he says,

> But soft! what light through yonder window breaks?
> It is the east, and Juliet is the sun. . . .
> See! how she leans her cheek upon her hand:
> O! that I were a glove upon that hand,
> That I might touch that cheek.

If those lines are recited well, Romeo addresses them softly to himself with all his mental concentration upon Juliet. The result is that even members of the audience who are sitting in the very last row do not feel distant from the stage. Similarly, when the liturgical speaker focuses his or her remarks on the wedding couple, or on the baby about to be baptized, or even on some imaginary parishioner sitting in the front row, rather than on the masses assembled anonymously "out there," a different feeling tone results. That warmer tone is not always desirable, of course: The liturgy features grand announcements as well as intimate invitations, so I am not arguing for any single way of saying everything.

> ✹ **The important point is the elusive influence of space, register, and focus as the determining factors to the way the liturgical lines are heard. Not only what we say, but how we say it, matters; and part of how we say things is not just the register we employ but also the way we focus remarks on particular others rather than on everyone all at once.**

The concept of focus is as simply grasped as it is normally overlooked. Performing artists practice it; so do athletes, courtroom lawyers, and expert speakers and debaters. Architects and interior decorators consider focus too when they arrange spaces for the people who will occupy them.

For performers, focus is the practice of mental concentration. Some performances—a pianist's recital, for example—require focus on the particular piece being played. In like fashion, a batter focuses complete attention on the ball being pitched, and a tennis pro waits in absolute awareness of an anticipated serve. In these instances, focus is directed at a particular blueprint of anticipated action—at the musical score about to be interpreted or the aerial course of a ball about to be returned with bat or racquet. Focus is the ability to filter out all extraneous thoughts and perceptions, and to sharpen the center of your awareness at the expense of the periphery.

Some performances require focus not on the blueprint of action alone, but on the people for whom the action is about to be performed.

At issue are two forms of communication. Communication involves a sender, a receiver, and a message. A telegraph operator sending a message in Morse code can completely ignore the receiver on the other end, but may have to focus on the message being transcribed into code. A pianist, too, largely ignores the audience but pays close attention to the musical score that is being encoded into a musical message. Both the telegraph operator and the pianist are engaged in the first kind of communication: action by a sender, but no immediate feedback from the receiver.

Now consider two lovers in intimate conversation about their relationship. Though what they say matters a great deal, their focus is on each other even more than it is on the message of their words together. True, they worry about saying the right thing, but more important than the words they use is getting across the information that they are speaking directly and personally to each other, not daydreaming off in space even as they profess their love. That kind of necessary focusing on the receiver as well as the message is what characterizes courtroom argumentation and parliamentary debate—or a stand-up comedian, who may even interrupt the evening's standard repertoire to inquire of an unresponsive audience, "Are you out there?" In this second kind of communication pattern, the speaker—the message sender—focuses on a person or persons representative of the whole audience, talking directly to them and looking, at the very least, for some eye contact or other sign that they have received the message.

In the baptism and wedding examples, the child and the couple constitute the obvious focal receivers (although it is surprising how many clergy fail to talk to the child being baptized). They make the mistake instead of addressing their impersonal theological remarks to the roomful of people in general. In a large assembly of people—a Sabbath liturgy, for example—the sermon has to be delivered, not to everyone indiscriminately, but to each person present. That is why a practiced speaker focuses first on one and then another specific listener, looking each one in the eyes long enough to establish contact before moving on. Unpracticed speakers make the mistake of thinking they are talking to everybody all at once: They either look into the impersonal distance or let their eyes wander around the room, darting from one person to the next, but never focusing on anyone. Regardless of the content of their message, their speech fails.

In these examples, focus is the practice of concentration through space by a message sender to a message receiver. The message's receipt is acknowledged directly by the receiver, who nods, looks the receiver in the eye, smiles, or performs some similar response in body language unmistakable to the sender. Or sometimes, when the receiver cannot have understood the message (say, the baby at the baptism, who is probably either sleeping or crying), the response is at least imagined. (The baby would be responding if he or she were old enough). The very fact that the baby is a point of focus for the speaker is sufficient to establish it as a point of focus for everyone else at the same time. Even though the baby cannot acknowledge the message's receipt, the congregation's common attention is enough to establish positive feedback to the speaker that the message is getting through. Getting everyone's attention on a single point in space is called *fused focus*. Since worship is a group event, not merely a series of individuals going through their motions in serial fashion until the script is done, successful public prayer depends at times on developing fused focus. We know it is working when it is readily apparent that the attention of all the participants is riveted together on a momentary event that they all can share in common.

Actors on a stage depend on fused focus also. They know they can provide the illusion called for by the script only if they work together to fuse the focus of the audience on the dramatic action. That is why, in an extended monologue, a cardinal rule is not to upstage the speaker; the other actors hold their pose and remain stock-still, their attention riveted on the speaker. Because all the characters on stage fuse their focus on the central point of action, they draw the focus of the onlookers there as well.

Of the many things that go into fusing congregational focus, space ranks among the highest. If you doubt it, take a look at the knick-knacks on your mantel or window sill. Every decorator knows that if you group the various objects together here and there, rather than space them out one by one at regular intervals, the room will look balanced and orderly, inviting attention rather than defusing it. Similarly, every teacher knows that some classrooms support classroom attention and some do not. The same is true of worship spaces. They either draw our attention together or they diffuse it. There is nothing mystical about it.

> ⚘ **Successful lawyers sway the members of a jury by getting their combined rapt attention fused on that all-important final argument. Good teachers arrange the seating so that their class will work together. Winning football teams fuse their members' individual focus on a single moment of common challenge. And worshipers who want to experience a shared moment of public prayer require a fused focus also.**

In rituals, the fusion of the worshiping group's focus is enhanced when individuals are led to concentrate on a central, visible object of attention. Sometimes a person being addressed fulfills that role; sometimes it is an object, like the skull Hamlet lifts up before he says, "Alas! poor Yorick. I knew him, Horatio." Most religions use their own set of significant objects to accomplish this end: the raising of the wine cup; the procession with a Bible, cross, or candle; the Torah scroll carried around the room. All of these are to their own sacred scripts what the skull is to Hamlet's graveyard: visible points of focus for the group.

It is easy to forget the role of liturgical props in facilitating the fused focus that successful worship demands. Jews, for example, have a beautiful ceremony for ending the Sabbath, called *Havdalah*. It features a spicebox, a cup of wine, and a tall braided candle. No one could ask for a more attractive possibility for a ritual. Some rabbis understand the magical quality inherent in the *Havdalah* symbolism: It is twilight

Saturday evening, the sun is setting, and the room is getting dark. The candle, wine, and spicebox sit on an unobtrusive central table, around which people stand shoulder to shoulder, in almost intimate distance from one another. Together they recite the appropriate blessings and sing the traditional songs for the occasion. They pass the sweet-smelling spices from hand to hand and watch the bright flame of the candle dance in the darkening room. Staring intently at this common focal point, they fuse their focus into a common spiritual goal. As the ritual moves toward its high point, the ritual moment, they are usually moved to hold hands around the circle. At the end, with the last song sung, the candle's flame doused in the remaining wine, the ritual moment behind them, they turn warmly to their neighbors, people who just a few moments before were strangers, and embrace them with the traditional greeting, "A good week!" They too have experienced the network effect.

Too many rabbis do everything wrong at *Havdalah*, starting with their failure to use the ritual props as a common focusing point. Instead, they put the objects on a table near the front of the room, where they can hardly be seen. Then, standing at public distance from the worshipers, they adopt a frozen style of speech and explain the cognitive meaning of the symbols, which then cease being symbols and become mere signs, about which no one in the room cares one whit. People leave the room with a brilliant opportunity for worship wasted.

Spatial Analogues and Cultural Ecosystems　✸

Specialized spaces provide the opportunity for specialized activities, or so they should. If we are not careful, they may equally well militate against them. Robert Sommer, a psychologist specializing in the influences of spatial design on behavior, studied schools, bars, hospitals, and airports to see how each one constituted what he called a *cultural ecosystem*—an arrangement of people in a particular way designed to accomplish certain ends consistent with the environment. Nature's own ecosystems are determined by a give-and-take between the evolutionary requirements of a species and the environment's ability to support those requirements. In human society our needs are not just physical, but cultural. We design environments to support some activities and discourage others.

A women's ward of a long-term state hospital, for example, featured halls with long rows of chairs where more than fifty residents could sit at one time. But even with all the chairs filled, Sommer rarely noted more than two conversations in progress. The paucity of dialogue was due to the fact that people do not converse when they have to sit shoulder to shoulder. Such a row design of furniture is called *sociofugal* (like the word "centrifugal"), meaning that it orients people away from each other. Chairs in airports function similarly to discourage waiting passengers from talking to each other. The same is true of lunch counters and bars; the media display bars as happy places where people wander in to meet strangers over drinks (as in the television show *Cheers*, where "everyone knows your name"). But the reality is otherwise. Bars where people engage in animated conversation depend on the fact that the clientele resides in the neighborhood, already has much in common, often knows each other, and has become accustomed to meeting in this particular central watering hole. Most bars, Sommer points out, the ones where strangers go to drink, feature "lonely men sitting speechless on a row of bar stools, with their arms triangled on the bar before a bottle of beer. . . . If anyone speaks to his neighbor under these circumstances, he is likely to receive a suspicious stare." If people want to talk together in bars, they go to booths, where they can sit across from each other at tables. Table seating plans are the opposite of sociofugal. They are *sociopetal*, that is, they focus people's attention toward the center and encourage social interaction around a common fused focus. When Sommer rearranged the hospital ward so that the residents had small, attractive square tables at which to meet, conversations doubled.

Straight lines of chairs, especially hard, unmovable ones bolted to the floor—which Sommer calls *hard architecture*—epitomize the very opposite of what we called community. Airports, he says, feature a sociofugal seating pattern in order to drive people out of the waiting areas into the shops and restaurants; the hospital preferred the row-by-row design because it was easier for the maintenance staff to clean the floors that way; bars find rows of stools profitable because their goal is not to encourage long conversations by people nursing a single drink, but to get them to order round after round unencumbered by interruptive socializing. In other words, hospitals, airports, and bars may seem inefficient by discouraging personal interaction. But the law of systems that we looked at in chapter 3 is operative. Most institutions are mostly efficient most of the time; if they appear to be inefficient, we are probably not looking at what they do efficiently.

People respond to furniture arrangements in predictable ways partially for physiological reasons. Chairs arranged side by side make people twist their heads on a ninety-degree angle if they want to converse with the people beside them. But there is more to the phenomenon than physiology. People learn to associate spatial arrangements with particular emotions and activities. They use successful instances of negotiating behavior in old, familiar environments as cues to what may be expected of them in new and unfamiliar ones. Straight rows once encountered tell us what to do when we find straight rows a second time.

❀ **When one environment with which we are familiar serves as a model for what to do in an environment new to us, the model environment is called a *cultural analogue*.**

A monumental impediment to fulfilling worship in our churches and synagogues is the insidious effect of the cultural analogues that condition people to act in certain prescribed ways during worship. Our houses of worship were designed with the European model of transcendence in mind. Worshipers were to be overwhelmed by their lonely, finite creatureliness and their absolute dependence on a God before whom they could only stand in awe. Our cathedral style sanctuaries still combine the baroque theater model with this ideal of a distant and transcendent God, to make worship space into the most sociofugal environment imaginable.

Eventually, those grand worship spaces became too expensive, and other architectural models became popular. But they too distanced worshipers from each other and from the liturgy. They operated with a model where the sacred action occurs in a "picture box" stage design. Worshipers sit in rows of pews stretching out endlessly through a long hall. Our cultural analogues for this layout include theaters and movies—or, if soloists are featured, an opera. People are thus encouraged to sit quietly and passively in rows designed for watching but not for interacting either with each other or with the drama of prayer. They know better than to participate. Even if they are told to sing along, the metacommunication of the stage design contradicts the verbal message, which they take with a grain of salt.

The pews themselves are troublesome. Normally, they are long wooden benches permanently installed in the floor—hard architecture, for sure. To make matters worse, there are no designated individual seats on pews, so that in crowded conditions, people will be jammed together in a way that magnifies the difficulty of turning to look at the person beside them. When Sommer experimented with these conditions by forcing students to sit close together in classroom rows, he observed them engaging in "escape behavior"—asking their teacher to move the class outdoors, for example. People who cannot physically escape develop internal escape mechanisms—like the crowded elevator phenomenon described above. They ignore each other, pretending that no one is around. They pass the time by counting the panels in the ceiling, making up mental shopping lists, reviewing the birth dates of their great-uncles in Europe, or turning their attention to any other task that will effectively remove them from the proceedings "on stage." They will not make the same mistake of sitting here next time. Instead, they will prefer watcher spots on the aisles at the back, where, even though they cannot see or hear the preacher, they can at least tune out and move out if necessary. They develop what Sommer calls "passivity in the face of an environment" that makes undue demands on them, but which is not their own to change—"prisonitis, hospitalism, and institutional neurosis," he calls it. If he had studied churches and synagogues, would he have recognized "sanctuary neurosis" as well?

The problem is that people relate to institutions as if they rent the space there, not as if they own it. "They accept the idea," says Sommer, "that the existing arrangement is justified according to some mysterious principle known only to the space owners." In our case, we can call it "the mysterious principle of theology," which relegates the worshipers to the status of temporary non-owners of worship space. It is only a short distance from that assumption to the idea that they are non-owners of the liturgy as well.

To be sure, this distancing message of pews may once have been functional. Certainly Reform Jews worked very hard in the nineteenth century to do away with the medieval lay involvement in the liturgy. Worshipers then were noisy, individualistic, and unappreciative of the higher artistry that characterized western aesthetics. But we have come a long way from that position. If worship today requires community, if God is known as present among us, then the metacommunication implicit in synagogue and church architecture may be the first thing we should question. The people charged with worship need to remain ever watchful for the cues people offer regarding their comfort or discomfort about the spaces in which they pray. We should not assume that the nonprofessionals who cannot walk around and who have not internalized theological reasons for their spaces share the clergy's positive attitudes toward even the most beautiful sanctuary; or even if they say they do, that they mean it; or even if they mean it, that we know what they mean by it. They think that the sets for productions of the Metropolitan Opera are gorgeous also. And never having experienced really compelling worship, they may unwittingly be telling us that they are willing to settle for poor opera in church or synagogue as the best of a series of bad options.

The theologians themselves would be appalled to think that worship was confused with opera, of course. But spatial concerns are only partially responsible for that misunderstanding. An entire worship system with the wrong understanding of how words work, the wrong music, the wrong register, and the wrong space collude to produce the undesired affect. But changing the system is possible. In the earlier discussion of sending messages (chapter 4), I broached the subject of systemic change. It is time now to return to it.

Ritual Check List　　　⊛

Words and Concepts You Should Know

- **How we label and arrange space** determines whether space works for or against us.
- **Space provides a nonverbal argument** for our religious values. The argument is of necessity silent. Precisely for that reason, it is beyond discussion, powerful in its very givenness, and more effective than any verbal rhetoric could be.
- **Themes are the eternal truths** that lie behind our religious stories, images, and metaphors. They are what the religion is all about. Religious artists apply contemporary styles to traditional conventions to express themes that tell timeless truths.
- **Renovating space means balancing** beauty, effectiveness, and tradition.
- **Space is fixed, semifixed, or personally negotiable.** Fixed space is whatever cannot be altered without massive structural revision. Semifixed space is moveable. Personally negotiable space is the way individuals move through the spaces that they

have. Innovative worship requires overcoming fixed space, altering semifixed space, and negotiating personal space to cross old boundaries—such as when a preacher leaves the pulpit to draw closer to the congregation, or a musician walks into the assembled congregation to invite group singing.

- **We perceive distances** as intimate, personal, social, or public. Each distance comes with its own style of speaking, which we call register. Rather than let the space dictate our register, we can alter our register to change the way people perceive distance.

- **Group ritual is enhanced** when the worshiping group is focused on a central, visible object of attention. Liturgical props (like Bibles, crosses, and Torah scrolls) provide visible points for a fused focus, which transforms disparate individuals into a single group.

- **Space can be sociofugal** (separating people from each other) or sociopetal (connecting people with each other). Hard architecture, straight lines of pews, social distance between people, and lecturelike seating arrangements designed for frontal presentations drive people away from each other and discourage a sense of community.

Conversation Points for Making Worship Work   ⊛

1 ▪ When a spatial arrangement with which we are familiar serves as a model for another space that is new to us, the model environment is called a cultural analogue. Most churches and synagogues were designed with fixed space, hard architecture, and social distance to maximize a congregant's sense of being alone before a mighty, transcendent God of distance. Some liturgical services may still require that attitude, but most demand just the opposite: a sense of care, love, interdependence, and knowledge of a God who is intimately present among us.

List the atypical worship occasions that you have attended over the past year (for holidays, for instance) and rate each according to the degree of intimacy or grandeur it requires. How is God to be known in each case?

Take an average Sabbath service, and rate it according to the degree of intimacy and grandeur that it ought to have in general. Do the same with its various parts (from the moment of gathering to the final song or hymn).

Now do an inventory of your space. Is your worship space better outfitted for the grand transcendent parts of the service or for the intimate personal parts?

2 ▪ The limitations of space can be conquered by taking advantage of personally negotiated space, register, and fused focus. Take a single part of your service that has always been led a certain way, and decide how to do it differently. If, for instance, the part of the liturgy that you choose ought to be personal in nature, how can you alter it so that the personal presence of God is manifest even if the fixed spatial pattern that you have is architecturally hard and sociofugal?

nine

Fixing the System to Make Worship Work

It is time to return to where we began: the twin axes of worship that create the focus of worship systems. Group prayer reaches out horizontally to the worshiping community and vertically to the divine.

Community is how individual worshipers are drawn together into a single unified group. The group galvanizes our commitment to the vision of an alternative world. It establishes the ultimacy of our own group and its right to demand our allegiance. The ritual must therefore be compelling. When we go through the ritual script, we should be proud to accept its ideals as our own.

But all of this, however successfully accomplished, does not count as worship if we do not connect with the presence of God beyond ourselves. It must be clear, in other words, that when we gather in worship, we are really praying, not just meeting for some other reason. I do not mean just relatively trivial ends, like marking the close of the bowling season or sitting around a campfire. Worship has to stand out equally from other religious staples like Bible class or Torah study, where we learn about God, but, presumably, do not invoke God's presence in the same way that we do in public prayer.

God's presence today, however, is more likely to be evident in the intimacy of community than in the awesome grandeur that marked

European-based worship styles. That says less about God, mind you, than it does about ourselves. I do not mean to make any philosophical assumptions about God when I pass judgment on styles of prayer; God is, after all, beyond being captured in any particular sensory guise. What is at issue is the cultural lens through which we filter reality. The formative age for both Christianity and Rabbinic Judaism projected everything outward. It magnified distance between people, classes, and nations, and it posited supernatural beings called angels, and heavens upon heavens, with God at the very outer edge of cosmic space.

We, on the other hand, have exchanged those , lenses for eyeglasses that make everything nearer than our ancestors imagined. Ours is the language of introjection, not projection. True, increasing numbers of Americans tell pollsters that they believe in angels, but the angels in whom they believe are like good friends and neighbors who drop in on you when you are sick. They are intimate acquaintances, hardly the distant creatures of the *K'dushah* or the *Sanctus:* the angelic bands of Isaiah's vision. The language of Americans is peppered with the interior life of the soul, not the exterior realms of the cosmos. We do not bat an eye when people speak of their conscience, soul, inner life, and private thoughts—all part of an internal landscape that American spirituality takes for granted. Raised on Freud, we do not cry foul if someone tells us we have an id, ego, or superego in that increasingly crowded space inside ourselves. Our language is a far cry from the biblical poets and sages who thought it was the outer world where a million angels and demons resided. Their problems began precisely when a demon from "out there" decided improperly to take up housing within a human being. Christianity developed a rite of exorcism for such cases. By contrast, we welcome inner voices, but distrust prophets who say they heard a voice outside themselves. Our whole way of thinking has been reversed. No wonder people find it hard to image a God "out there" but readily concede that "God is within us all."

Scientifically too, the last fifty years have brought distant horizons closer and imploded the expanse of space. We've landed astronauts on the moon and our spacecraft have reached Jupiter and beyond. The Hubble telescope has radioed back pictures of what we once thought was the end of our galaxy. Down here on earth, meanwhile, television brings us instantaneous images of distant wars and faraway cultures, as the world becomes what Marshall McLuhan called a global village. But for the oft-whispered possibility of life on Mars, the universe without angelic hosts has become endless and empty, whereas the miracle of human contact beckons every time we open a newspaper, turn on the television, or click on a chat room. No wonder we look for God among us, not just beyond us any more. For Christians, the incarnation describes our best bet of discovering the divine. And Jews cite their own stories of God's visits here on earth—the many tales of the *Sh'khinah*, for example, God's earthly presence, which accompanied Israel into exile and cried with the Jewish People when the Temple was destroyed.

We begin to think we are more apt to run into God, not in the endless reaches of space and time, but in a global town meeting, along with the other villagers who inhabit the immediate place we call home. Thus is born a new master image, as I called it, a vision of God in keeping with the cultural backdrop of our age and dependent on a new symbolic vocabulary as well: God who inhabits no chariot in the sky, God who abandons space and takes up residence alongside us or who speaks with us through the love of another human being.

Expanding the concept of *vocabulary* to include more than lists of words led us to think through the message of the words we use, the songs we sing, and the space we call sacred, all of which combine to make public prayer possible. Words, music, and space are like three parallel channels of communication that come together in public prayer to connect worshipers with their religious tradition and to bond them together in a way that makes God's presence manifest.

Moral Urgency   ❁

I have spoken of worship as if it were simply a matter of appropriate artistic skill: the competent management of space, words, and music; the appreciation of symbols, not just signs; and the willingness to think systemically rather than to scapegoat handy would-be villains in our churches and synagogues. To a great extent, that is exactly the case. Our cultural bias toward spontaneity may delude us into thinking that real prayer happens spontaneously, but that is rarely the case, except, perhaps, in traditions that await the visitation of the Holy Spirit: Quaker meetings, or Pentecostal speaking in tongues. But even there, rules exist to help the Spirit find its way to the assembled worshipers. Certainly liturgical faiths that depend on a script for prayer need to know how to make that script come alive. Very frequently, worship fails because those charged with its presentation lack the requisite skills to do so, usually because they have never even considered what those skills should be. Attending to the way we speak, sing, and arrange our space does not in itself make worship less authentic any more than planning a wedding with care makes the marriage suspect.

On the other hand, it should be quite clear that authentic worship goes well beyond mere artistic entertainment. *Elmer Gantry* was a great American novel that explored the possibility of what can happen when worship is manipulated for the emotional effect it can have on worshipers. Every once in a while, the news brings us images of modern-day Elmer Gantrys, of cult leaders who divorce artistic competence from integrity. We all know that ritual without morality can become downright demonic: Witness the marches of the Ku Klux Klan and the rallies of the Nazi Party. But ritual with morality has just as much power to enhance the world's good. In fact, it can be argued that morality without ritual is relatively powerless—or at least severely hobbled—compared to what it would be if it were supported by regular liturgical celebration that commits believers to the finest lives possible.

It is precisely the capacity of public prayer to produce a better world that makes it necessary to pass judgment on dysfunctional worship systems. I have no interest in promoting wholesale change for the sake of mere emotional gratification. Revisiting our worship with a view toward making it more compelling comes with a moral urgency because such causes as helping the needy, disavowing abuse, controlling human violence, and saving our planet, are more likely to be taken seriously if public prayer promotes them as matters of moment.

The likelihood that public prayer will impact positively on public morality becomes clear if we revisit the comparison of liturgy to theater, thinking once again of worship as sacred drama. Like any great play, the liturgical dramas are compelling (to begin with) just by virtue of the insights in their scripts. Prayer books can, after all, be read and studied for their messages of the human condition, just as great plays can be. If we are moved to read or to sing our religious dramas with conviction, it is partly for the same reason that brilliant scripts invite great acting.

The analogy of great theater is not entirely adequate, however. Think of how a play comes into being. A playwright expresses his or her own vision of the human situation, hoping that it will convince audiences of its truth. The burden of proof is entirely on the playwright. Of a thousand new plays every year, only a handful are produced, and of those, only one or two, at the most, prove powerful enough to warrant being called great drama. Our liturgies, however, are largely unchanged through the ages. Not that new prayers aren't added with some regularity; they are. But the editors of new prayers and prayer books know that they must demonstrate not only the literary adequacy of what they have written, but also how they are consistent with their received traditions. A new eucharistic prayer must be more than good poetry; it must also be good theology. That is why composing new prayers is entrusted to committees, while writing new plays never is. Prayer is the concern of the community whereas ordinary theater is the concern of the individual artist.

Artists, however, do not work in a vacuum. They are part of an artistic tradition in much the same way that liturgical committees depend on religious traditions. In music, for example, one composer may self-consciously produce a variation on a theme used by another composer. In films, once a great director (like Alfred Hitchcock) experiments with a novel presentation (say, the shower scene in *Psycho*), any number of later directors will try variations on it. Archibald MacLeish could not have composed *J.B.* had he not read Job first—not as a book of the Bible, mind you, but as a human theme in world literature. *J.B.* makes no pretense at being sacred writ, but it is an artistic variation on an earlier piece of artistry. In time, we get schools of music and fine art, baroque as opposed to romanticism, say, or cubism as opposed to impressionism. Theater too has its own set of internal traditions, so that a given play is not just theater: it might be theater of the absurd, or a modern American musical.

Still, purely theatrical or artistic traditions differ from religious traditions in this all-important respect: They do not come packaged with a very strong moral demand upon us to adopt them as our own. Culturally sophisticated parents may instruct their children to develop a taste for Beckett, Brecht, and Bach; but if they opt instead for the "Mad Dog Raving Rock Band," the most they are guilty of is bad taste—a sin only somewhat higher than preferring fast food to French cuisine and considerably lower than such moral indiscretions as marital infidelity and stock manipulation.

In sum, religious traditions differ from artistic ones not because they are not artistic, but because they are not purely so; they share the moral imperative associated not with the arts, but with ethics. The drama of liturgy establishes an alternative world in which we find more than the personal insight of a particular artist working from within a particular artistic tradition. It is possible, and maybe even probable, that we will be more likely to swear off alcohol after seeing Tennessee Williams's *Cat on a Hot Tin Roof.* Williams was himself an alcoholic who poured all the pathos of his own torments into the character of Brick, who says of life, "I want to dodge away from it." But however well Williams portrayed his own tragedies, his purely artistic presentation is just that: a presentation. Religious visions claim to be more. The drama of a liturgy makes demands on us that purely artistic visions do not. We have a right, at least, to attend the theater, to be moved by the performance, and then to move on with life unaffected by what we have seen. We have no such right when it comes to our worship. The whole point of public prayer is that the principles it espouses are supposed to make a difference in how we lead our lives. Even religions that hold cigarette smoking to be an addiction, not a sin, expect parishioners who hear a sermon on the subject to help stop billboard advertising that encourages teenagers to smoke.

> **Liturgies that work do more than entertain; they make moral demands on us that transcend the similar claim of dramas in general. We are expected to take the liturgical message home with us, internalized in our psyche. The liturgical drama doesn't end with the final song or benediction. Our day to day lives testify to liturgical success when we act out the message of our prayers in moral behavior.**

It will be helpful to imagine a scale on which we choose behaviors according to their degree of moral value. It ranges from pure taste at the bottom to absolute obligation at the top. Food tastes are low down in the scale. You either like artichokes or you don't; and if you want to spend a lot of time growing them, studying them, and cooking with them, even going to the point of joining the local branch of the National Artichoke League, the only quarrel I can have with you is that I may fail to see how you can spend all your leisure time that way instead of in the Society of Tomato Growers, which attracts my allegiance.

Higher up on the ladder is artistic taste, where different taste cultures tend to hold each other guilty for their bad judgment. The history of rock music, for example, demonstrates how musical taste can even go so far as to signify social conflict. Early British rock drew on reggae music that had grown out of the black emigration from the West Indies; by the 1970s, lower-class, white "Teddy Boys" in England erupted in waves of violence against blacks and against the sound of the rock music that was then popular. The rest of the decade saw a bewildering assortment of successive styles: mods, skinheads, glam-rock, teenybop, and the punk rock of the Sex Pistols. These were movements, not just sounds. They demonstrated how tastes in art carry baggage that goes well beyond that of tastes in food.

At the highest rung, however, is religion, which formulates morals and demands that we take stands to make the world over in our own religious image. We saw early on in this book that, generically speaking, everything from "the one true church" to "godless communism" can be a religion in this sense, as each tries to implement its own vision on a world in process.

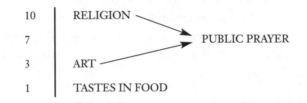

Fig. 9.1. Public Prayer at Interface of Art and Religion.

Insofar as the ritual of public prayer is drama, it is art; insofar as it is a religious drama that makes obligatory demands on those who attend it, it is religion. It therefore occupies the interface between art and religion, using the force of artistic presentation to enforce the imperatives of the religious vision. And here is where our right to be judgmental in behalf of religious drama enters in.

◉ **Tampering with worship is not just fooling around with an old recipe for parsnips; it is more, even, than upgrading old music or dramatic style in pursuit of current fad or fashion. It is the necessary task we undertake from**

time to time to ensure that the power of our religious vision will make it through to the next generation, rather than be lost for lack of attention.

There is urgency, then, to liturgical reform. It cannot wait until we have time to do it right. If public prayer is failing, we need to find time to do it right, and we must do it right away. The naturally conservative side of religion always warns us against hurrying, but if any sin is to be feared, it is the sin of temporizing—of doing too little, not too much.

Blending Past and Present:
The Chances for Success ◉

Worship always balances continuity and innovation, past and present. Tradition bequeaths to us its time-honored chants, age-old prayers, standard deployment of space, and familiar sacred objects. But we cannot avoid filtering these through the prism of contemporary style. Style, remember, is an aesthetic preference that cuts across society at any time and place and impacts all religious traditions to some degree or other. Ancient Judaism had a sacrificial cult, for instance, but so did pagan religion. The Jewish temple looked pretty much like the others, with an inner sanctum and a courtyard where the sacrifices occurred. John Wesley's eighteenth-century Methodism was a unique creation, but at the same time it exemplified a larger cultural style that has been called "religion of the heart." Roman Catholics in France and even Jews as far away as Poland had their own version of the new phenomenon that swept through Europe. The Baal Shem Tov, who started Chasidism, was not all that unlike Wesley. Both men preached in the countryside, spoke to the simple folk, and emphasized God's preference for inner piety over outer rigor. Today too, stylistic considerations influence the way Jews and Christians alike think about their acts of public prayer.

Style is similar to what I called cultural backdrop. Here and there, we may find people are immune to the need for caring communities to take the place of the extended families and close-knit neighborhoods that once characterized the landscapes of our lives. But most of us cannot long escape the realities of a social life that is progressively more bereft of natural communities. And it is doubtful whether limited liability communities that traffic in signs but not in symbols can evoke the sure knowledge that God is among us.

With regard to the vertical axis of worship, then, I cannot emphasize enough the need for symbolic communication that enhances the sense of community in which God's presence is manifest, rather than the nineteenth-century sense of awe that projected God into the distant void.

We need spaces that do not separate laity from clergy; music that collapses social distance; accessible, warm melodies and poetically touching texts. In addition, we must avoid such messages as sexist language that excludes those about whom we say we care. We must rearrange seats in sanctuaries so that people can see each other; encourage people to know who sits beside them; extend the liturgical action into the congregation or assembly; make regulars aware of the concerns of watchers; and let the people themselves do the praying by singing, reciting, and acting out the script in the sure knowledge that it is *theirs*, not the guarded turf of professionals who are there to do it for them. We must discover the joy of knowing how it feels to be part of a closely knit fabric of people in touch with one another in an environment of absolute care and compassion. This is what we called a community of total liability, for it is there that we find God.

Our failure to accomplish these ends is only partly explainable by our persistent refusal to adopt the right communication. Only partially can we lay our failure at the door of "someone else"—professionals who are ill-equipped, poorly trained, or pathologically immune to altering age-old habits; or "people nowadays," who seem spiritually impregnable in a cultural fortress of rampant materialism. Scapegoating will not do. To be sure, those planning the liturgy, both professionals and laypeople, require a sense of public prayer as art. They need to appreciate how worship works and to consider the music they use, the texts they read, the space they occupy, and the props they handle. But even if we were all individually to master the art of worship, claiming competence as well in all its various component arts, we would still have no guarantee that *together* our efforts would succeed. That is because people working together are a system. Vested interests conspire to preserve the system we have, no matter how poorly it functions. True to the law of systems that we postulated earlier, dysfunctional systems that are not very good at worship are quite effective at doing something else. The solution to our worship problems must go deeper than the art of worship alone. It must tackle the systemic nature of the church or synagogue in which the worship occurs, so that all its parts cooperate to make the system work for us, not against us. We call such systemic problem solving *systems intervention*.

Systems Intervention for Action, Care, and Creativity 🏵

Systems intervention is a common strategy of professional change managers who are hired from outside an organization to tackle a problem that seems intractable from within. But there is no reason that the people from within cannot use it themselves. It involves coming to terms with our corollary to the law of systems. All institutions have two sets of defined goals. One is publicly proclaimed as official; the other is never even acknowledged. When the two are in conflict, the unofficial one is the only one that counts.

When Freud first studied human nature, he shocked the world by revealing that individual men and women are at war with themselves in just this way. As individuals, we too have conflicting agendas: not just the official goals and standards that we say motivate us, but the unofficial ones as well. Further study led Freud to see that we adopt complex rules of behavior ostensibly designed to accomplish our official goals, but which work in just the opposite way. Rather than make it more likely that we will succeed at our officially defined tasks, they become defense mechanisms that seal in all the neuroses that stand in the way.

The Compulsive Executive

A compulsive executive has worked for a company for over forty years and has never thrown out a single piece of paper. As everyone in the office knows, he spends so much time filing that he never has a chance to consult anything that he has already put away. He *says* that some day he will write a great case study of the corporation where he works, and he wants to have all the paperwork ready for his research. But he will never get around to the research; he will die, still filing. That, in fact, is the point of the whole exercise. It's not the official point, but it is the unofficial one, and it is the only one that counts. He is afraid to start writing for fear of failure. So with the presumed good intention of making writing easier, he actually makes it impossible. He is his own worst enemy.

▦ **Institutions are like people. They just require a little more tacit collusion among their parts. They can become their own worst enemy by erecting a series of procedures designed to make things work efficiently, but which actually stand in the way of real success. Their actual function is to protect the vested interests of unofficial goals that are never acknowledged. The only way to get beyond them is to break down the collusion. And the only way to do that is to get the people doing the colluding to ask basic questions together about why they do what they do.**

Examples of institutional collusion abound, even in corporate giants that look from the outside as if they are magnificent examples of purely rational decision making. It seems ludicrous to imagine that the Fortune 500 firms are riddled with inefficient bumblers, but they are. Every once in a while, a mammoth miscalculation comes to our attention—an Edsel, say, which no one wants to buy. And then we wonder, "How could Ford have produced that thing?" What we do not so readily note are the little things that prevent full productivity every single day: offices that cannot function, paperwork that gets done wrong, bureaucratic bungling that comes our way only after being converted into higher prices passed along to the consumers.

Thomas J. Peters and Robert H. Waterman Jr. studied America's best-run companies to see what made them excellent. They concluded that our ideal of a totally rational corporate management is a giant piece of fiction. In *The Search For Excellence*, they chronicle case after case where rational decision makers armed with postgraduate degrees work long hours designing more mathematically sound projections at the cost of losing the competitive edge in the real world; or where overly rule-conscious managers with a rule for everything do not realize that the rules they invent to grease the corporate machine are really slowing it down to a crawl.

These investigations should lead us to think more nervously about the claims of churches and synagogues, for it is a truism that religious institutions have adopted corporate models for their own structure and operation. We have boards, committees, elections, and even that elusive thing called "company culture," the hard-to-define element that makes one church different from another. The woman who belonged to "Fort Baptist" knew what it was to affiliate with a religious corporation in which a senior pastor was elected as the chief executive officer and charged with selling the product—religion—to a larger and larger market share. There are problems with corporate religion, to be sure. It fosters competition among churches and synagogues that would do better cooperating; it evokes scapegoating by professionals who do not want to shoulder all the blame for poor performance levels; it distances lay boards from their own religious journeys by making them into oversight commissions for the money side of the operation—as if they do the paying and the clergy do the praying. So I am not advocating a higher degree of corporate style.

But when royal courts were in fashion, churches were like palaces and bishops were like princes. I understand, then, why twentieth-century religion adapted itself to corporate America. To the extent that it is now changing that identity, it is because, in part, corporations themselves are changing. Even corporations are flirting with spirituality. As I look at what we have been doing until now, however, it seems to me that insofar as we have been corporations, then within the bounds of our ethics and principles, we should at least have gotten good at it. We should have been among the ones Peters and Waterman cite as worth emulating.

How would your church or synagogue have fared in the study?

- *Action:* Good corporations have a bias for action rather than for multiplying paperwork that pretends to be action, but really stifles it.
- *Care:* Good corporations care deeply for the customer.
- *Creative risk:* Good corporations value creative souls, whom Peters and Waterman call "product champions."

 Excellence requires action, care, and creative risk.

Action is not the same as busyness. Most churches and synagogues are busy; they have one program after another. They churn out paperwork announcing what is happening, and then more paperwork telling people that it did happen. Real action is activity that is driven by somebody's vision of "doing church or synagogue better." Their visions, however, have to correlate somehow to the underlying mandate of the institution where they work. That means coming to terms with the purpose for which the church or synagogue exists in the first place, and then turning people loose to try out all the ways they can of doing it better. The first thing, then, is knowing the reason that a church or synagogue even exists. Would it matter if it ceased functioning tomorrow? In Irvine, California, Rick Warren created the Saddleback megachurch, where about ten thousand worshipers attend every Sunday. He describes his success in a book whose title sums up the alternative to busyness. It is called *The Purpose Driven Church*.

Every church and synagogue will have to determine its own purpose, depending on how it reads its biblical or rabbinic mandate.

> ❀ **Action, care, and creativity follow a religious institution's decision not to be all things to all people, and to focus all its energy on realizing its purpose instead.**

The underlying presumption of this book has been that the purpose of worship is to connect worshipers with the presence of God (the vertical axis), and to bond them together in sacred community (the horizontal axis), in common pursuit of the alternative universe that their religion spells out as their moral imperative. If the busyness around worship has nothing to do with those goals, if time is spent in empty ritualizing, then the people planning worship are guilty of inaction.

There is also the question of care, not just whether people are cared for, but also if they *know* they are cared for. Rabbi Akiba is said to have advised, "Happy are you, O Israel, for God loves you; happier still are you because you know that God loves you." I know of no priest, pastor, or rabbi who says, "I do not love my people." But I know of many people who do not know they are so loved. The ambiance of the church and synagogue often advertises patent and thorough unconcern. Telephone answering machine menus are impersonal; guards scowl at people who enter; sanctuaries are locked; regulars ignore watchers; it is hard to find the clergy office, and harder still to find the clergy.

Worship especially ought to advertise care: the care of God. And it ought to do so by modeling that care in everything it does. As things stand now, watchers are afraid to be too visible lest they are embarrassed on account of what they do not know and what they do not know how to do. Services attend carefully to detail of the rite, the finest music, and a proper sermon, but show little concern for the people who are confused, sung at, spoken at, and read to. Worship should not be something people stay away from because they are tired or hurting; it should be something they cannot stay away from precisely because it is a place where they have at least a chance of feeling revived and healed.

No activity and care will ever happen without the willingness to take creative risks. If the professionals and regulars never try out new ideas and do things differently; if you find an innate conservatism that would squelch any product champion in a maze of committee red tape; if you find yourself always saying, "The people aren't ready for it," or "We can't move too quickly here," and the like, then face it: Your house of prayer is suffering from institutional defense mechanisms equally as deleterious as those Freud found in his neurotic patients. Nothing will change until the system comes to terms with itself.

That, then, is the first and all-important step: coming to terms with what we are. It is a charge that should not sound foreign to people engaged in religion! Should we not demand of ourselves a fair accounting of what we do wrong? If we do not ask that hard question, we will emerge from committee meetings on our worship with the "sound" decision that this or that scapegoated element in our midst is at fault, whereas the real culprit is the institution itself, which has yet to get as far as Pogo, who knew that he had met the enemy and "the enemy is us."

Needed: A Worship Care Committee   ◉

Only people inside a church or synagogue can say what is going wrong with their own worship. They may be unconsciously protecting an old status quo rather than experimenting with novelty. They may be protecting their flank against a new wave of members with different values or goals. Any one of a million things may lurk behind the worship dysfunction. The only way to figure out what it is to constitute a *worship care committee*, a group that is willing to ask hard questions in the certain knowledge that no one will be scapegoated and everyone will be safe, no matter what the problems turn out to be.

Not unlike a patient in therapy, members of the worship care committee will have to learn how to be open with each other in a free-wheeling stream of consciousness that addresses many topics until the pieces fall into place, pointing to a sense of the truth about why the committee's church or synagogue has ended up the way it has. Like therapy, this will require mutual understanding and acceptance of the foibles that plague us all. And in that trusting atmosphere, individual members of the committee will be moved to see how they personally may have colluded unwittingly for all sorts of reasons. One person is afraid of change in general; another thinks that a new way of worship threatens his values; a third would do things differently, if she had been trained to; a fourth really doesn't care what the watchers think and would rather not co-opt their help for fear that help leads to empowerment.

All the systems in a synagogue or church are involved. The Sunday school may have to move the annual event of honoring its teachers out of the sanctuary and back into the classroom. The scouts may have to give up Scouting Sabbath. The rabbi or minister may have to move the pulpit where preaching is done down to the pew level to enhance dialogue with congregants. The cantor may have to find new music, hire a flutist, and learn to teach congregational singing. The board may have to vote the money so the cantor can attend a summer institute where this latter skill is taught, and, in the meantime, be supportive of all the other things that the cantor does well, as he or she pursues professional retooling. The sanctuary lighting may have to be changed, and the seating redesigned. Only a community engaged in honest self-evaluation will have the answers. And these will come slowly, after long and patient struggle, in a caring and supporting network of community members who have come together because they believe worship can work.

Signs of Success: Pastoral, Prophetic, and Priestly   ✺

Ironically, just the effort to create such a committee will go a long way toward solving the problem, if only because such a group best exemplifies the spiritual and caring community of total liability which, we said, must take the place of extended families and functioning neighborhoods.

I have rarely seen liturgical problems that are not really, at a deeper level, communal problems. Solve the problem of the absence of community, and we go a long way toward solving the problem of the absence of genuine prayer. I do not know if (as the old saying used to go) "the family that prays together stays together," but I am convinced that a community of souls who are so accepting of each other that they want to stay together will probably also want to pray together. And then it will be true that their successful liturgical celebration of community—and of God in their midst—will further enhance their chances of staying together. For their worship will be just that: theirs, born of their mutual self-discovery that they are a people of God, charged with a mission to care for one another and, together, to care for the world. They will discover their communal bonds even as they sink roots deeply into their communal past, linking them to generations long gone by and generations yet to come. Through it all, they will find, in their own way, the presence of God, calling them to that sense of meaning in their lives that only the art of worship gives. In the charged atmosphere of discovery, age-old liturgical signs will become symbols; empty ritualizations will become rituals; and, emerging with luminous clarity, in sanctuaries once best known as "bare ruined choirs," will be the ritual moments for which we yearn. At bottom, this quest to celebrate human meaning is a religious quest, and it is never too late for that quest to begin.

Once begun, the quest is endless—and endlessly satisfying, even if it never reaches a final destination where everything is perfect and nothing else need be done. I end, then, with signs of being on the right track. There are obvious things: an ambiance of activity, care, and creativity, as I said above; and the kinds of changes in the service that I detailed in the previous paragraph. But over the long run, three criteria should haunt your every observation of where your change is leading you. I have said a lot about what worship should not be; and I have looked at what it should be, in terms of the specifics related to things like symbols, communication, words, music, and space. All of these specifics go into developing public prayer that is pastoral, prophetic, and priestly.

Pastoral worship soothes the aches within us. It offers us sure knowledge that in God's eyes we matter; that we are not alone; that whatever ails us, we are part of a story going back through time and extending far beyond where human ken can take us. In the pastoral mode of prayer, we are prayed for, and we pray for others. We connect with those around us, we know the healing balm of human love, and we feel the infinite assurance from on high that everything will turn out well—in this life, perhaps, or in the next, whatever that may mean. The helping hand of God is felt in the outstretched arms of those around us. Worship should be pastoral; it should be healing.

Having self-help in mind, Hillel the Elder asked, "If I am not for myself, who will be for me?" But he quickly added, "Being for myself, however, what am I?" The pastoral moment of being helped must be accompanied by the prophetic moment of helping others who are not even part of this worshiping community. The prophets consistently faulted Israel's worship when it consisted of sacrifice alone, not ethics as well. They never opposed the cult, but they did rail against a cult that was not concerned with social evils. In the original eucharist, those in attendance went forth to feed others, not just themselves. To this day, the Passover Seder begins by inviting "all who are hungry" to come and eat. Churches and synagogues cannot be closed-off enclaves sealed hermetically against the wider world outside their doors. If cries from without are not heard within, prayers from within are not heard on high.

Prophetic worship fires us up. It reminds us of our responsibility and sends us forth to do our duty. It tells us we are in a long-term battle for justice and for good. We know we matter. We overcome doubt, denounce despair, ally with others, and then sign up for the causes that demand our help. Pastoral worship is properly concerned with self. Prophetic worship prevents the self from becoming self-centered. Worship must heal the aching heart while at the same time move mind and heart to responsibility.

In the end, however, worship must be priestly. Some strands of Jewish and Christian tradition dispensed with priests a long time ago. Others retain a priesthood, but only as an honorary body. Others still have priests who matter. Whatever the case, priestly worship captures the ultimate task of making manifest the presence of God. That is what this book has been about: how once again to know the reality of God in sanctuaries that seem emptied of any hint of such a presence. Pastoral or prophetic worship without God is not whole. When all is said and done, we want to know that this thing called religion is of ultimate value, that we human beings are not alone either in our pain or in our acts of justice. Worship must be priestly, in that it must invoke God.

A simple way of measuring how far we have come is to ask occasionally, "To what extent is any given worship service evidence of pastoral care, of prophetic commitment, and of priestly invocation of the presence of God?" Ask the watchers too, not just the regulars. Keep your eye on this threefold purpose of public prayer. Change everything that gets in the way of realizing these ends. Remember always that a paragraph here, a song there, the usual entrance, the traditional way of doing it (whatever "it" is)—these are petty concerns compared to ultimate commitment to our pastoral, prophetic, and priestly mandate. Be sure your worship is increasingly pastoral, prophetic, and priestly, and you will again know the magic of worship.

Ritual Check List ❀

Words and Concepts You Should Know

- **Effective worship does more than entertain;** it makes moral demands on us. The liturgical drama doesn't end with the final song or benediction. Our day-to-day lives testify to liturgical success when we act out the message of our prayers in moral behavior.

- **Tampering with worship is necessary from time to time** to ensure that the power of our religious vision will make it through to the next generation rather than be lost for lack of attention to it.

- **When it comes to liturgical reform,** the naturally conservative side of religion always warns us against hurrying, but if any sin is to be feared it is the sin of temporizing, of doing too little, not too much.

- **Worship blends inherited tradition with contemporary style.** Style is the aesthetic preferences that cut across society and affect all religious traditions to some degree. Style today dictates that we need spaces that do not separate laity from clergy; music that collapses social distance; accessible, warm melodies and poetically touching texts.

- **Institutions are like people.** They just require slightly more tacit collusion among their parts. They too become their own worst enemy if they erect procedures that are designed to make things work efficiently, but which actually impede success. Their actual function is to protect the vested interests of the unofficial goals that are never even acknowledged. The only way to get beyond them is to break down the collusion. And the only way to do that is to have the people doing the colluding ask basic questions together about why they do what they do. We call such action systems intervention.

- **Excellence** requires action, care, and creative risk, all linked to religious vision.

- **Liturgical problems are often communal problems.** Solve the problem of the absence of community, and we go a long way toward solving the problem of the absence of prayer.

Conversation Points for Making Worship Work ✦

1 ▪ Establish a worship care committee and begin the task of systems intervention. Listen carefully to each other in an atmosphere where anyone can say anything but no one may be scapegoated.

2 ▪ Go over a recent worship service and rate it on a scale of one to ten with regard to its success as pastoral, prophetic, and priestly. Isolate those moments when you knew it succeeded at any of these, and ask what contributed to that success. Was it the music? The use of space? A particular text or action? Also ask which moments failed and why. Build on success by doing more of what worked. Be sure to ask strangers and watchers what they felt. If you are a regular or a professional, do not trust your own judgment. You may be the last to know what is really going on.

For Further Reading

This book draws on twenty years of studying liturgy and ritual, a combination of subjects that has only relatively lately come about. For most of the period of time in which scientific study has existed, neither liturgy nor ritual was even considered a discipline. Jewish liturgy was subsumed under the category of Talmud or Rabbinics, while Christian liturgy was considered a branch of theology. Ritual was usually studied as anthropology or psychology, not on its own terms. It is hard to say who the first "liturgist" was, as it is equally hard to credit the first person who recognized ritual as a multi-faceted human endeavor deserving an interdisciplinary approach of its own. What is clear is that despite earlier pioneers in the field, the impetus to put the two subjects together emerged mostly from the increasing interest in worship occasioned by the 1960s and '70s. On the international front, Vatican II demanded a complete revision of Catholic worship worldwide. Catholic efforts were quickly matched by Protestants and Jews, who were influenced less by Catholic models than by the forces of change that swept across North America in the wake of those tumultuous decades in which traditional loyalties to synagogue and state were eroded by the coming of age of the baby boomers who were becoming social critics.

I had studied liturgy in the 1960s. By the mid-1970s, I encountered a group of colleagues, mostly Catholic, who had mastered their own liturgy, as I had mine, but who were exploring the interface between liturgy and the social sciences. At some point early on, it occurred to me that instead of liturgy, I was now studying worship, by which I mean the public services that liturgy becomes when a community of the faithful meet to pray. For more than a quarter of a century, this act of public prayer has been my focus, as I have tried to help worshiping communities apply insights from the study of ritual to their worship. This book is the latest result of that study.

Looking back now, it is a little hard to know precisely where each and every idea of mine emerged. A full listing of everything I have read and profited from would take another entire volume. Where, however, I am aware of authors or works whose insights were directly germane to the ideas expressed here, I wish to give them credit. One purpose of this bibliography, then, is to thank the people who came before me and who nurtured my own study insofar as that study resulted in this guide to public prayer. Another is to allow readers who are interested in one chapter or another to go deeper into the thought of the people from whom my own thinking here has profited. (In that regard, I have also listed some further work of my own that expands on themes found in this book.) Since this book is a synoptic work—a summary of twenty-five years of thinking—rather than a single project of primary research for which scholars keep copious notes of what books and articles they look up as the research progresses, I fear I will inevitably have left people out of my retrospective reckoning. Sometimes the most important influences on one's thoughts become so second-nature that they are easily overlooked decades after the fact. To all my teachers and colleagues whose work rightly belongs here but who were inadvertently omitted, I apologize.

Introduction

Geertz, Clifford. *Islam Observed: Religious Development in Morocco and Indonesia*. Chicago: University of Chicago Press, 1971.

Turnbull, Colin M. *The Human Cycle*. New York: Simon and Schuster, 1983.

1 ▪ Structuring Time

Arnheim, Rudolf. *Entropy and Art: An Essay on Disorder and Order.* Berkeley, CA: University of California Press, 1983.

Bellah, Robert N. "Civil Religion in America" and "American Civil Religion in the 1970's," in *American Civil Religion,* edited by Russell E. Richey and Donald G. Jones. New York: Harper and Row, 1974.

Driver, Tom F. *The Magic of Ritual.* New York: HarperSanFrancisco, 1991.

Erikson, Erik. *The Life Cycle Completed: A Review.* New York: W.W. Norton, 1998.

Grimes, Ronald, *Beginnings on Ritual Studies.* Lanham, MD: University Press of America, 1982.

Hall, Edward T. *The Silent Language.* New York: Doubleday Anchor, 1973.

_____. *Beyond Culture.* New York: Doubleday Anchor, 1977.

Hobsbawn, Eric, and Terence Ranger. *The Invention of Tradition.* Cambridge: Cambridge University Press, 1983.

Imber-Black, Evan and Janine Roberts. *Rituals For Our Times.* New York: HarperCollins, 1992.

Kertzer, David I. *Ritual, Politics, and Power.* New Haven and London: Yale University Press, 1989.

Maslow, Abraham H. *Religions, Values and Peak Experiences.* New York: Viking, 1994.

Novak, Michael. *The Joy of Sports.* Lanham, MD: Madison Books, 1993.

O'Meara, Thomas F. "Field of Grace," *Notre Dame Magazine* (Fall, 1991): 12-14.

Rappaport, Roy. *Ecology, Meaning and Religion.* Berkeley: North Atlantic Books, 1979.

Sered, Susan Starr. *Women as Ritual Experts.* New York and Oxford: University of Oxford Press, 1992.

Schmidt, Leigh Eric. *Consumer Rites: The Buying and Selling of American Holidays.* Princeton, NJ: Princeton University Press, 1995.

2 ▪ Lost Symbols

Fink, Peter E. "Theoretical Structures for Liturgical Symbols," *Liturgical Ministry 2* (Fall, 1993): 125-137

Hickman, Hoyt L., Don E. Saliers, Laurence Hull Stookey, and James F. White. *Handbook of the Christian Year.* Nashville, TN: Abingdon Press, 1986.

Jung, C. G., with M. L. Von Franz Joseph Henderson. *Man and His Symbols.* New York: Doubleday, 1998.

Langer, Susanne. *Philosophy in a New Key.* New York: Mentor, 1948.

Leach, Edmund R. *Culture and Communication: The Logic by Which Symbols are Connected.* Cambridge: Cambridge University Press, 1976.

Ricoeur, Paul. *Figuring the Sacred: Religion, Narrative and Language* [Marc Wallace, ed.] Minneapolis: Fortress Press, 1995.

Sill, Gertrude Grace. *A Handbook of Symbols in Christian Art.* New York: Simon & Schuster, 1996.

Turner, Victor. *The Forest of Symbols.* Ithaca, NY: Cornell University Press, 1967.

Wetzler, Robert and Helen Huntington. *Seasons and Symbols: A Handbook on the Church Year.* Minneapolis: Augsburg Fortress Publishers Publishing House, 1962.

3 ▪ Worship Systems *and*
4 ▪ Mistaking the Code, Mixing Messages, and Managing Change

Bateson, Gregory. *Steps to an Ecology of Mind.* New York: Ballantine Books, 1972.

Kantor, David and William Lehr. *Inside the Family: Toward a Theory of Family Process.* San Francisco: Jossey-Bass, 1975.

Koestler, Arthur. *Ghost in the Machine.* Chicago: Henry Regnery Company, 1990.

Koestler, Arthur and J.R. Smythies. *Beyond Reductionism: New Perspectives in the Life Sciences.* Boston: Beacon Press, 1971.

Scheflen, Albert E. with Alice Scheflen. *Body Language and the Social Order: Communication As Behavioral Control.* Englewood Cliffs, NJ: Prentice-Hall, 1972.

Von Bertalanffy, Ludwig, et. al. *General System Theory: Foundations, Development, Applications.* New York: George Braziller, Inc., 1976.

5 • The Presence of God at Worship

Bateson, Gregory. *Mind and Nature: A Necessary Unity*. New York: Dutton, 1988.

Bernstein, Basil, ed. *Class, Codes and Control*. New York: Routledge, 1973.

Douglas, Mary. *Natural Symbols: Explorations in Cosmology*. New York: Routledge, 1996.

Durkheim, Emile and Karen Fields, trans. *The Elementary Forms of Religious Life*. New York: Free Press, 1995.

Dykstra, Craig and Sharon Parks. *Faith Development and Fowler*. Birmingham: Religious Education Press, 1986.

Eliade, Mircea. *The Sacred and the Profane*. New York: Harcourt Brace and World, 1959.

Erikson, Erik. *Childhood and Society*. New York: W.W. Norton and Company, 1993.

Otto, Rudolf and John W. Harvey, trans. *The Idea of the Holy*. London: Oxford University Press, 1923.

Rennie, Bryan S. *Reconstructing Eliade*. Albany, NY: State University of New York Press, 1996.

Smart, Ninian. *Dimensions of the Sacred: An Anatomy of the World's Beliefs*. Berkeley and Los Angeles: University of California Press, 1996.

Stein, Maurice R. *The Eclipse of Community*. Princeton: Princeton University Press, 1960.

Suttles, Gerald D. *The Social Construction of Communities*. Chicago and London: University of Chicago Press, 1972.

Turner, Victor. *The Ritual Process: Structure and Anti-Structure*. Chicago: Aldine de Gruyter, 1995.

_____. *Dramas, Fields, and Metaphors: Symbolic Action in Human Society*. Ithaca and London: Cornell University Press, 1975.

6 • The Script of Prayer: Words Spoken

Austin, J.L. Edited by Marina Sbisa and J. O. Urmsson. *How to Do Things with Words*. Cambridge: Harvard University Press, 1975.

Ayer, A.J. *Wittgenstein*. Chicago: University of Chicago Press, 1986.

Berger, Peter L. and Thomas Luckmann. *The Social Construction of Reality: A Treatise in the Sociology of Knowledge*. New York: Doubleday, 1967.

Culler, Jonathan. *Ferdinand de Saussure*. Ithaca, NY: Cornell University Press, 1986.

Donovan, Peter. *Religious Language*. New York: Hawthorn Books, 1976.

Geertz, Clifford. *Interpretation of Cultures*. New York: Basic Books, 1977.

Gilbert, Margaret. *On Social Facts*. Princeton: Princeton University Press, 1989.

Hartnack, Justus. *Wittgenstein and Modern Philosophy*. Notre Dame: University of Notre Dame Press, 1985.

Hawkes, Terence. *Structuralism and Semiotics*. Berkeley: University of California Press, 1989.

Hirsch, E.D. *Validity in Interpretation*. New Haven and London: Yale University Press, 1967.

Janik, Allan and Stephen Toulmin. *Wittgenstein's Vienna*. Chicago: Ivan R. Dee, Inc., 1996.

Levi-Strauss, Claude and Doreen Weightman, trans. *Naked Man (Mythologiques, Vol. 4)*. Chicago: University of Chicago Press, 1990.

Philips, D.Z. *The Concept of Prayer*. New York: Seabury Press, 1981.

Saussure, Ferdinand de, et al., translated by Wade Baskin. *Course in General Linguistics*. New York: McGraw-Hill, 1983.

Searle, John R. *Speech Acts: An Essay in the Philosophy of Language*. Cambridge: Cambridge University Press, 1970.

_____. *The Construction of Social Reality*. New York: Free Press, 1995.

Stevick, Daniel B. *Language in Worship*. New York: Seabury Press, 1970.

Van Buren, Paul M. *The Edges of Language*. New York: Macmillan, 1972.

7 ▪ The Script of Prayer: Words Sung

Copland, Aaron. *What to Listen for in Music*. New York: Mentor Books, 1989.

Dasilva, Fabio, Anthony Blasi, and David Dees. *The Sociology of Music*. Notre Dame: University of Notre Dame Press, 1984.

Foley, Edward. *Foundations of Christian Music: The Music of Pre-Constantinian Christianity*. Gramcote and Nottingham: Grove Press, 1992.

Gans, Herbert J. *Popular Culture and High Culture: An Analysis and Evaluation of Taste*. New York: Basic Books, 1974.

Gelineau, Joseph. *The Liturgy Today and Tomorrow*. London: Darton, Longman and Todd, 1978.

Hoffman, Lawrence A. "Musical Traditions and Tensions in the American Synagogue," in *Music and the Experience of God: Concilium 222*, edited by David Power, Mary Collins, and Mellonee Burnim. Edinburgh: T. and T. Clark, Ltd., 1989: 30-38.

_____ and Janet Walton. *Sacred Sound and Social Change*. New York and London: University of Notre Dame Press, 1993.

Silins, Gershon, Lawrence A. Hoffman and Ben Steinberg. "The Discussion of Music in Lawrence A. Hoffman's *The Art of Public Prayer*," *CCAR Journal* (Summer, 1991): 1-22.

Speck, Ross V. and Carolyn L. Attneave. *Family Networks*. New York and Toronto: Random House, 1973.

8 ▪ Sacred Space: The Message of Design

Bouyer, Louis. *Liturgy and Architecture*. Notre Dame: University of Notre Dame Press, 1967.

Davies, J. G. *New Westminster Dictionary of Liturgy and Worship*. Philadelphia: Westminster Press, 1986.

Hall, Edward. *Hidden Dimension*. Landover Hills, MD: Anchor, 1990.

Hoffman, Lawrence A. *Sacred Places and the Pilgrimage of Life (Meeting House Essays, #1)*. Chicago: Liturgy Training Publications, 1991.

Sommer, Robert. *Personal Space*. Englewood Cliffs, NJ: Prentice-Hall, 1969.

_____. *Tight Spaces: Hard Architecture and How to Humanize It*. Englewood Cliffs, NJ: Prentice-Hall, 1974.

Wilder, Thornton. "Preface" to *Three Plays*. New York: HarperPerennial Library, 1998.

Lakoff, George, and Mark Johnson. *Metaphors We Live By*. Chicago: University of Chicago Press, 1980.

Vosko, Richard S. *Designing Future Worship Spaces (Meeting House Essays, #8)*. Chicago: Liturgy Training Publications, 1996.

9 ▪ Fixing the System to Make Worship Work

Berger, Peter. *The Sacred Canopy*. New York: Doubleday Anchor, 1969.

Campbell, Ted A. *The Religion of the Heart: A Study of European Religious Life in the Seventeenth and Eighteenth Centuries*. Columbia, SC: University of South Carolina Press, 1991.

Duby, Georges and Elanor Levieux, trans. *The Age of the Cathedrals: Art and Society, 980-1420*. Chicago: University of Chicago Press, 1983.

Goodman, Nelson. *Ways of Worldmaking*. Indianapolis: Hacket Publishing Co., 1978.

Hebdige, Dick. *Subculture: The Meaning of Style*. London and New York: Methuen and Co., Ltd., 1979.

Martland, Thomas R. *Religion As Art: An Interpretation*. Albany: State University of New York, 1981.

Nisbet, Robert. *The Sociological Imagination*. New York: Basic Books, 1966.

_____. *Sociology As an Art Form*. London, Oxford and New York: Oxford University Press, 1976.

Palmer, Parker, J. *The Courage to Teach*. San Francisco: Jossey-Bass, 1998.

Panofsky, Erwin. *Gothic Architecture and Scholasticism: An Inquiry into the Analogy of the Arts, Philosophy and Religion in the Middle Ages*. New York: World Publishing Company, 1957.

Peters, Thomas J. and Robert H. Waterman, Jr. *In Search of Excellence: Lessons from America's Best-Run Companies*. New York: Warner Books, 1988.

Putnam, Hilary. *The Many Faces of Realism*. LaSalle, IL: Open Court Publishing, 1987.

Sharpe, R.A. *Contemporary Aesthetics: A Philosophical Analysis*. New York: St. Martin's Press, 1983.

Warren, Rick. *The Purpose Driven Church*. Grand Rapids: Zondervan Publishing Co., 1995.

Index

About SKYLIGHT PATHS Publishing

Through spirituality, our religious beliefs are increasingly becoming *a part of* our lives, rather than *apart from* our lives. Nevertheless, while many people are more interested than ever in spiritual growth, they are less firmly planted in *traditional* religion. To deepen their relationship to the sacred, people want to learn from their own and other faith traditions, in new ways.

SkyLight Paths sees both believers and seekers as a community that increasingly transcends traditional boundaries of religion and denomination. Many people want to learn from each other, *walking together, finding the way.*

The SkyLight Paths staff is made up of people of many faiths. We are a small, highly committed group of people, a reflection of the religious diversity that now exists in most neighborhoods, most families. We will succeed only if our books make a difference in your life.

We at SkyLight Paths take great care to produce beautiful books that present meaningful spiritual content in a form that reflects the art of making high quality books. Therefore, we want to acknowledge those who contributed to the production of this book.

PRODUCTION
Bridgett Taylor & David Wall

EDITORIAL & PROOFREADING
Jennifer Goneau & Martha McKinney

COVER DESIGN
Bridgett Taylor

PRINTING AND BINDING
Lake Book, Melrose Park, Illinois

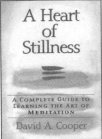

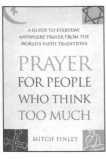

Other Interesting Books—Spirituality

WHO IS MY GOD?
An Innovative Guide to Finding Your Spiritual Identity
Created by *the Editors at SkyLight Paths*
Introduction by *Dr. John Berthrong, author of* The Divine Deli

An innovative guide to spiritual self-discovery.

This dynamic resource is designed to help you discover your own spiritual identity, providing a helpful framework to begin or deepen your spiritual growth. Begin by taking the unique spiritual identity self-test; tabulate your results; then explore one, two or more of the 34 faiths/spiritual paths represented.

6" x 9", 156 pp. Quality Paperback Original, ISBN 1-893361-08-X **$15.95**

SPIRITUAL MANIFESTOS
Visions for Renewed Religious Life in America from Young Spiritual Leaders of Many Faiths
Edited by *Niles Elliot Goldstein*
Preface by *Martin E. Marty*

Discover how our faith traditions are being transformed by today's young spiritual leaders, who are beginning to remove the reasons why so many people have kept organized religion at arm's length. Here, ten contributors, most in their mid-thirties, who span the spectrum of religious traditions—Protestant, Catholic, Jewish, Buddhist, Unitarian Universalist—present the innovative ways they are transforming our spiritual communities and our lives.

"These ten articulate young spiritual leaders engender hope for the vitality of 21st-century religion."
—Forrest Church, Minister of All Souls Church
in New York City

6" x 9", 256 pp. Hardcover, ISBN 1-893361-09-8 **$21.95**

THE NEW MILLENNIUM SPIRITUAL JOURNEY
Change Your Life—Develop Your Spiritual Priorities with Help from Today's Most Inspiring Spiritual Teachers
Created by *the Editors at SkyLight Paths*

A life-changing resource for reimagining your spiritual life.

What better time than now to refocus ourselves on what is most important in life? This book will allow you to set your own course of self-examination, reflection and spiritual transformation—with the help of self-tests, spirituality "exercises," sacred texts from many traditions, time capsule pages, and helpful suggestions from more than 20 spiritual teachers.

7" x 9", 144 pp. Quality Paperback Original, ISBN 1-893361-05-5 **$16.95**

Spirituality from Jewish Lights

SOUL JUDAISM
Dancing with God into a New Era
by *Rabbi Wayne Dosick*

An easy to read introduction to Jewish spirituality, this do-it-yourself approach provides simple exercises and suggestions for connecting personally with the divine.

"A very helpful, considerate introductory manual to a richer Jewish life."
—Rodger Kamenetz, author of *Stalking Elijah*

5½" x 8½", 304 pp. Quality Paperback, ISBN 1-58023-053-9 **$16.95**

THE JEWISH GARDENING COOKBOOK
Growing Plants & Cooking for Holidays & Festivals
by *Michael Brown*

Wherever you garden—a city apartment windowsill or on an acre—with the fruits and vegetables of your own labors, the traditional repasts of Jewish holidays and celebrations can be understood in many new ways!
Gives easy-to-follow instructions for raising foods that have been harvested since ancient times. Provides carefully selected, tasty and easy-to-prepare recipes using these traditional foodstuffs for holidays, festivals, and life cycle events. Clearly illustrated with more than 30 fine botanical illustrations. For beginner and professional alike.

6" x 9", 224 pp. HC, ISBN 1-58023-004-0 **$21.95**

GOD & THE BIG BANG
Discovering Harmony Between Science & Spirituality
by *Daniel C. Matt*

Mysticism and science: What do they have in common? How can one enlighten the other? By drawing on modern cosmology and ancient Kabbalah, Matt shows how science and religion can together enrich our spiritual awareness and help us recover a sense of wonder and find our place in the universe.

"This poetic new book...helps us to understand the human meaning of creation."
—Joel Primack, leading cosmologist, Professor of
Physics, University of California, Santa Cruz

•AWARD WINNER•

6" x 9", 216 pp. Quality Paperback, ISBN 1-879045-89-3 **$16.95**; HC, ISBN-1-87904548-6 **$21.95**

MINDING THE TEMPLE OF THE SOUL
Balancing Body, Mind, & Spirit through Traditional Jewish Prayer, Movement, & Meditation
by *Tamar Frankiel* and *Judy Greenfeld*

This new spiritual approach to physical health introduces readers to a spiritual tradition that affirms the body and enables them to reconceive their bodies in a more positive light. Relying on Kabbalistic teachings and other Jewish traditions, it shows us how to be more responsible for our own psychological and physical health. Focuses on the discipline of prayer, simple Tai Chi–like exercises and body positions, and guides the reader throughout, step-by-step, with diagrams, sketches and meditations.

7" x 10", 184 pp. Quality Paperback Original, illus., ISBN 1-879045-64-8 **$16.95**

Audiotape of the Blessings, Movements & Meditations (60-min. cassette) **$9.95**
Videotape of the Movements & Meditations (46-min. VHS) **$20.00**

From Our Friends at Jewish Lights

Spirituality from Jewish Lights

EYES REMADE FOR WONDER
A Lawrence Kushner Reader
Introduction by *Thomas Moore*

A treasury of insight from one of the most creative spiritual thinkers in America. Whether you are new to Kushner or a devoted fan, you'll find inspiration here. With samplings from each of Kushner's works, and a generous amount of new material, this is a book to be savored, to be read and reread, each time discovering deeper layers of meaning in our lives. Offers something unique to both the spiritual seeker and the committed person of faith.

6" x 9", 240 pp. Quality PB, ISBN 1-58023-042-3 **$16.95**; HC, ISBN 1-58023-014-8 **$23.95**

INVISIBLE LINES OF CONNECTION
Sacred Stories of the Ordinary
by *Lawrence Kushner*

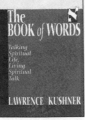

Through his everyday encounters with family, friends, colleagues and strangers, Kushner takes us deeply into our lives, finding flashes of spiritual insight in the process.

5½" x 8½", 160 pp. Quality Paperback, ISBN 1-879045-98-2 **$15.95**
HC, ISBN 1-879045-52-4 **$21.95**

•AWARD WINNER•

NEW ANNIVERSARY EDITION

HONEY FROM THE ROCK
An Introduction to Jewish Mysticism
by *Lawrence Kushner*

"Quite simply the easiest introduction to Jewish mysticism you can read."

An introduction to the ten gates of Jewish mysticism and how it applies to daily life.

6" x 9", 176 pp. Quality Paperback, ISBN 1-58023-073-3 **$15.95**

THE BOOK OF WORDS
Talking Spiritual Life, Living Spiritual Talk
by *Lawrence Kushner*

In the incomparable manner of his extraordinary *The Book of Letters*, Kushner now lifts up and shakes the dust off primary religious words we use to describe the spiritual dimension of life. For each word Kushner offers us a startling, moving and insightful explication. He concludes with a short exercise that helps unite the spirit of the word with our actions in the world.

6" x 9", 160 pp., 2-color text, Quality PB, ISBN 1-58023-020-2 **$16.95**; HC, ISBN 1-879045-35-4 **$21.95**

THE BOOK OF LETTERS
A Mystical Hebrew Alphabet
by *Rabbi Lawrence Kushner*

In calligraphy by the author. Folktales about and exploration of the mystical meanings of the Hebrew Alphabet. Draws from ancient Judaic sources, weaving Talmudic commentary, Hasidic folktales, and kabbalistic mysteries around the letters.

• **Popular Hardcover Edition** 6" x 9", 80 pp. HC, two colors, inspiring new Foreword. ISBN 1-879045-00-1 **$24.95**
• **Deluxe Gift Edition** 9" x 12", 80 pp. HC, four-color text, ornamentation, in a beautiful slipcase. **$79.95**

•AWARD WINNER•

• **Collector's Limited Edition** 9" x 12", 80 pp. HC, gold-embossed pages, hand-assembled slipcase. With silkscreened print. **Limited to 500 signed and numbered copies.** ISBN 1-879045-04-4 **$349.00**

Spirituality from Jewish Lights

GOD WAS IN THIS PLACE & I, i DID NOT KNOW
Finding Self, Spirituality & Ultimate Meaning
by *Lawrence Kushner*

Who am I? Who is God? Kushner creates inspiring interpretations of Jacob's dream in Genesis, opening a window into Jewish spirituality for people of all faiths and backgrounds.

6" x 9", 192 pp. Quality Paperback, ISBN 1-879045-33-8 **$16.95**

THE RIVER OF LIGHT
Spirituality, Judaism, Consciousness
by *Lawrence Kushner*

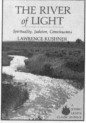

A "manual" for all spiritual travelers who would attempt a spiritual journey in our times. Taking us step by step, Kushner allows us to discover the meaning of our own quest: "to allow the river of light—the deepest currents of consciousness—to rise to the surface and animate our lives."

6" x 9", 192 pp. Quality Paperback, ISBN 1-879045-03-6 **$14.95**

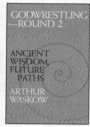

•AWARD WINNER•

GODWRESTLING—ROUND 2
Ancient Wisdom, Future Paths
by *Arthur Waskow*

This 20th-anniversary sequel to a seminal book of the Jewish renewal movement deals with spirituality in relation to personal growth, marriage, ecology, feminism, politics, and more.

6" x 9", 352 pp. Quality Paperback, ISBN 1-879045-72-9 **$18.95**

HC, ISBN 1-879045-45-1 **$23.95**

ECOLOGY & THE JEWISH SPIRIT
Where Nature & the Sacred Meet
Edited and with Introductions by *Ellen Bernstein*

What is nature's place in our spiritual lives?

A focus on nature is part of the fabric of Jewish thought. Here, experts bring us a richer understanding of the long-neglected themes of nature that are woven through the biblical creation story, ancient texts, traditional law, the holiday cycles, prayer, *mitzvot* (good deeds), and community.

6" x 9", 288 pp. HC, ISBN 1-879045-88-5 **$23.95**

BEING GOD'S PARTNER
How to Find the Hidden Link Between Spirituality and Your Work
by *Jeffrey K. Salkin*; Introduction by *Norman Lear*

Will challenge people of every denomination to reconcile the cares of work and soul. A groundbreaking book about spirituality and the work world, from a Jewish perspective. Offers practical suggestions for balancing your professional life and spiritual self.

6" x 9", 192 pp. Quality Paperback, ISBN 1-879045-65-6 **$16.95**

HC, ISBN 1-879045-37-0 **$19.95**

Spirituality from Jewish Lights

MEDITATION FROM THE HEART OF JUDAISM
Today's Teachers Share Their Practices, Techniques, and Faith
Edited by *Avram Davis*

A "how-to" guide for both beginning and experienced meditators, it will help you start meditating or help you enhance your practice.

Twenty-two masters of meditation explain why and how they meditate. *A detailed compendium of the experts' "Best Practices"* offers practical advice and starting points.

6" x 9", 256 pp. Quality Paperback, ISBN 1-58023-049-0 **$16.95**; HC, ISBN 1-879045-77-X **$21.95**

DISCOVERING JEWISH MEDITATION
Instruction & Guidance for Learning an Ancient Spiritual Practice
by *Nan Fink Gefen*

Helps readers of any level of understanding learn the practice of Jewish meditation on their own, starting you on the path to a deep spiritual and personal connection to God and to greater insight about your own life. An accessible, comprehensive introduction to a time-honored spiritual practice.

6" x 9", 208 pp. Quality PB Original, ISBN 1-58023-067-9 **$16.95**

SELF, STRUGGLE & CHANGE
Family Conflict Stories in Genesis and Their Healing Insights for Our Lives
by *Norman J. Cohen*
How do I find greater wholeness in my life and in my family's life?

The people described by the biblical writers of Genesis were in situations and relationships very much like our own. We identify with them. Their stories still speak to us because they are about the same problems we deal with every day. Here a modern master of biblical interpretation brings us greater understanding of the ancient text and of ourselves in this intriguing re-telling of conflict between husband and wife, father and son, brothers, and sisters.

6" x 9", 224 pp. Quality Paperback, ISBN 1-879045-66-4 **$16.95**; HC, ISBN 1-879045-19-2 **$21.95**

VOICES FROM GENESIS
Guiding Us through the Stages of Life
by *Norman J. Cohen*

A brilliant blending of modern *midrash* and the life stages of Erik Erikson's developmental psychology. Shows how the pathways of our lives are quite similar to those of the leading figures of Genesis who speak directly to us, telling of their spiritual and emotional journeys.

6" x 9", 192 pp. HC, ISBN 1-879045-75-3 **$21.95**

ISRAEL—A SPIRITUAL TRAVEL GUIDE
A Companion for the Modern Jewish Pilgrim
by *Rabbi Lawrence A. Hoffman*
Be spiritually prepared for your journey to Israel.

A Jewish spiritual travel guide to Israel, helping today's pilgrim tap into the deep spiritual meaning of the ancient—and modern—sites of the Holy Land. Combines in quick reference format ancient blessings, medieval prayers, biblical and historical references, and modern poetry. The only guidebook that helps readers to prepare spiritually for the occasion. More than a guide book: It is a spiritual map.

•AWARD WINNER•   4¾" x 10", 256 pp. Quality Paperback Original, ISBN 1-879045-56-7 **$18.95**

Spirituality from Jewish Lights

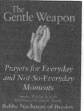

Healing/Recovery/Wellness from Jewish Lights

Experts Praise *Twelve Jewish Steps to Recovery*

"Recommended reading for people of all denominations."
—*Rabbi Abraham J. Twerski, M.D.*

TWELVE JEWISH STEPS TO RECOVERY
A Personal Guide to Turning from Alcoholism & Other Addictions...Drugs, Food, Gambling, Sex...
by *Rabbi Kerry M. Olitzky & Stuart A. Copans, M.D.*
Preface by *Abraham J. Twerski, M.D.*; Intro. by *Rabbi Sheldon Zimmerman*; "Getting Help" by *JACS Foundation*

A Jewish perspective on the Twelve Steps of addiction recovery programs with consolation, inspiration and motivation for recovery. It draws from traditional sources and quotes from what recovering Jewish people say about their experiences with addictions of all kinds. Inspiring illustrations of the twelve gates of the Old City of Jerusalem introduce each step.

6" x 9", 144 pp. Quality Paperback, ISBN 1-879045-09-5 **$13.95**

Recovery from Codependence: A Jewish Twelve Steps Guide to Healing Your Soul
by Rabbi Kerry M. Olitzky
6" x 9", 160 pp. Quality Paperback Original, ISBN 1-879045-32-X **$13.95**; HC, ISBN -27-3 **$21.95**

Renewed Each Day: Daily Twelve Step Recovery Meditations Based on the Bible
by Rabbi Kerry M. Olitzky & Aaron Z.
6" x 9", Quality Paperback Original **V. I**, 224 pp., ISBN 1-879045-12-5 **$14.95**
V. II, 280 pp., ISBN 1-879045-13-3 **$16.95**

One Hundred Blessings Every Day: Daily Twelve Step Recovery Affirmations, Exercises for Personal Growth & Renewal Reflecting Seasons of the Jewish Year
by Rabbi Kerry M. Olitzky
4½" x 6½", 432 pp. Quality Paperback Original, ISBN 1-879045-30-3 **$14.95**

HEALING OF SOUL, HEALING OF BODY
Spiritual Leaders Unfold the Strength and Solace in Psalms
Edited by *Rabbi Simkha Y. Weintraub, CSW, for The Jewish Healing Center*

A source of solace for those who are facing illness, as well as those who care for them. The ten Psalms which form the core of this healing resource were originally selected 200 years ago by Rabbi Nachman of Breslov as a "complete remedy." Today, for anyone coping with illness, they continue to provide a wellspring of strength. Each Psalm is newly translated, making it clear and accessible, and each one is introduced by an eminent rabbi, men and women reflecting different movements and backgrounds. To all who are living with the pain and uncertainty of illness, this spiritual resource offers an anchor of spiritual comfort.

"Will bring comfort to anyone fortunate enough to read it. This gentle book is a luminous gem of wisdom."

—*Larry Dossey, M.D., author of* Healing Words:
The Power of Prayer & the Practice of Medicine

6" x 9", 128 pp. Quality Paperback Original, illus., 2-color text, ISBN 1-879045-31-1 **$14.95**

Life Cycle from Jewish Lights

GRIEF IN OUR SEASONS
A Mourner's Kaddish Companion
by *Rabbi Kerry M. Olitzky*

Strength from the Jewish tradition for the first year of mourning.

Provides a wise and inspiring selection of sacred Jewish writings and a simple, powerful ancient ritual for mourners to read each day, to help hold the memory of their loved ones in their hearts. It offers a comforting, step-by-step daily link to saying *Kaddish.*

"A hopeful, compassionate guide along the journey from grief to rebirth from mourning to a new morning."
  —*Rabbi Levi Meier, Ph.D., Chaplain, Cedars–Sinai Medical Center, Los Angeles*

4½" x 6½", 448 pp. Quality Paperback Original, ISBN 1-879045-55-9 **$15.95**

MOURNING & MITZVAH
• WITH OVER 60 GUIDED EXERCISES •
A Guided Journal for Walking the Mourner's Path Through Grief to Healing
by *Anne Brener, L.C.S.W.*
Foreword by *Rabbi Jack Riemer;* Introduction by *Rabbi William Cutter*

"Fully engaging in mourning means you will be a different person than before you began." **For those who mourn a death, for those who would help them,** for those who face a loss of any kind, Brener teaches us the power and strength available to us in the fully experienced mourning process. Guided writing exercises help stimulate the processes of both conscious and unconscious healing.

"A stunning book! It offers an exploration in depth of the place where psychology and religious ritual intersect, and the name of that place is Truth."
  —*Rabbi Harold Kushner, author of* When Bad Things Happen to Good People

7½" x 9", 288 pp. Quality Paperback Original, ISBN 1-879045-23-0 **$19.95**

A TIME TO MOURN, A TIME TO COMFORT
A Guide to Jewish Bereavement and Comfort
by *Dr. Ron Wolfson*

A guide to meeting the needs of those who mourn and those who seek to provide comfort in times of sadness. While this book is written from a layperson's point of view, it also includes the specifics for funeral preparations and practical guidance for preparing the home and family to sit *shiva.*

"A sensitive and perceptive guide to Jewish tradition. Both those who mourn and those who comfort will find it a map to accompany them through the whirlwind."
  —*Deborah E. Lipstadt, Emory University*

7" x 9", 336 pp. Quality Paperback, ISBN 1-879045-96-6 **$16.95**

WHEN A GRANDPARENT DIES
A Kid's Own Remembering Workbook for Dealing with Shiva and the Year Beyond
by *Nechama Liss-Levinson, Ph.D.*

Drawing insights from both psychology and Jewish tradition, this workbook helps children participate in the process of mourning, offering guided exercises, rituals, and places to write, draw, list, create and express their feelings.

"Will bring support, guidance, and understanding for countless children, teachers, and health professionals."
  —*Rabbi Earl A. Grollman, D.D., author of* Talking about Death

8" x 10", 48 pp. HC, illus., 2-color text, ISBN 1-879045-44-3 **$15.95**

From Jewish Lights—The Art of Jewish Living Series for Holiday Observance

THE SHABBAT SEDER
by *Dr. Ron Wolfson*

A concise step-by-step guide designed to teach people the meaning and importance of this weekly celebration, as well as its practices.

Each chapter corresponds to one of ten steps which together comprise the Shabbat dinner ritual, and looks at the *concepts, objects,* and *meanings* behind the specific activity or ritual act. The blessings that accompany the meal are written in both Hebrew and English, and accompanied by English transliteration. Also included are craft projects, recipes, discussion ideas and other creative suggestions for enriching the Shabbat experience.

"A how-to book in the best sense...."
—*Dr. David Lieber, President, University of Judaism, Los Angeles*

7" x 9", 272 pp. Quality Paperback, ISBN 1-879045-90-7 **$16.95**

Also available are these helpful companions to *The Shabbat Seder*:
- Booklet of the Blessings and Songs   ISBN 1-879045-91-5 $5.00
- Audiocassette of the Blessings   DNO3 $6.00
- Teacher's Guide   ISBN 1-879045-92-3 $4.95

HANUKKAH
by *Dr. Ron Wolfson*
Edited by *Joel Lurie Grishaver*

Designed to help celebrate and enrich the holiday season, *Hanukkah* discusses the holiday's origins, explores the reasons for the Hanukkah candles and customs, and provides everything from recipes to family activities.

There are songs, recipes, useful information on the arts and crafts of Hanukkah, the calendar and its relationship to Christmas time, and games played at Hanukkah. Putting the holiday in a larger, timely context, "December Dilemmas" deals with ways in which a Jewish family can cope with Christmas.

"Helpful for the family that strives to induct its members into the spirituality and joys of Jewishness and Judaism...a significant text in the neglected art of Jewish family education."
—*Rabbi Harold M. Schulweis, Cong. Valley Beth Shalom, Encino, CA*

7" x 9", 192 pp. Quality Paperback, ISBN 1-879045-97-4 **$16.95**

THE PASSOVER SEDER
by *Dr. Ron Wolfson*

Explains the concepts behind Passover ritual and ceremony in clear, easy-to-understand language, and offers step-by-step procedures for Passover observance and preparing the home for the holiday.

Easy-to-Follow Format: Using an innovative photo-documentary technique, real families describe in vivid images their own experiences with the Passover holiday. **Easy-to-Read Hebrew Texts:** The Haggadah texts in Hebrew, English, and transliteration are presented in a three-column format designed to help celebrants learn the meaning of the prayers and how to read them. **An Abundance of Useful Information:** A detailed description of how to perform the rituals is included, along with practical questions and answers, and imaginative ideas for Seder celebration.

"A creative 'how-to' for making the Seder a more meaningful experience."
—*Michael Strassfeld, co-author of* The Jewish Catalog

7" x 9", 336 pp. Quality Paperback, ISBN 1-879045-93-1 **$16.95**

Also available are these helpful companions to *The Passover Seder*:
- Passover Workbook   ISBN 1-879045-94-X $6.95
- Audiocassette of the Blessings   DNO4 $6.00
- Teacher's Guide   ISBN 1-879045-95-8 $4.95

Theology/Philosophy from Jewish Lights

A LIVING COVENANT
The Innovative Spirit in Traditional Judaism
by *David Hartman*

The Judaic tradition is often seen as being more concerned with uncritical obedience to law than with individual freedom and responsibility. Hartman challenges this approach by revealing a Judaism grounded in a covenant—a relational framework—informed by the metaphor of marital love rather than that of parent-child dependency.

"Jews and non-Jews, liberals and traditionalists will see classic Judaism anew in these pages."
—*Dr. Eugene B. Borowitz, Hebrew Union College–Jewish Institute of Religion*

•AWARD WINNER•

6" x 9", 368 pp. Quality Paperback, ISBN 1-58023-011-3 **$18.95**

THE SPIRIT OF RENEWAL
Finding Faith after the Holocaust
by *Edward Feld*

To address the question of faith after the Holocaust, explores three key cycles of destruction and recovery in Jewish history, each of which radically reshaped Jewish understanding of God and the world.

"A profound meditation on Jewish history [and the Holocaust]. . . . Christians, as well as many others, need to share in this story."
—*The Rt. Rev. Frederick H. Borsch, Ph.D., Episcopal Bishop of L.A.*

•AWARD WINNER•

6" x 9", 224 pp. Quality Paperback, ISBN 1-879045-40-0 **$16.95**

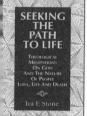

SEEKING THE PATH TO LIFE
Theological Meditations On God
and the Nature of People, Love, Life and Death
by *Rabbi Ira F. Stone*

For people who never thought they would read a book of theology—let alone understand it, enjoy it, savor it and have it affect the way they think about their lives. In 45 intense meditations, each a page or two in length, Stone takes us on explorations of the most basic human struggles: Life and death, love and anger, peace and war, covenant and exile.

•AWARD WINNER•   "A bold book. . . . The reader of any faith will be inspired. . . ."
—*The Rev. Carla V. Berkedal, Episcopal Priest*

6" x 9", 132 pp. Quality Paperback, ISBN 1-879045-47-8 **$14.95**; HC, ISBN-17-6 **$19.95**

•CLASSICS BY ABRAHAM JOSHUA HESCHEL•

The Earth Is the Lord's: The Inner World of the Jew in Eastern Europe
1/2" x 8", 112 pp, Quality Paperback, ISBN 1-879045-42-7 **$13.95**

Israel: An Echo of Eternity with new Introduction by Susannah Heschel
1/2" x 8", 272 pp, Quality Paperback, ISBN 1-879045-70-2 **$18.95**

Passion for Truth: Despair and Hope in Hasidism
1/2" x 8", 352 pp, Quality Paperback, ISBN 1-879045-41-9 **$18.95**

•THEOLOGY & PHILOSOPHY...Other books—Classic Reprints•

Aspects of Rabbinic Theology by Solomon Schechter, with a new Introduction by Neil Gillman 6" x 9", 448 pp, Quality Paperback, ISBN 1-879045-24-9 **$18.95**

The Last Trial: On the Legends and Lore of the Command to Abraham to Offer Isaac as a Sacrifice by Shalom Spiegel, with a new Introduction by Judah Goldin x 9", 208 pp, Quality Paperback, ISBN 1-879045-29-X **$17.95**

Judaism and Modern Man: An Interpretation of Jewish Religion by Will Herberg; new Introduction by Neil Gillman 5.5" x 8.5", 336 pp, Quality Paperback, ISBN 1-879045-87-7 **$18.95**

Tormented Master: The Life and Spiritual Quest of Rabbi Nahman of Bratslav by Arthur Green 6" x 9", 416 pp, Quality Paperback, ISBN 1-879045-11-7 **$18.95**

Your Word Is Fire Ed. and trans. with a new Introduction by Arthur Green and Barry W. Holtz 6" x 9", 160 pp, Quality Paperback, ISBN 1-879045-25-7 **$14.95**

Life Cycle from Jewish Lights

TEARS OF SORROW, SEEDS OF HOPE
A Jewish Spiritual Companion for Infertility and Pregnancy Loss
by *Rabbi Nina Beth Cardin*

Many people who endure the emotional suffering of infertility, pregnancy loss, or stillbirth bear this sorrow alone. Rarely is the experience of loss and infertility discussed with anyone but close friends and family members. Despite the private nature of the pain, many women and men would welcome the opportunity to be comforted by family and a community who would understand the pain and loneliness they feel, and the emptiness caused by the loss that is without a face, a name, or a grave.

Tears of Sorrow, Seeds of Hope is a spiritual companion that enables us to mourn infertility, a lost pregnancy, or a stillbirth within the prayers, rituals, and meditation of Judaism. By drawing deeply on the texts of tradition, it creates readings and rites of mourning, and through them provides a wellspring of compassion, solace—and hope.

6" x 9", 192 pp. HC, ISBN 1-58023-017-2 **$19.95**

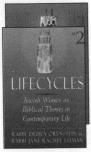

•AWARD WINNER•

LIFECYCLES
V. 1: Jewish Women on Life Passages & Personal Milestones
Edited and with Introductions by *Rabbi Debra Orenstein*
V. 2: Jewish Women on Biblical Themes in Contemporary Life
Edited and with Introductions by
Rabbi Debra Orenstein and Rabbi Jane Rachel Litman

This unique multivolume collaboration brings together over one hundred women writers, rabbis, and scholars to create the first comprehensive work on Jewish life cycle that fully includes women's perspectives.

V. 1: 6" x 9", 480 pp. Quality Paperback, ISBN 1-58023-018-0 **$19.95**
HC, ISBN 1-879045-14-1 **$24.95**

V. 2: 6" x 9", 464 pp. Quality Paperback, ISBN 1-58023-019-9 **$19.95**
HC, ISBN 1-879045-15-X **$24.95**

LIFE CYCLE— The Art of Jewish Living Series for Holiday Observance
by Dr. Ron Wolfson

Hanukkah—7" x 9", 192 pp. Quality Paperback, ISBN 1-879045-97-4 **$16.95**

The Shabbat Seder—7" x 9", 272 pp. Quality Paperback, ISBN 1-879045-90-7 **$16.95**;
Booklet of Blessings **$5.00**; Audiocassette of Blessings **$6.00**; Teacher's Guide **$4.95**

The Passover Seder—7" x 9", 336 pp. Quality Paperback, ISBN 1-879045-93-1 **$16.95**;
Passover Workbook, **$6.95**; Audiocassette of Blessings, **$6.00**; Teacher's Guide, **$4.95**

• LIFE CYCLE...Other Books •

A Heart of Wisdom: Making the Jewish Journey from Midlife Through the Elder Years
Ed. by Susan Berrin 6" x 9", 384 pp. Quality Paperback, ISBN 1-58023-051-2, **$18.95**;
HC, ISBN 1-879045-73-7 **$24.95**

Bar/Bat Mitzvah Basics: A Practical Family Guide to Coming of Age Together
Ed. by Cantor Helen Leneman 6" x 9", 240 pp. Quality Paperback, ISBN 1-879045-54-0 **$16.95**

Embracing the Covenant: Converts to Judaism Talk About Why & How
Ed. and with Intros. by Rabbi Allan L. Berkowitz and Patti Moskovitz
6" x 9", 192 pp. Quality Paperback, ISBN 1-879045-50-8 **$15.95**

For Kids—Putting God on Your Guest List: How to Claim the Spiritual Meaning of Your Bar or Bat Mitzvah by Rabbi Jeffrey K. Salkin
6" x 9", 144 pp. Quality Paperback Original, ISBN 1-58023-015-6 **$14.95**

The New Jewish Baby Book: Names, Ceremonies, Customs—A Guide for Today's Families by Anita Diamant 6" x 9", 336 pp. Quality Paperback, ISBN 1-879045-28-1 **$16.95**

Putting God on the Guest List, 2nd Ed.: How to Reclaim the Spiritual Meaning of Your Child's Bar or Bat Mitzvah by Rabbi Jeffrey K. Salkin
6" x 9", 224 pp. Quality Paperback, ISBN 1-897045-59-1 **$16.95**; HC, ISBN 1-879045-58-3 **$24.95**

So That Your Values Live On: Ethical Wills & How to Prepare Them
Ed. by Rabbi Jack Riemer & Professor Nathaniel Stampfer
6" x 9", 272 pp. Quality Paperback, ISBN 1-879045-34-6 **$17.95**

Spirituality from Jewish Lights

PARENTING AS A SPIRITUAL JOURNEY
Deepening Ordinary & Extraordinary Events into Sacred Occasions
by *Rabbi Nancy Fuchs-Kreimer*

A perfect gift for the new parent, and a helpful guidebook for those seeking to re-envision family life. Draws on experiences of the author and over 100 parents of many faiths. Rituals, prayers, and passages from sacred Jewish texts—as well as from other religious traditions—are woven throughout the book.

6" x 9", 224 pp. Quality Paperback, ISBN 1-58023-016-4 **$16.95**

STEPPING STONES TO JEWISH SPIRITUAL LIVING
Walking the Path Morning, Noon, and Night
by *Rabbi James L. Mirel & Karen Bonnell Werth*

How can we bring the sacred into our busy lives?

Transforms our daily routine into sacred acts of mindfulness. Chapters are arranged according to the cycle of each day—and the cycle of our lives—providing spiritual activities, creative new rituals, meditations, acts of *kavannah* (spiritual intention) and prayers for any lifestyle.

6" x 9", 240 pp. HC, ISBN 1-58023-003-2 **$21.95**

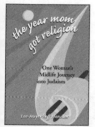

THE YEAR MOM GOT RELIGION
One Woman's Midlife Journey into Judaism
by *Lee Meyerhoff Hendler*

A frank, thoughtful, and humorous "spiritual autobiography" that will speak to anyone in search of deeper meaning in their religious life. The author shares with the reader the hard lessons and realizations she confronted as a result of her awakening to Judaism, including how her transformation deeply affected her lifestyle and relationships. Shows that anyone, at any time, can deeply embrace faith—and face the challenges that occur.

6" x 9", 208 pp. Quality Paperback, ISBN 1-58023-070-9 **$15.95**
HC, ISBN 1-58023-000-8 **$19.95**

MOSES—THE PRINCE, THE PROPHET
His Life, Legend & Message for Our Lives
by *Rabbi Levi Meier, Ph.D.*

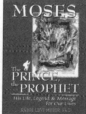

How can the struggles of a great biblical figure teach us to cope with our own lives today? A fascinating portrait of the struggles, failures and triumphs of Moses, a central figure in Jewish, Christian and Islamic tradition. Draws from Exodus, *midrash*, the teachings of Jewish mystics, modern texts and psychotherapy. Offers new ways to create our own path to self-knowledge and self-fulfillment—and face life's difficulties.

6" x 9", 224 pp. Quality Paperback, ISBN 1-58023-069-5 **$16.95**
HC, ISBN 1-58023-013-X **$23.95**

ANCIENT SECRETS
Using the Stories of the Bible to Improve Our Everyday Lives
by *Rabbi Levi Meier, Ph.D.*

Drawing on a broad range of Jewish wisdom writings, distinguished rabbi and psychologist Levi Meier takes a thoughtful, wise and fresh approach to showing us how to apply the stories of the Bible to our everyday lives. The courage of Abraham, who left his early life behind and chose a new, more difficult and more rewarding path; the ability of Joseph to forgive his brothers; Moses' over-powering grief over the loss of his sister—the quests and conflicts of the Bible are still relevant, and still have the power to inform and change our lives.

5½" x 8¼", 288 pp. Quality Paperback, ISBN 1-58023-064-4 **$16.95**

Children's Spirituality from Jewish Lights

A PRAYER FOR THE EARTH
The Story of Naamah, Noah's Wife

For ages 4 and up

by *Sandy Eisenberg Sasso*
Full-color illustrations by *Bethanne Andersen*

NONDENOMINATIONAL, NONSECTARIAN

This new story, based on an ancient text, opens readers' religious imaginations to new ideas about the well-known story of the Flood. When God tells Noah to bring the animals of the world onto the ark, God *also* calls on Naamah, Noah's wife, to save each plant on Earth.

9" x 12", 32 pp. HC, Full-color illus., ISBN 1-879045-60-5 **$16.95**

•AWARD WINNER•

THE 11TH COMMANDMENT
Wisdom from Our Children

For all ages

by The Children of America

MULTICULTURAL, NONDENOMINATIONAL, NONSECTARIAN

"If there were an Eleventh Commandment, what would it be?"

Children of many religious denominations across America answer this question— in their own drawings and words—in *The 11th Commandment*.

•AWARD WINNER•

8" x 10", 48 pp. HC, Full-color illus., ISBN 1-879045-46-X **$16.95**

FOR HEAVEN'S SAKE

For ages 4 and up

by *Sandy Eisenberg Sasso*
Full-color illustrations by *Kathryn Kunz Finney*

MULTICULTURAL, NONDENOMINATIONAL, NONSECTARIAN

People said "for heaven's sake" to Isaiah a lot. Everyone talked about heaven: "Thank heavens." "Heaven forbid." "For heaven's sake, Isaiah." But no one would say what heaven was or how to find it. So Isaiah decided to find out. After seeking answers from many different people, he learns that heaven isn't so difficult to find after all.

9" x 12", 32 pp. HC, Full-color illus., ISBN 1-58023-054-7 **$16.95**

•AWARD WINNER•

SHARING BLESSINGS
Children's Stories for Exploring the Spirit of the Jewish Holidays

For ages 6 and up

by *Rahel Musleah* and *Rabbi Michael Klayman*
Full-color illustrations by *Mary O'Keefe Young*

What is the spiritual message of each of the Jewish holidays? How do we teach it to our children? Many books tell children about the historical significance and customs of the holidays. Now, through engaging, creative stories about one family's spiritual preparation, *Sharing Blessings* explores ways to get into the *spirit* of 13 different holidays.

7" x 10", 64 pp. HC, Full-color illus., ISBN 1-879045-71-0 **$18.95**

THE BOOK OF MIRACLES
A Young Person's Guide to Jewish Spiritual Awareness

For ages 9–13

by *Lawrence Kushner*

From the miracle at the Red Sea to the miracle of waking up this morning, this intriguing book introduces kids to a way of everyday spiritual thinking to last a lifetime. Kushner, whose award-winning books have brought spirituality to life for countless adults, now shows young people how to use Judaism as a foundation on which to build their lives.

6" x 9", 96 pp. HC, 2-color illus., ISBN 1-879045-78-8 **$16.95**

Children's Spirituality from Jewish Lights

For ages 8 and up

BUT GOD REMEMBERED
Stories of Women from Creation to the Promised Land
by *Sandy Eisenberg Sasso*, Full-color illus. by *Bethanne Andersen*

NONDENOMINATIONAL, NONSECTARIAN

A fascinating collection of four different stories of women only briefly mentioned in biblical tradition and religious texts. Award-winning author Sasso vibrantly brings to life courageous and strong women from ancient tradition. All teach important values through their faith and actions.

9" x 12", 32 pp. HC, Full-color illus., ISBN 1-879045-43-5 **$16.95**

•AWARD WINNER•

IN GOD'S NAME
by *Sandy Eisenberg Sasso*
Full-color illustrations by *Phoebe Stone*

Selected as Outstanding by Parent Council, Ltd.™

For ages 4 and up

MULTICULTURAL, NONDENOMINATIONAL, NONSECTARIAN

Like an ancient myth in its poetic text and vibrant illustrations, this modern fable about the search for God's name celebrates the diversity and, at the same time, the unity of all the people of the world.

9" x 12", 32 pp. HC, Full color illus., ISBN 1-879045-26-5 **$16.95**

WHAT IS GOD'S NAME?

•AWARD WINNER•

An abridged board book version, for children ages 0–4.

5" x 5", 20 pp. Board, Full color illus., ISBN 1-893361-10-1 **$7.95**

GOD IN BETWEEN

For ages 4 and up

by *Sandy Eisenberg Sasso*
Full-color illustrations by *Sally Sweetland*

NONDENOMINATIONAL, NONSECTARIAN, MULTICULTURAL

If you wanted to find God, where would you look?

A magical, mythical tale that teaches that God can be found where we are: within all of us and the relationships between us.

9" x 12", 32 pp. HC, Full-color illus., ISBN 1-879045-86-9 **$16.95**

•AWARD WINNER•

IN OUR IMAGE
God's First Creatures
by *Nancy Sohn Swartz*
Full-color illustrations by *Melanie Hall*

Selected as Outstanding by Parent Council, Ltd.™

For ages 4 and up

NONDENOMINATIONAL, NONSECTARIAN

For ages 4 and up

A playful new twist to the Creation story. Celebrates the interconnectedness of nature and the harmony of all living things.

9" x 12", 32 pp. HC, Full-color illus., ISBN 1-879045-99-0 **$16.95**

•AWARD WINNER•

GOD'S PAINTBRUSH

For ages 4 and up

by *Sandy Eisenberg Sasso*
Full-color illustrations by *Annette Compton*

MULTICULTURAL, NONDENOMINATIONAL, NONSECTARIAN

Invites children of all faiths and backgrounds to encounter God openly in their own lives. Wonderfully interactive, provides questions adult and child can explore together at the end of each episode.

11" x 8½", 32 pp. HC, Full-color illus., ISBN 1-879045-22-2 **$16.95**

•AWARD WINNER•

Also Available! **Teacher's Guide: A Guide for Jewish & Christian Educators and Parents**

8½" x 11", 32 pp. PB, ISBN 1-879045-57-5 **$6.95**

AVAILABLE FROM BETTER BOOKSTORES.
TRY YOUR BOOKSTORE FIRST.

SkyLight Paths—Spirituality

HOW TO BE A PERFECT STRANGER, In 2 Volumes
A Guide to Etiquette in Other People's Religious Ceremonies

Edited by *Arthur J. Magida* & *Stuart M. Matlins*

BEST REFERENCE BOOK OF THE YEAR

Two books that belong in every living room, library and office!

Explains the rituals and celebrations of North America's major religions/denominations, helping an interested guest to feel comfortable, participate to the fullest extent possible, and avoid violating anyone's religious principles. Answers practical questions from the perspective of *any* other faith.

VOL. 1: North America's Largest Faiths

VOL. 1 COVERS: Assemblies of God • Baptist • Buddhist • Christian Church (Disciples of Christ) • Christian Science • Churches of Christ • Episcopalian/Anglican • Greek Orthodox • Hindu • Islam • Jehovah's Witnesses • Jewish • Lutheran • Methodist • Mormon • Presbyterian • Quaker • Roman Catholic • Seventh-day Adventist • United Church of Canada • United Church of Christ

6" x 9", 432 pp. Quality Paperback, ISBN 1-893361-01-2 **$19.95**

VOL. 2: Other Faiths in North America

VOL. 2 COVERS: African American Methodist Churches • Baha'i • Christian and Missionary Allian • Christian Congregation • Church of the Brethren • Church of the Nazarene • Evangelical Fr Church • International Church of the Foursquare Gospel • International Pentecostal Holiness Chur • Mennonite/Amish • Native American/First Nations • Orthodox Churches • Pentecostal Church God • Reformed Church • Sikh • Unitarian Universalist • Wesleyan

6" x 9", 416 pp. Quality Paperback, ISBN 1-893361-02-0 **$19.95**

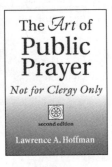

The *Art* of **Public Prayer**

Not for Clergy Only

second edition

Lawrence A. Hoffman

THE ART OF PUBLIC PRAYER
Not for Clergy Only

by *Lawrence A. Hoffman*

A resource for worshipers today looking to change hardened worship patterns that stand in the way of everyday spirituality

Written for laypeople and clergy of any denomination. This ecumenical int duction to meaningful public prayer is for everyone who cares about relig today.

6" x 9", 288 pp. Quality Paperback, ISBN 1-893361-06-3 **$17.95**

Or phone, fax or mail to: **SKYLIGHT PATHS** Publishing
Sunset Farm Offices, Route 4 • P.O. Box 237 • Woodstock, Vermont 05091
Tel: (802) 457-4000 • Fax: (802) 457-4004 • www.skylightpaths.com
Credit card orde (800) 962 4544 ET Monday–Friday)
Generous discounts on q *Prices subject to change.*